Praise for *Libraries and Sanctuary*

'The first book in a very welcome new series from Facet Publishing, *Libraries and Social Justice*, John Vincent's volume is a timely reminder, sadly, of the essential contribution libraries have made – and must continue to make – in supporting refugees and other new arrivals.

Commendably accessible and well-researched, it outlines the recent debates around new arrivals, challenging some of the language used to describe these people, and gives historical and contemporary context for the reasons why people may become displaced and the multiple barriers that new arrivals face. Whilst the author gives us an overview of what libraries have done in the last seventy years to practically address the needs of new arrivals, as well as highlighting the academic research that has often informed this work, this book is ultimately a very readable and practical guide for library staff to consider their own service development – right now – for all new arrivals, offering useful examples and case studies from the UK and elsewhere.'
Dave Percival, Library and Archive Services Manager, Portsmouth

'The Libraries of Sanctuary movement simply would not have been possible without John. His in-depth knowledge of libraries and how they can be a place of welcome and solidarity has been pivotal in setting up the Libraries of Sanctuary programme and supporting its growth into the flourishing network that it is today. If you want to know why libraries have to be at the centre of the movement of creating welcome for all, you need this book.'
Sian Summer-Rees, City of Sanctuary Chief Officer

'Libraries are a vital part of our society, offering access to information and knowledge to everyone and a welcome to people newly arrived in the country, signposting them to national and local services, and hosting them to meet and share their experiences with others. Yet libraries are often regarded as "easy targets" for cuts and closures, disregarding the enormous positive impact they have on people's lives.

This important new book explores some of the historical background and shows both how society has responded to new arrivals to this country and how libraries have developed their provision to meet changing needs, often in difficult circumstances.

We need more libraries, not fewer!'
Peter Tatchell, Peter Tatchell Foundation

Libraries and Sanctuary

Libraries and Social Justice

Series Editor: John Vincent
Independent writer, researcher and trainer on libraries, museums and archives

Social justice can be defined as including the equality of access to resources, equity, participation, diversity and human rights. It is a direct response to historical and contemporary challenges in communities and in society, and is a topic which garners much passion and discussion. Where the latter is frequently lacking, however, is in libraries where we are all meant to feel welcome. Libraries serve the community but in order to do so properly, they must support and represent everyone, whether that be people seeking sanctuary, people who identify as LGBTQ+, young people in care, those living in poverty and/or with mental health issues, as just a few examples.

This pioneering series examines how areas of social justice are dealt with by all types of library and information service, with the purpose of making this information easily accessible to all those interested. Consisting of practical and digestible guides, the series will become an important reference for people wishing to explore, read around or start in a particular area of work. In addition to practical advice, topics are provided a historical and political context, together with case studies to ensure that the *Libraries and Social Justice* series encourages good practice across the library and information sectors.

The Editor welcomes submissions from practitioners and scholars from across the information sector, including librarianship, archives, recordkeeping, classification, knowledge management and beyond.

Libraries and Sanctuary
Supporting Refugees and Other New Arrivals

John Vincent

© John Vincent 2022

Published by Facet Publishing
7 Ridgmount Street, London WC1E 7AE
www.facetpublishing.co.uk

Facet Publishing is wholly owned by CILIP: the Library and Information Association.

The author has asserted his right under the Copyright, Designs and Patents Act 1988 to be identified as author of this work.

Except as otherwise permitted under the Copyright, Designs and Patents Act 1988 this publication may only be reproduced, stored or transmitted in any form or by any means, with the prior permission of the publisher, or, in the case of reprographic reproduction, in accordance with the terms of a licence issued by The Copyright Licensing Agency. Enquiries concerning reproduction outside those terms should be sent to Facet Publishing, 7 Ridgmount Street, London WC1E 7AE.

Every effort has been made to contact the holders of copyright material reproduced in this text, and thanks are due to them for permission to reproduce the material indicated. If there are any queries please contact the publisher.

British Library Cataloguing in Publication Data
A catalogue record for this book is available from the British Library.

ISBN 978-1-78330-500-1 (paperback)
ISBN 978-1-78330-501-8 (hardback)
ISBN 978-1-78330-502-5 (PDF)
ISBN 978-1-78330-528-5 (EPUB)

First published 2022

Text printed on FSC® accredited material.

Every purchase of a Facet book helps to fund CILIP's advocacy, awareness and accreditation programmes for information professionals.

Typeset from author's files by Flagholme Publishing Services in
10/13 pt Palatino Linotype and Open Sans.
Printed and made in Great Britain by CPI Group (UK) Ltd, Croydon, CR0 4YY.

Contents

About the author	**xi**
Acknowledgements	**xii**
Abbreviations	**xiii**
Introduction	**xv**

1 Definitions and Scope of the Book: When We Talk About 'Refugees and Other New Arrivals', Who Exactly Do We Mean? — **1**

Introduction	1
Refugees and other new arrivals – seeking sanctuary	2
Refugees and asylum seekers	5
Refugee resettlement programmes	7
International agreements	9
Other reasons for seeking safety and sanctuary	11
Irregular migrants	16
Unaccompanied children and young people	17
Trafficking/modern slavery	18
The lifetime impact of seeking sanctuary	20
Other new arrivals	20

2 What Has Been the Response in the UK? — **23**

Immigration and the UK – and has there always been a welcome?	24
Institutional racism	28
Immigration and the UK – a summary of who is coming (and going)	29
Immigration and the UK – growing hostility	30
The 'refugee crisis'	31
The hostile environment	32
The Equality Act 2010	35
The Windrush scandal	36
Brexit	40
Where are we now?	42
Where are we now in the UK?	45

3 What Does Any of This Have to Do with Libraries? — **63**

Statements of ethics by library associations	63
Library workers – journeys to the UK	66
Library workers – offering support	71

viii   LIBRARIES AND SANCTUARY

4   Libraries' Responses in the UK – Historical Background   **73**
Introduction   73
The 1940s and 1950s   76
The 1960s and 1970s   76
The 1980s   84
The 1990s   87
2000 onwards   93

5   What Barriers are There to the Take-Up of Library Services by New   **101**
Arrivals? And How Can We Begin to Dismantle These?
Introduction   101
Overcoming barriers: personal and social   101
Overcoming barriers: perception and awareness   102
Overcoming barriers: environmental   102
Overcoming barriers: institutional   103

6   How Are Libraries Responding Today? And What More Can We Do?   **105**
Some Practical Ideas ...
Introduction   105
Learn   105
Embed   111
Share   123
Case Studies   126
   Case study 1: Wirral Schools' Library Service Library of Sanctuary Scheme   126
   Case study 2: Music and new arrivals   127
   Case study 3: Lambeth Libraries and the Polish community   130
   Case study 4: Promoting diversity and multicultural blending through the   132
   Conversation Café initiative

7   And What Can We Learn From Elsewhere?   **139**
Academic libraries: 'Project Welcome'   139
ECHO Mobile Library   141
Toronto Public Library   143

8   Conclusions   **145**
Introduction   145
Responses to people seeking sanctuary and other new arrivals   145
Libraries and new arrivals   146
So, what can go wrong?   146
What can we do to start to make things right?   147

Appendices   **149**
Appendix 1: Main countries of origin of people seeking asylum   149
Appendix 2: Immigration status   150
Appendix 3: A note on funding   152
Appendix 4: A brief look at the supply of library materials   158
Appendix 5: Outline for a course, 'Working with New Arrivals'   162
Appendix 6: Some sources of information about new arrivals locally   163
and regionally
Appendix 7: Effective communications   164
Appendix 8: Community cohesion   166

Endnotes	169
References	189
Index	233

About the Author

John Vincent has worked in the public sector since the 1960s, primarily for Hertfordshire, Lambeth and Enfield public library services, including as a young people's librarian and senior manager.

In 1997, he was invited to become part of the team that produced the UK's first review of public libraries and social exclusion, from which 'The Network – tackling social exclusion in libraries, museums, archives and galleries' originated and which he now coordinates. As part of this, John runs courses and lectures, writes, produces regular newsletters and e-bulletins, and lobbies for greater awareness of the role that libraries, archives, museums, and the cultural and heritage sector play in contributing to social justice.

John is particularly interested in supporting work with people seeking sanctuary and other 'new arrivals' to the UK; with young people in care, and with LGBTQ+ people. This has involved participating in the Welcome To Your Library project (2004–7); working with Libraries Connected West Midlands and partners to produce the *Libraries of Sanctuary Resource Pack* (2021); developing the 'Access to Books and Reading Projects for Young People in Public Care: the librarians' training kit' project (2004); and co-chairing the CILIP LGBTQ+ Network Steering Group. He is also currently the Chair of the CILIP Benevolent Fund.

John is co-author of *Public Libraries and Social Justice* (2010), and author of *LGBT People and the UK Cultural Sector* (2014). In 2018, his report *Libraries Welcome Everyone: six stories of diversity and inclusion from libraries in England* was published by Arts Council England.

In 2014, John was awarded the CILIP CDEG Special Diversity Award, and in September 2014, became an Honorary Fellow of CILIP.

Acknowledgements

I am immensely grateful to everyone who has shared their work and knowledge with me and given me advice. I hope I haven't missed anyone!

Mag Astill, Briony Birdi, Vickery Bowles, Colin Bray, Donal Brennan, Helen Carpenter, Bertha Calles Cartas, Norah Carr, Suzanne Carroll, Simon Cloudesley, Patricia Coleman, Louise Cooke-Escapil, Emma Corless, John Dolan, Nathaniel Dziura, Dylan Fotoohi, Andrew Grave, Ash Green, Robin Green, Linda Harding, Iain Harris, Kevin Harris, Aidan Harte, Karen Huxtable, Ayub Khan, Allison Kirby, Wendy Kirk, Catriona MacIsaac, Julie Mckirdy, Catherine McNally, Kirsten MacQuarrie, Geoff Mills, Geoff Mitchell, Dawn Murray, Molly Newcomb, Tim O'Dell, Ann-Marie Parker, John Pateman, Jolanta Peters, Louise Rice, Valerie Samuel, Katharine Seymour, Silvia Spaltro, Pierrette Squires, David Stokes, Julian Taylor, Vickie Varley, Deborah Varenna, Toni Velikova, Dawn Winter, Lydia Wright, Keri Yearwood.

Thanks too to Dawn Beaumont and staff at Birmingham Library Service, the Reading Rooms teams at the British Library, the team at City of Sanctuary and staff at CILIP.

Also very special thanks to Andrew Scrogham and Stella Thebridge for reading and commenting on drafts of the book. I am also indebted to KS for inspiring me in the first place, just missing his input . . .

I couldn't have written this without continuing support from Robert, thank you.

Finally, my thanks to Pete Baker at Facet Publishing, whose support and encouragement – and unflappability! – throughout this process has been immense.

Abbreviations

ACET	Adult Continuing Education and Training
AGM	annual general meeting
ARAP	Afghan Relocations and Assistance Policy
BME	Black and Minority Ethnic
BTCDC	Barton and Tredworth Community Development Centre
CILIP	Chartered Institute of Librarians and Information Professionals (now CILIP: the Library and Information Association)
CILLA	Cooperative of Indic Language Library Authorities
CISSY	Campaign to Impede Sex Stereotyping in the Young
CLEAR	City Life Education and Action for Refugees
CTPSR	Centre for Trust, Peace and Social Relations
DCMS	Department for Digital, Culture, Media and Sport
DOTW	Doctors of The World
EAL	English as an Additional Language
EEA	European Economic Area
EHRC	Equality and Human Rights Commission
EIA	Equality Impact Assessment
EMAG	Ethnic Minority Achievement Grant
ESOL	English for Speakers of Other Languages
EU	European Union
EUSS	EU Settlement Scheme
FE	Further education
GARAS	Gloucestershire Association for Refugees and Asylum Seekers
GRT	Gypsy, Roma and Traveller
HMPS	Her Majesty's Prison Service
HSR	Hastings Supports Refugees
ICT	information and communications technology

IFLA	International Federation of Library Associations and Institutions
ILR	Indefinite Leave to Remain
JCWI	Joint Council for the Welfare of Immigrants
LAASLO	Local Authority Asylum Support Liaison Officer
LASER	London and South East Region library interlending bureau
LGBTQ+	lesbian, gay, bisexual, trans, queer/questioning (with + equalling all the other people within this umbrella term)
LSEE	London School of Economics and Political Science Research on South Eastern Europe
MBC	metropolitan borough council
MEAS	Minority Ethnic Achievement Service
MENA	Middle East and North Africa
NGO	nongovernmental organisations
NHS	National Health Service
NRPF	no recourse to public funds
NUI	National University of Ireland
ONS	Office for National Statistics
PEP	Political and Economic Planning
PHF	Paul Hamlyn Foundation
PLA	public library authority
PSED	Public Sector Equality Duty
RCO	Refugee Community Organisation
RNLI	Royal National Lifeboat Institution
RTÉ	Raidió Teilifís Éireann
SCONUL	Society of College, National and University Libraries
SEALS	SElection, Acquisition and Loan System
SGBV	sexual and gender-based violence
SLS	Schools Library Service
SOGICA	Sexual Orientation and Gender Identity Claims of Asylum
SWRLS	South Western Regional Library Service
TPL	Toronto Public Library
UKIP	United Kingdom Independence Party
UN	United Nations
UNESCO	United Nations Educational, Scientific and Cultural Organisation
UNHCR	United Nations High Commissioner for Refugees
WTYL	Welcome To Your Library
YOI	Her Majesty's Young Offender Institution

Introduction

This book is the first in a new series from Facet Publishing, 'Libraries and Social Justice'. Books in this series are intended to be introductions to each topic, looking briefly at the background, then at how libraries have responded in the past and, particularly, at what provision libraries – of all types – are making now. They will be practical guides, the key idea being that you can take away ideas to develop your own service provision, find out more about the topic, and discover sources should you wish to read more widely.

This title, *Libraries and Sanctuary: Supporting Refugees and Other New Arrivals*, sadly, could not be more timely. As I write, the after-effects of the humanitarian crisis in Afghanistan are still very much with us, and war has broken out as Russia invades Ukraine, causing millions of people to flee their country.

How can libraries (and library and information workers) respond? This book intends to provide some practical starting points.

The book begins by looking at terminology (many of the terms we use have considerable 'baggage') and at the range of reasons why people may be forced to flee their countries. This includes people being forced to flee conflict and persecution; people migrating to avoid changing climates, environmental degradation and the lack of work, education and other opportunities; and people coming to the UK for other reasons. New arrivals to the UK can include people seeking sanctuary (refugees, asylum seekers); people coming to the UK to work; international students; people coming to the UK for family reunion/reunification; returning UK citizens; and 'irregular' migrants – there will be more on all these groups later, and, in looking at this, it introduces aspects of political responses in the UK.

One of the common factors shared by the people included in this book is that they have all faced hostility, possibly because of the colour of their skin, or their language, or their supposed behaviour – or because of some new prejudice, such as anti-Chinese, anti-east and southeast Asian feelings and anti-Semitism in the wake of the coronavirus pandemic (see, for example: Parveen and Huynh, 2021; Qian, 2021; Dawson, 2021; Ng, 2021; Human Rights Watch, 2020; Detzler, 2020); and anti-Russian feelings following the invasion of Ukraine (Qureshi, 2022), what the Institute of Race Relations (and others) have called xenoracism (Fekete, 2001).

At the time of writing, there is renewed interest in terminology, particularly around the increasingly disliked term 'BAME' (Black, Asian and Minority Ethnic), and, interestingly, drawn from debates and a survey, Inc Arts (as part of their #BAMEOver campaign) have drafted A Statement for the UK which challenges a lot of shortcuts in describing people – and also suggest:

> Too many words? Want an easy acronym? A simple collective term?
> There isn't one. We choose not to be reduced to an inaccurate grouping.
> But what we have in common is that we are . . .
> 'People who experience racism'. This term will require you to then articulate who you are referring to, and may, depending on context, refer to Western Asian people, Irish people, Jewish people and others whose oppression is not captured by current terminology. Please use with awareness the phrase 'people who experience racism', and don't make it an acronym ever.
>
> (Inc Arts, 2020, 3– 4)

So, 'people who experience racism' is an additional term that I will use to describe whom we are talking about in this book.

It is clear that there is no easy term that encompasses all this. Having looked at terms used by other organisations, I have opted for 'global migration and mobility' as my overall description, with more specific terms as required – shorthanded to 'new arrivals'.

Chapter 2 then looks at the UK's responses to new arrivals from the 1950s onwards: has the UK always provided a welcome? And what effect has our past had on our responses today? This chapter highlights some particularly significant issues (such as the tension between welcome and hostility), institutional racism, the idea of the 'hostile environment', the Windrush scandal, and the impact of Brexit, before summarising what the position in the UK is today.

Chapter 3 asks 'What does any of this have to do with libraries?'. At a formal level, it includes policy responses, but also has personal accounts from three library workers, setting out the impact on their lives and work of being 'new arrivals' at some points in their lives.

Chapter 4 outlines the historical response from libraries, starting with an introduction to libraries' relationship with the idea of sanctuary, primarily since the 19th century, and then focusing on library initiatives since the 1940s, looking briefly at some of the work around welcoming new arrivals in the 1960s and 1970s, and highlighting significant pieces of work from the 1980s until now.

Chapter 5 outlines the barriers there are to the take-up of library services by new arrivals and begins to set out ways in which we can start to dismantle these.

Chapter 6 then looks at what libraries are doing today. This is set within the context of the Libraries of Sanctuary's key components, summarised as Learn, Embed and Share – these are used to shape this chapter. This is full of practical examples and case studies, very much the heart of the book.

Chapter 7 looks at what we can learn from elsewhere, drawing particularly on academic libraries' 'Project Welcome'; the ECHO Mobile Library; and work at Toronto Public Library.

Chapter 8 tries to draw conclusions from all this and looks at some ways forward.

This is supported by a number of appendices, including the main countries of origin of people seeking asylum; a note on immigration status; a note on funding (mainly historical, but with strong reminders of what we can learn from the past); a brief look at the supply of library materials (again mostly historical); a suggested training course outline; some sources of information about new arrivals locally and regionally; a note on effective communications; and an outline of what 'community cohesion' is and where the term came from.

From my experience of having written about, discussed and run courses on migration for many years, it is also clear that some people – and some people in libraries – are just not aware of the realities of life for people who have experienced global migration and mobility, who are seeking sanctuary in the UK and/or who have experienced racism. I will discuss this later, particularly in the section of the book that looks at the current migration position in the UK.

Finally, throughout the book, I have referred to 'library staff' – by that I mean all people involved with libraries, including paid staff at all levels and volunteers.

1

Definitions and Scope of the Book: When We Talk About 'Refugees and Other New Arrivals', Who Exactly Do We Mean?

Introduction

At the time of writing, much of the world is acknowledging (again) just what a grip racism (and political populism) have, and so it is also timely to confront a major issue around migration to the UK: are there some people who seem to be welcome and some who are not? Is this based solely on skin colour, or is there more to it? And does this level of welcome fluctuate?

Writers have acknowledged the perception that some people are seen as 'Good Immigrants' (i.e. those who seem to fit in) (see, for example: Hirsch, 2018; Shukla, 2017) – what makes some new arrivals 'good' and others not? New arrivals from Hong Kong are an example.[1] As journalist Jeevan Vasagar argues, the view of them is partly based on stereotypes:

> Immigration has always been a contentious issue in Britain. So why, as the UK opens a path to citizenship for millions of Hong Kong residents, is it different this time?
>
> Hong Kong Chinese are seen as a model minority, successors to the status of Ugandan Asians: a 'thrifty', 'entrepreneurial' and 'family-oriented' community who will skimp to send their children to private schools and boost Britain's economic fortunes, while quietly demonstrating that other ethnic minorities could be equally successful if they worked a little harder.
>
> (Vasagar, 2021)

We have seen this even more clearly with the welcome offered by the UK – albeit haphazardly – to people fleeing Ukraine, yet people seeking sanctuary from other countries are not provided with the same level of support (see for example Sajjad, 2022).

In addition, the perception of refugees is often very limited and/or stereotyped: '. . . everything made about refugees is by someone else and they are represented in offensive ways. Either refugees are criminals or saints. There is no mention of the challenges people go through, things aren't black and white.' (Mračević, 2020)

Refugees and other new arrivals – seeking sanctuary

Introduction

People have migrated – for a variety of reasons – ever since the development of the earliest societies. However, the concept of 'asylum' (helping people to seek refuge and offering them protection) developed more recently, originally as a religious obligation, but later taken on by nation states (Wikipedia, 2021c; Lock, 2020; Asylum Insight, 2016).

Historical background

After the end of World War 1 (1914–18):

> . . . the international community steadily assembled a set of guidelines, laws and conventions to ensure the adequate treatment of refugees and protect their human rights. The process began under the League of Nations in 1921.
>
> (United Nations High Commissioner for Refugees, 2011, 1)

There were further efforts to clarify the position of people fleeing for their lives after World War 2:

> In July 1951, a diplomatic conference in Geneva adopted the Convention relating to the Status of Refugees ('1951 Convention'), which was later amended by the 1967 Protocol. These documents clearly spell out who is a refugee and the kind of legal protection, other assistance and social rights a refugee is entitled to receive. It also defines a refugee's obligations to host countries and specifies certain categories of people, such as war criminals, who do not qualify for refugee status. Initially, the 1951 Convention was more or less limited to protecting European refugees in the aftermath of World War II, but the 1967 Protocol expanded its scope as the problem of displacement spread around the world.
>
> (United Nations High Commissioner for Refugees, 2011, 1)

Current position

At the present time, around the world, more people than ever are being forced to flee to seek safety and sanctuary elsewhere.

Many of these people would be covered by the formal United Nations Convention definition of a refugee – a person who has '. . . a well-founded fear of being persecuted for reasons of race, religion, nationality, membership of a particular social group or political opinion . . .' (Refugee Council, 2020).

However, there are also people seeking safety and sanctuary for other reasons, including:

- changing climates and environmental degradation
- lack of work, education and other opportunities
- their sexuality and/or gender identity.

Terminology – and the problems with binary definitions

City of Sanctuary[2] recommend using the term 'people seeking sanctuary' rather than defining people by their immigration status. This is a positive, useful point; however, to understand more about what people in different categories face, we are going to look here at the terms and how they define people's status, as this has an impact on what services they require and how able they are to access them, as well as some of the attitudes taken towards them.

This issue is explored further in Rebecca Hamlin's book, *Crossing* (Hamlin, 2021), in which she argues that we often oversimplify things by using binary divisions, for example (in relation to border crossing) safe/dangerous, planned/spontaneous, desirable/threatening, legal/illegal, deserving/undeserving, genuine/fraudulent, citizen/alien . . . and migrant/refugee:

> If we look closely at migration, we see that people with multiple and various motivations use the same routes and defy categorization at every turn. To be sure, some border crossers are totally forced and some are purely voluntary, some are solely economically motivated and some are exclusively politically motivated, some may be morally deserving of assistance and some may not be. But these distinctions fall along continua and elude clear-cut binaries.
>
> (Hamlin, 2021, 3)

Rebecca Hamlin argues that this leads to making false assumptions, and she highlights three:

> Refugees and migrants have distinct and distinguishable motivations for crossing borders (p. 9)

4 LIBRARIES AND SANCTUARY

> Refugees are the neediest among the world's border crossers (p. 13)
> True refugees are rare (p. 16)

These oversimplifications in turn lead to further issues – as an example:

> So, people who cross borders to save themselves from starvation, for example, are sometimes labeled 'survival migrants' to whom very little is owed . . . (p. 4)

Here, Rebecca Hamlin has drawn on work by political scientist Alexander Betts, who has questioned the existing definitions:

> In the context of the changing nature of forced displacement, who should have an entitlement to cross an international border and seek asylum? Given that the refugee regime was a product of its time and mainly provides protection to only a narrow group of people fleeing targeted persecution, how can we conceptualize the broader category of people who today cross an international border and are in need of protection because of serious human rights deprivations? If 'refugee' is a legal-institutional category defined by state practice, how can we stand apart from that and render visible the situation of the many millions of people crossing borders in failed and fragile states such as Zimbabwe, Democratic Republic of Congo, and Somalia, people who are often in desperate need of protection and yet frequently fall outside the refugee framework? Should these people also be entitled to asylum?
>
> (Betts, 2013, 10)

Because of these wider issues (environmental change; food insecurity; state fragility), Alexander Betts has argued that we need a new term, 'survival migration':

> This book therefore chooses to adopt a new term for the broader category of people who should have a normative entitlement to asylum based on human rights grounds. It does so in order to render visible a population that is not currently recognized as refugees within the dominant interpretation of a refugee in international law, and yet are outside their country of origin because of a very serious threshold of human rights deprivations.
>
> (Betts, 2013, 22)

Other writers have also questioned the logic of having a binary approach, for example HOPE not Hate's Joe Mulhall:

The reasons that people make the journey are extremely complex. Overwhelmingly, though, the primary 'push factors' are conflict and economic migration. The latter is often greeted with scepticism in Europe, framing these migrant stories as a simple economic 'choice', yet the truth is usually more complicated, as Jusselme from the [UN's International Organisation for Migration] explains: 'It is indeed a choice, but within your economic migration, what part is a choice and what part is you being forced to actually move?'

(Mulhall, 2021, 256)

At the same time, it is vital that the political background to migration is not lost (or hidden), otherwise the result may be a depoliticised narrative (Sergi, 2021). In a piece written in February 2022, researcher Seb Rumsby argued that migration was a result of global inequality:

So if we really want to reduce migration, we must treat it as an inevitable by-product of inequality and address the root causes – instead of simply blaming smugglers or washing our hands of the migrants' plight.

(Rumsby, 2022)

It is worth beginning by also briefly considering 'sanctuary'. 'Sanctuary is struggle' is how Alison Phipps[3] powerfully described it in her keynote presentation (Phipps, 2020) on the first day of the Universities of Sanctuary Conference 2020 – she went on to talk about sanctuary being both inside ourselves (finding a place of safety) and within our institutions (which may be a struggle to find). If anyone had a view that sanctuary is somehow cosy, this talk changed minds.[4]

The next section of this chapter looks at some of the key definitions.

Refugees and asylum seekers

According to the United Nations High Commissioner for Refugees, a refugee is:

A person who owing to a well-founded fear of being persecuted for reasons of race, religion, nationality, membership of a particular social group or political opinion, is outside the country of his [sic] nationality and is unable or, owing to such fear, is unwilling to avail himself [sic] of the protection of that country; or who, not having a nationality and being outside the country of his [sic] former habitual residence as a result of such events, is unable or, owing to such fear, is unwilling to return to it.

(Refugee Council, 2020)[5]

6 LIBRARIES AND SANCTUARY

A person seeking asylum is:

> A person who has left their country of origin and formally applied for asylum in another country but whose application has not yet been concluded.
>
> (Refugee Council, 2020)

However, in the UK:

> . . . a person becomes a refugee when government agrees that an individual who has applied for asylum meets the definition in the Refugee Convention[:] they will 'recognise' that person as a refugee and issue them with refugee status documentation. Usually refugees in the UK are given five years' leave to remain as a refugee. They must then must apply for further leave, although their status as a refugee is not limited to five years.
>
> (Refugee Council, 2020)

At the time of writing, there is continued discussion around accepting people seeking asylum in the UK; as Refugee Action emphasises:

> The right to seek asylum is a legal right we all share. It isn't illegal to seek asylum, because seeking asylum is a legal process. It also isn't illegal to be refused asylum – it just means you haven't been able to meet the very strict criteria to prove your need for protection as a refugee.
>
> (Refugee Action, 2016)

However:

> . . . there is no obligation on refugees to claim asylum in the first safe country they reach, although many in fact do. The UK receives a tiny number of refugees compared to other countries in the EU and beyond. There are multiple reasons why refugees might want to move on from refugee camps or travel to find family members or better prospects. If they do so, and would face a well founded fear of being persecuted in their home country, they are still refugees.
>
> (Yeo, 2019)

There is information about the main countries from where people claim asylum in Appendix 1 and on the different levels of immigration status in Appendix 2.

DEFINITIONS AND SCOPE OF THE BOOK   7

Refugee resettlement programmes

> Resettlement is the transfer of refugees from an asylum country to another State that has agreed to admit them and ultimately grant them permanent settlement.
>
> (United Nations High Commissioner for Refugees, 2020)

> Unlike asylum seekers, who can apply for asylum only in the UK, resettled refugees are identified abroad by the UN, and then transferred to the UK.
>
> (Walsh, 2021, 3)

In the period 1 January 2010 to 31 December 2020 some 29,500 refugees were resettled in the UK:

> . . . 75% were citizens of Middle Eastern countries, and 18% were citizens of sub-Saharan African countries. Most were nationals of Syria: 68%.
>
> (Walsh, 2021, 13)

However, the humanitarian crisis in Afghanistan from August 2021 onwards also meant that there were calls for a new resettlement route to be agreed for Afghans who have worked for British forces[6] – even though the UK's record on taking Afghan refugees is variable, as Open Democracy claim that: 'The Home Office has rejected at least 76 Afghan nationals' requests for asylum in 2021 alone – including ten women and a girl' (Williams, 2021).

There has been considerable discussion about the terms under which Afghan refugees are able to enter the UK. According to BBC News coverage, the then Foreign Secretary, Dominic Raab, did not confirm how many Afghan refugees would be able to come to the UK but said the UK was 'a big-hearted nation' (Morton, 2021). However, this statement has been criticised, for example by journalist Amelia Gentleman, who said that:

> This is not a picture which many Afghan asylum seekers in the UK will recognise. Over the past 20 years, the Home Office has gone to extreme lengths to return thousands back to the country which they had risked their lives to flee.
>
> British officials have faced repeated criticism from international refugee organisations for the frequency with which young Afghan asylum seekers have been denied formal refugee status when they turn 18, despite having spent large parts of their childhood in the UK; many have subsequently been forcibly returned to the country they left years earlier.
>
> (Gentleman, 2021b)

8 LIBRARIES AND SANCTUARY

At the time of writing, changes to these lifelines for Afghan refugees were being made regularly: for example, in Dec 2021, further changes to immigration rules were announced, which:

> . . . narrow the criteria for being accepted onto the ARAP scheme, and are retrospective. In other words, they apply to all decisions made after 16:00 on 14 December 2021. As a result, people who were advised by UK government officials (sometimes very highly placed) to make ARAP applications, and reassured that they should qualify, may not now be eligible – even if they have already lodged that application.
>
> (Pinder, 2021)[7]

To conclude, here are the words of journalist Akhtar Mohammad Makoii:

> I have made a career reporting on war, but what I always wanted to report on was peace. Peace is an emotional word for every Afghan; we have no sense of how it would actually look. It is in every Afghan's destiny to witness war. A deadly guarantee to every generation.
>
> (Makoii, 2021)

Since February 2022, the conflict in Ukraine (after Russian forces invaded the country) has dominated the news. By the end of March 2022, some 4.1 million people have left Ukraine, and an estimated 6.5 million people have been displaced within the country (Wikipedia, 2022a). A similar situation with regard to people seeking sanctuary appears to exist, with, as *Guardian* journalist Simon Jenkins described it, the refugees encountering the hostile environment:

> When the surge began Johnson won headlines by promising to let in 200,000 'eligible' Ukrainians. It turned out that 'eligible' meant only those with direct, immediate relatives, though even this didn't include the parents of anyone over 18. Only after an eruption in the House of Commons did Johnson make what he presented as a grand concession, to include grandparents. By the weekend it emerged that of 5,535 laboriously completed online applications, just 50 had been granted. More than 1000 have already entered the much smaller Republic of Ireland.
>
> (Jenkins, 2022)

International agreements
The United Nations Refugee Convention

The UK is a signatory to the 1951 United Nations Refugee Convention and also to the amendments made via the 1967 Protocol (United Nations High Commissioner for Refugees, n.d.-b).

> Initially, the 1951 Convention was more or less limited to protecting European refugees in the aftermath of World War II, but the 1967 Protocol expanded its scope as the problem of displacement spread around the world.
>
> (United Nations High Commissioner for Refugees, 2011, 1)

The UNHCR states that:

> The core principle is non-refoulement, which asserts that a refugee should not be returned to a country where they face serious threats to their life or freedom. This is now considered a rule of customary international law.
>
> (United Nations High Commissioner for Refugees, n.d.-a)

Therefore, in terms of being a signatory to the Convention:

> When a State accedes to the 1951 Convention:
> - it demonstrates its commitment to treating refugees in accordance with internationally recognized legal and humanitarian standards;
> - it gives refugees a possibility to find safety;
> - it helps to avoid friction between States over refugee questions. Granting asylum is a peaceful, humanitarian and legal act rather than a hostile gesture, and should be understood by the refugee's country of origin as such;
> - it demonstrates its willingness to share the responsibility for protecting refugees; and it helps UNHCR to mobilize international support for the protection of refugees.
>
> (United Nations High Commissioner for Refugees, 2011, 7)

Rebecca Hamlin (whose work has been cited earlier) also reminds us that the United Nations Refugee Convention was very much a product of its time and place, but has not necessarily been adopted by all nations in the Global South, which '. . . is often characterized by scholars and advocates in the North as noncompliance by Global South states . . . Many host states or adjacent states to conflict and displacement are not signatories to the Refugee Convention, notably Lebanon, Jordan, Iraq, Saudi Arabia, India, Pakistan, Indonesia, Malaysia, and Thailand.' (Hamlin, 2021, 95)

10 LIBRARIES AND SANCTUARY

She describes the UN Convention as being viewed as part of the Global North's colonial legacy and reminds us that the South has also created refugee Conventions, which is why I am including a short introduction to these here.

Organisation of African Unity Convention

The Organisation of African Unity (OAU)[8] was established in 1963 (and was succeeded by the African Union in 2002).

In 1969, the OAU drew up its Convention[9] which came into force on 20 June 1974. According to the UNHCR:

> The OAU Convention is a regional complement to the 1951 United Nations Convention. It broadens the definition of a refugee and offers legal protection to a wider category of people in response to the growing refugee problem in the continent. The wider definition has made it possible for the Convention to be applicable to groups of refugees as well as to individual refugees. This significant distinction will be appreciated when formal aspects or recognition of refugee status on an individual or collective basis are being considered . . .
>
> Through the Convention the Member States of the OAU undertake not to reject refugees at the frontier, return or expel them to the country of origin.
>
> (United Nations High Commissioner for Refugees, 1992)

Colloquium on the International Protection of Refugees in Central America, Mexico and Panama: Cartagena Declaration

Similarly, in Latin America, key stakeholders met in Cartagena de Indias, Colombia, in November 1984 to discuss the international protection of refugees:

> The meeting, which grew from the recognition that the region lacked the institutional infrastructure and legal norms to deal with such crises, resulted in the Cartagena Declaration on Refugees, hailed by experts as a progressive milestone in refugee-protection law. The declaration established a protection framework that the region continues to employ today, and which several countries have enshrined in law.
>
> (Esthimer, 2016)

The key introduction via the Declaration[10] was:

> . . . the definition or concept of a refugee to be recommended for use in the region is one which, in addition to containing the elements of the 1951 Convention and

the 1967 Protocol, includes among refugees persons who have fled their country because their lives, safety or freedom have been threatened by generalized violence, foreign aggression, internal conflicts, massive violation of human rights or other circumstances which have seriously disturbed public order.

(United Nations High Commissioner for Refugees, 1984, 36)

Other reasons for seeking safety and sanctuary
Changing climates and environmental degradation
As political ecologist Scott Leatham describes it:

> As impacts have increased, such as in droughts and floods, fires and crop failures, they have fallen unequally across the world, hitting the poorest hardest. Those least responsible, with the fewest resources to adapt or build back, are in the most immediate danger.

(Leatham, 2020, 26)

Dina Ionesco (Head of the Migration, Environment and Climate Change Division at IOM, the UN Migration Agency) reports:

> In 2018 alone, 17.2 million new displacements associated with disasters in 148 countries and territories were recorded [Internal Displacement Monitoring Centre] and drought displaced 764,000 people in Somalia, Afghanistan and several other countries . . .
> Climate migrants have been invisible for many years on the migration and climate debates. Our work at IOM has been focused for over 10 years on bringing climatic and environmental factors to the light and on building a body of evidence proving that climate change affects – directly and indirectly – human mobility.

(Ionesco, 2019)

In February 2022, the most recent Intergovernmental Panel on Climate Change report was published (IPCC, 2022a). It warned that:

> Human-induced climate change is causing dangerous and widespread disruption in nature and affecting the lives of billions of people around the world, despite efforts to reduce the risks. People and ecosystems least able to cope are being hardest hit . . .

(IPCC, 2022b)

In September 2021, City of Sanctuary noted that:

> Since 2008, weather-related hazards have displaced an average of 41 people every minute, and this humanitarian crisis is only going to deepen as the climate breaks down further.
>
> (City of Sanctuary UK, 2021)

At the current pace of tackling the climate emergency, then, we are likely to be seeing more and more environmentally driven migration.

Lack of work, education and other opportunities

Migration as a result of the lack of work and education (and other opportunities) is of growing significance. As a 2021 International Labour Organisation report states: 'International migrant workers constitute nearly 5 per cent of the global labour force and are an integral part of the world economy.' (International Labour Organisation, 2021, 5). Importantly: 'In destination countries with aging populations, their contribution can be important in meeting labour shortages, rejuvenating the labour force and supporting the social security system' (p. 16).

There is also evidence that a lack of educational opportunities – or a desire to seek educational improvement and better job prospects – may also lead people to migrate (see, for example, Browne, 2017). As the Kino Border Initiative[11] says on its website: 'Lack of access to quality education is a root cause of poverty and economic hardship which in turn drive people to choose migration as a means of seeking job opportunities and improving their lives' (Kino Border Initiative, 2018).

Poverty is explored further by Oluwayemisi Adeleke (a researcher based at Redeemer's University, Nigeria) who writes that:

> In 2019, 70% of the world poor was in Africa, and this has increased from 50% five years ago, with Nigeria being the first on the list. This is also supported by the world bank poverty report, which states that Nigeria has overtaken India, a country with a population seven times larger than Nigeria, as the country with the most extreme poor people in the world in the year[s] 2018 and 2019. Nigeria had the largest extreme poverty population, whereby 86.9 million Nigerians are now living in extreme poverty and this represents nearly 50% of its estimated 180 million population . . .
>
> (Adeleke, 2021, 2)

Migration because of the lack of work and education (and other opportunities) and because of poverty seems also likely to grow, especially where these are linked closely to environmental disaster.

Sexuality and/or gender identity

People who identify as LGBTQ+ face discrimination, both in their home country and, often, when they flee abroad. For example:

> In July 2020, researchers from the University of Sussex found a pervasive 'culture of disbelief' against LGBT+ asylum seekers both in the UK and across Europe. It followed a 2019 revelation that the UK had refused at least 3,100 people who had fled nations where being queer is illegal, and were seeking asylum on this basis.
>
> LGBT+ people seeking asylum have faced mockery and derision during Home Office processes, been told they 'aren't gay enough' to warrant asylum or couldn't possibly be lesbian because they are also Christian.
>
> (Smith, 2021)

Jane Traies highlighted some of these issues in her collection of 'refugee stories' – as she said in the introduction:

> If [a woman who has fled from persecution in her home country] is claiming asylum on the grounds of her sexual orientation, she will be required to prove to the British authorities that she is, indeed, a lesbian . . .
>
> How can anyone 'prove' their sexual orientation? LGBTQ+ people are just as diverse as the rest of the population . . . Yet some of the women whose stories appear in this book have been told by the Home Office that they 'don't look like' lesbians.
>
> (Traies, 2021, 13–14)

Many people also face enormous legal battles, for example to convince UK courts that their asylum claims are valid (see, for example: Baldwin, 2021; Davies, 2021).

Asylos[12] documents such cases, including the following:

> Scared of returning to Serbia and facing renewed assault, J filed an asylum application in the UK, but the British authorities denied his asylum application on several grounds. Firstly, and fundamentally, the Home Office questioned whether J was actually homosexual. Secondly, they pointed to alleged improvements in the treatment of the LGBTQ+ community in Serbian society: Serbia had its first openly gay prime minister and the Serbian government had

recently tolerated a Gay Pride event in Belgrade. According [to] the Home Office's evidence, the climate for gay individuals in Serbia was better than ever.

(Pohl, 2019)

One of Jane Traies's interviewees, Chipo, described her experience:

I had my interview at the Home Office. It was six or seven hours long. They wanted to know everything: 'When did you start to feel like a lesbian? When did you start to feel those feelings? How did you live?' everything that I went through, my marriage, everything. It felt just horrible. And then the court . . .

They sent a refusal. The reason for the refusal was that they didn't believe I was a lesbian. That was the main argument, that I was not a lesbian.

(Traies, 2021, 67)

Trans people seeking sanctuary face additional issues, as 'Nisha's story' shows:

She knew she could not return to India. Her family had made violent threats against her, and she was scared about what would happen if she went back. She would also not have access to the medical care she needed. Instead, Nisha claimed asylum. She was released from detention but claiming asylum was not a quick or easy process for her.

Nisha lived on her friends' sofa for 2 years while she waited for her asylum decision. When her initial claim was refused, she then went through the process of appeal. This time was very difficult for Nisha, she says: 'I had to revert back to where I was. I couldn't work. I had to hide my identity, because my friends who are helping if they knew my trans identity, they would not help me.'

When Nisha's appeal was dismissed by the Tribunal, she was sent back to detention, 'the second time I got detained,' Nisha says 'I suffered a lot.' Nisha describes detention as 'horrible,' categorising her experience in detention as both unsafe and dangerous.

Similar to many other trans people entering detention, the Home Office failed to recognise Nisha's correct gender identity and she was detained in a male facility. Research by Rainbow Migration and Stonewall has found that LGBTQI+, and particularly trans people, face systematic discrimination, harassment and violence in detention, both from staff and other detainees. This was true for Nisha too, Nisha says that for trans people 'when you are in detention centres, you are always vulnerable'.

(Rainbow Migration, n.d.)

However, some LGBTQ+ people are now talking about this, publishing and recording their life stories, for example artist Youcef Hadjazi:

> Being a queer person, a migrant from the age of eight and of Muslim background are all basepoints that almost dictate the way I artistically work, particularly on a project like Queer Journeys. I arrived in the UK in 2013 from Kuwait, where I grew up, after (almost) fleeing Algeria with my family and its socioeconomic struggles. Having come from two equally homophobic countries, I thought I could finally live my sexuality with less fear, prejudice and repression. However, in parallel, I had forgotten I had arrived in a country, hypothetically, tens if not hundreds of years ahead of where I came from in terms of sexual tolerance, and hardly had any clue as to how I would initiate defining my sexuality and gender.
>
> (Hadjazi, 2021)

and, fortunately, some of these horrendous stories do achieve a happy ending – although Victor's experience is not likely to become the norm within a system that insists on an unrealistic burden of proof with regard to someone's sexuality:

> Having come from a well-off family and launching his own business after studying mechanical engineering at university, Victor thought his life was set.
>
> But growing up in Nigeria, where homosexuality is a crime, and with a strict religious family who believe it is a sin, he was left with no alternative.
>
> Victor endured conversion therapy, exorcisms, and a brush with death before he sought UK asylum in 2017 with the hope of living life freely as a gay man. But his struggles were far from over and he became homeless within two months.
>
> Fast-forward four years and Victor is now happily married living with his husband in Birmingham and fulfilled in his 'wonderful' work at Coventry Refugee and Migrant Centre.
>
> (Menendez, 2021)

Being a Gypsy, Roma or Traveller[13]

As Schools of Sanctuary state:

> ... whilst many Gypsies, Roma and Travellers are from the UK, some flee to the UK as refuge from policies and community maltreatment even worse than those they face [in] the UK. The Roma in particular, are often very poorly treated in a variety of countries in Europe and come to the UK to escape the daily discrimination they experience there. Whilst they may not be arriving in the UK

as asylum-seekers or refugees (at least pre-Brexit), that does not mean they are any less seeking sanctuary.

(Schools of Sanctuary, 2021)

Drawing on a number of pieces of research (European Union Agency for Fundamental Rights, 2016; Brown et al., 2016; Craig, 2011; Poole and Adamson, 2008), Migration Yorkshire argue that the reasons for Roma migration to the UK are complex, '. . . placed somewhere "between forced and voluntary" . . . and that their needs are more akin to those of people seeking sanctuary' (Jamroz, 2018, 9).

More recent research (Anti-Bullying Alliance and Families and Travellers Friends, 2020) also illustrated just how discriminated against they are, backed up by evidence from the House of Commons Women and Equalities Committee:

> Gypsy, Roma and Traveller people have the worst outcomes of any ethnic group across a huge range of areas, including education, health, employment, criminal justice and hate crime.
>
> (House of Commons. Women and Equalities Committee, 2019, 3)

Irregular migrants

According to The Migration Observatory:

> In the UK, there is no single legal or accepted definition of an 'irregular migrant', also known as an 'unauthorised', 'undocumented', 'non-registered', or 'illegal' immigrant. However, a definition in common usage is a person who is in the UK without a valid residence permit.
>
> (Walsh, 2020a, 3)

In terms of 'illegal immigration':

> Irregular migration is often referred to as illegal immigration. The use of the term illegal in this context is considered contentious, for two reasons. First, illegal immigration can suggest the breaching of criminal laws. In some countries, breaching immigration laws is an administrative rather than criminal matter . . . However, in the UK it is a criminal offence knowingly to enter or remain in the country without authorisation . . . though prosecutions are rare.
>
> The second objection is to the related term illegal immigrant, which is argued to be degrading because it implies that people can be illegal. Most international organisations, including the United Nations and the International Organization for Migration, specifically avoid the terms illegal immigration and illegal

immigrant for this reason, instead preferring irregular immigration and irregular migrant. The adjectives unauthorised and undocumented are also used to refer to the same phenomenon of illegal immigration, especially by researchers.

(Walsh, 2020a, 2)

There are also, according to The Migration Observatory, four main ways in which a person can become an irregular migrant:

1 Enter the UK regularly and breach the conditions upon which entry or stay was granted, such as by visa overstaying, doing work that is not permitted, or due to a criminal conviction.
2 Enter the UK irregularly or through deception, such as using forged documents or lying about the purpose of entry.
3 Do not leave the country after an application for asylum has been rejected and all rights of appeal exhausted.
4 Be born in the UK to parents who are irregular migrants, because the UK does not have birthright citizenship. (Some of these children can acquire citizenship directly. This category is included here because they are often included in estimates of the UK's irregular population).

(Walsh, 2020a, 5)

Unaccompanied children and young people

According to research by CoramBAAF:[14]

Most unaccompanied children are aged 15 or over, but many are younger. Most are boys. They come from many different countries – the particular mix of countries at any given time reflects the world's trouble spots. In recent years, most have come from Afghanistan, Iran, Eritrea, Sudan and Vietnam.

(Fursland and Lowe, 2020, 2)

CoramBAAF define these young people in the following way:

The children are 'unaccompanied' because they are under the age of 18 and there is no one with legal responsibility for them in the UK when they arrive. However, this does not necessarily mean that they travelled alone. Usually someone will have helped them to make the journey, perhaps an agent or someone posing as a member of the family . . .

Due to the circumstances in which they have been living, children and young people are, in many cases, in a poor physical state and suffering from emotional distress before they even begin their journey . . .

On arriving in the UK, the agent or other adult may deliver the child to a relative or some other contact or to a refugee organisation. However, in some cases – in spite of promises to the child's family – they may simply abandon the child to be discovered by the immigration authorities, police or local authority children's services.

(pp. 3– 4)

CoramBAAF quote Wellela, a 12-year-old Eritrean girl's reaction:

I am sure the man did not tell the people who paid him for our trip . . . that he would abandon us outside the Eritrean community centre once we got to London.

(p. 4)

Trafficking/modern slavery

In addition, there is increasing evidence of people being trafficked into the UK, often victims of modern slavery:

Modern slavery in the UK can take many forms, including forced sexual exploitation, domestic slavery or forced labour on farms, in construction, shops, bars, nail bars, car washes or manufacturing.

Forced labour is the most common form of slavery in the UK, fuelled by a drive for cheap products and services, with little regard for the people behind them.

A growing form of slavery is trafficking into crime. In the UK, it's fuelled by the trafficking of primarily British children, forced into 'county lines' drug trafficking and trafficking of Vietnamese nationals forced to work in cannabis production.

(Anti-Slavery International, 2021)

As the UK National Crime Agency states:

Many victims have been trafficked from overseas – frequently from eastern Europe, south east Asia, and Africa – and their exploitation often begins en route. British victims tend to have fallen on difficult times, making them vulnerable to the lure of well-paid work complete with decent accommodation, which proves a cruel lie.

(National Crime Agency, n.d.)[15]

Obviously, it is impossible to be sure of the numbers involved[16] but:

Estimates suggest there may be tens of thousands or more people enslaved in the UK. To make this figure feel real, that would be about 600–700 people in forms of direct slavery in a large city or a county. In 2018, almost 7000 people presented themselves to the official source of help, the National Referral Mechanism, now run by the Home Office. It is widely agreed that this is just the tip of the iceberg and this number is increasing significantly every year. The number may be close to 10,000 for 2019. Many victims of slavery won't report their situation to the NRM, however, because they fear either being retrafficked or being deported.

(Craig, 2020)

This is echoed by Adam Hewitt (Hope for Justice):

Modern slavery is thought to be the world's third-largest criminal enterprise. It is a hidden crime, but the best estimates say there are 40 million people in forced labour, forced marriage, sexual exploitation and domestic servitude.

In the UK, there were 10,613 potential victims identified in 2020, but since most victims are hidden from sight, the actual figure is thought to be more than 100,000.

(Hewitt, 2021)

CoramBAAF have looked in particular at Vietnam:

In the case of many Vietnamese children and young people, they may have been brought to the UK by traffickers to work against their will. It is estimated that thousands of Vietnamese children are trafficked into Europe every year. Poverty in certain areas of the country, particularly rural areas, lack of political freedom, environmental changes and lack of safe, legal migration routes make children vulnerable to deceit by traffickers. At all stages of the journey, they may be subjected to neglect, forced labour and sexual exploitation.

(Fursland and Bond, 2020, 3)

There have also been allegations about the treatment of fruit-pickers on UK farms:

'It doesn't matter how you look at it, every day I am here I feel like a slave.'

A group of migrant workers from Barbados is speaking out about the abuses they faced on British strawberry farms. They report being forced to work long hours for less pay than they were promised and charged for poor and dirty accomodation [*sic*].

They came to the UK in June as part of the government-backed UK Farm Labour Programme, but now want to return home after facing horrendous working conditions.

(Freedom United, 2021)

The lifetime impact of seeking sanctuary

Finally, in terms of background, it is worth emphasising that, just because someone finds sanctuary, this does not mean that life is smooth thereafter. For example, the lifetime after-effects of migration, including the ongoing sense of displacement, are also movingly caught by the writer Angela Qian (who is based in New York):

> Once, a friend asked me: 'How good are you at passing?' – that is, passing as Chinese-Chinese, not Chinese American. I wanted to pass, but like the many Asian Americans who, like me, have tried to go back to the motherland and find a place there, I could never 'pass' for long.
>
> (Qian, 2021)

and in the interview between '. . . an Anonymous Immigrant who is an indigenous Moroccan and a displaced black student in Britain, and Rumana Hashem, a displaced sociologist and an unestablished academic in the UK':

> Anonymous fled from Morocco with a hope that he would get education when he comes in the UK. But his experience as a 'Black refugee' from Morocco is 'depressing and unacceptable'. Although he has received a permanent residence permit, recurrent race inequalities, cruel comments on the high streets in London, deprivation and difficulty in accessing higher education, exclusion at work, and experiences of health inequalities relating to 'race' in the British National Health System (NHS) have made him vulnerable. Six years on asylum, his search for a safe home, a suitable job, income, wellness and passion for higher education have not ended.
>
> Anonymous finds himself as someone 'too Afrikan to be a Black-British in the UK'. His experiences are un-heard by most people of Black and Asian Minority Ethnicity (BAME), because their past and his past do not match. For Anonymous there is a 'serious issue with British values', which many BAME members embrace, but it is one that Anonymous recurrently confronted since his arrival in the UK.
>
> (Anonymous Immigrant and Hashem, 2020, 20)

Other new arrivals

As I noted in the Introduction, as well as seeking sanctuary, people have always come to the UK for a range of other reasons, including for work; as international students; for family reunion/reunification; and as returning UK citizens – there will be more on these, as appropriate, further on in the book.

I am also including people who had moved to the UK from the Caribbean (although this really merits a book of its own) particularly because the grim outcomes of the hostile environment and the Windrush scandal make this necessary.

As City of Sanctuary say:

Welcome is for everyone, not just those who have fled war and persecution.
(Filipova-Rivers, 2021)

2
What Has Been the Response in the UK?

This book is concentrating on responses post-World War 2. However, it is important to note the obvious – that immigration (and emigration) are not new phenomena:

> All the rhetoric that seeks to depict modern immigration into Britain as a hazard, putting at risk a thousand-year way of life, plays false with the historical truth: Britain has always accommodated strangers. One of the reasons why it has been able to absorb so many overseas citizens in recent times is that people have been settling here since time began.
>
> (Winder, 2013, 10)

Indeed, there are dangers in assuming otherwise: as the Mayor's Commission on African and Asian Heritage[17] found, assuming that migration has been solely a post-World War 2 phenomenon gives a distorted picture of the make-up of the UK, and '. . . diminish[es] the long-term presence of Africans and Asians in the country.' (The Mayor's Commission on African and Asian Heritage, 2005, 65)

However, since World War 2, immigration has taken on a new focus. Much has been written elsewhere about the historical, legislative and social approaches to migration, as well as the large number of legislative changes made in recent years (see for example Girvan, 2018) and their impact on different aspects of UK society and the welcome for new arrivals (Calò et al., 2021). As just one example, the enormous volume of legislation and policy changes since 2007 was highlighted during debates on the Immigration Bill in 2015:

... Lib Dem spokesman Alistair Carmichael said there had been seven immigration bills in the last eight years and 45,000 changes to the immigration rules since Mrs May became home secretary in 2010, but decision making by border agencies did not seem to have improved.

(BBC News, 2015)[18]

Immigration and the UK – and has there always been a welcome?

Here we will look at this background very briefly.

1940s–1950s

Firstly, there is something of a rose-tinted view of the welcome that the UK offered in the past (especially in relation to refugees arriving during and just after World War 2). It is salutary to remember, for example, that the government refused Jewish immigration at the start of World War 2;[19] that 'After giving safe harbour to thousands of people fleeing Nazi persecution in Europe, the British government decided that some of them could be a threat – and locked all of them up.' (Parkin, 2022)[20]

There were some more positive notes, however: '. . . by the end of 1949 some 150,000 Polish soldiers and their dependents had settled in the UK. Further family members arrived in the early 1950s by which time over 250,000 Poles had turned to Britain to start a new life.' (Moss, 2022)

Although, in principle, people from all over the British Empire could arrive to live in the UK, this right was written into law in the 1948 British Nationality Act, whereby people living in countries that had been, or were still, under British rule had the status of British subjects or Commonwealth citizens (see Great Britain, 1948).

Following the invitation from the post-war UK Government to people in the Caribbean and the encouragement of people from India and Pakistan to come to the UK to work, by 1958 there were some 125,000 West Indians and 55,000 Indians and Pakistanis in the UK (Fryer, 1984, 372–3).[21]

However, despite the invitations and encouragement from Government,[22] there was a growing backlash against immigration (for example from some trade unionists) and increasing levels of racism, all of which culminated in riots in 1958[23] (in some cases, spurred on by the media).

1960s–1970s

As part of the aftermath to this, there were increasing calls for immigration control, and, despite some prominent people acknowledging what was really happening – 'The real problem is not black skins, but white prejudice' (Tom Driberg, Labour Party Chair, quoted in Fryer, 1984, 380) – the fight against racism was temporarily lost; as Peter Fryer describes it:

> Between 1958 and 1968 black settlers in Britain watched the racist tail wag the parliamentary dog. It was a sustained triumph of expediency over principle. Fearful of being outflanked by fascists and each other, fearful of losing votes and seats, Tory and Labour politicians progressively accommodated themselves to racism.
>
> (Fryer, 1984, 381)

In 1968, the situation was further inflamed by Enoch Powell, Conservative MP for Wolverhampton South West, who delivered a speech which became known as the 'rivers of blood' speech,[24] '. . . suggesting that continued immigration and the enshrining of race equality legislation might cause future violence and unrest in the UK' (Runnymede Trust, n.d.-b).

This was despite the introduction of legislation intended to stop overt racism: the Race Relations Act 1965 '. . . banned racial discrimination in public places and made the promotion of hatred on the grounds of "colour, race, or ethnic or national origins" an offence'; this was followed by the Race Relations Act 1968 '. . . which made unlawful acts of discrimination within employment, housing and advertising.' (UK Parliament, 2021)

The 1960s and early 1970s also saw a flurry of legislation which was intended to curb further immigration, for example:

- The Commonwealth Immigrants Act 1962, which, although described by the then Labour Party leader, Hugh Gaitskell, as a 'miserable, shameful, shabby Bill' (Hansard, 1961), became law in 1962 and restricted the admission of Commonwealth settlers to those issued with employment vouchers.[25] Peter Fryer described it as '. . . a piece of discriminatory legislation . . . ' (Fryer, 1984, 383)
- The 1965 White Paper on Immigration from the Commonwealth, which followed on from the 1964 general election, where a candidate fought an openly racist campaign – see for example 'Britain's most racist election: the story of Smethwick, 50 years on' (Jeffries, 2014) – and which assumed that there was a problem with the number of people arriving from the Commonwealth.
- The revised Commonwealth Immigrants Act 1968, which, according to the Runnymede Trust '. . . amended sections of the Commonwealth Immigration Act 1962 [and] subjected all holders of UK passports to immigration controls unless they, their parents or a grandparent had

been born, adopted or naturalised in the United Kingdom.' This was in response to '. . . thousands of Kenyan Asians arriving in the UK to flee political turmoil.' (Runnymede Trust, n.d.-a)

- The Immigration Act 1971 which '. . . replaced employment vouchers with work permits, allowing only temporary residence. "Patrials" (those with close UK associations) were exempted from the Act. It also tightened the immigration control administration and made some provision for assisting voluntary repatriation.' (The National Archives, n.d.-a)[26]

On the same day as this Act came into force, 1 January 1973, the UK also joined the European Economic Community (EEC). This was to have a significant impact in all sorts of ways. As Wikipedia describes it:

> At the same time that immigration restrictions were confirmed for Commonwealth citizens (Africa, Asia, Caribbean, America's [sic] and Pacific) with a traditional allegiance to Britain, a new category of privilege was created for the European nationals who had formed the bulk of the work of the Immigrations Service for the preceding 50 years. This represented a dramatic racial exclusion in Freedom of Movement from one that was previously ethnically diverse that included nations from Africa, Asia, America's [sic], Caribbean and Pacific to white only European nations. This was a form of structural racism [which] involved the normalization and legitimization of an array of dynamics (historical, cultural, institutional and interpersonal), that routinely advantage white nations while producing cumulative and chronic adverse outcomes for people of non-white nations.
>
> (Wikipedia, 2021a)

In addition to legislative changes, new policies were also introduced in the 1960s and 1970s. One of these, for example, was 'bussing': 'Eleven Local Area Authorities (LEAs) decided there should be no more than 30% of immigrants at any one school. . . . It meant once that quota was reached, children were taken elsewhere.' (BBC News, 2017)

The impact of this was noted in 2021 by author Suhaiymah Manzoor-Khan: 'Three of the 11 councils that adopted this policy – Bradford, Huddersfield and Halifax – were in Yorkshire. Paraded as an "integration" project, the buses were soon termed "Paki buses" by local people, and children were taught in segregated sections of buildings.' She goes on to argue that: 'This exemplifies the paradoxical message that haunts us to this day: while we order you to integrate, we will continue to label you and punish you as outsiders.' (Manzoor-Khan, 2021)

However, it is also important to note that there was growing recognition in the 1970s that 'racial disadvantage' (and racism) was an issue. Following the production of a series of research reports by PEP[27] (Smith, 1974; 1975; 1976; McIntosh, 1974)[28] the findings were brought together in a ground-breaking book, *Racial Disadvantage in Britain* (Smith, 1977). This brought together valuable information about communities in the UK; identified discrimination in, for example, housing, education and employment; and also had some clear words of warning:

> Of course, the stereotyped thinking, the hostile and destructive tendencies which are capable of sustaining a racial conflict do exist, and can be manipulated by demagogues and political parties. The objective must be to prevent that from happening, and to allow the co-existent repertoire of constructive and tolerant attitudes to assert themselves. If we look after the facts, the attitudes will look after themselves.

> (Smith, 1977, 330)

Looking at this book some 45 years later, it is a reminder of just how much we knew then – and how much we have ignored.

1980s to date

From 1981 onwards, there was a series of enlargements of the EEC/EU. These included:

- 1981, which added Greece
- 1986, which added Spain and Portugal
- 1995, which added Austria, Finland and Sweden
- 2004, which added Cyprus, Czech Republic, Estonia, Hungary, Latvia, Lithuania, Malta, Poland, Slovakia, Slovenia
- 2007, which added Bulgaria, Romania
- 2013, which added Croatia.

Political concerns over numbers were mounting, and the Government passed the Immigration Act 2014. The reasons for introducing this Act were made very clear in a Home Office Factsheet (which also reiterated some of the same political tropes that have run through these debates):

> As things stand, it is too easy for people to live and work in the UK illegally and take advantage of our public services. The appeals system is like a never-ending game of snakes and ladders, with almost 70,000 appeals heard every year. The

winners are foreign criminals and immigration lawyers – while the losers are the victims of these crimes and the public. It is too difficult to get rid of people with no right to be here.

This is not fair to the British public and it is not fair to legitimate migrants who want to come and contribute to our society and economy.

(Home Office, 2013, 1)

The 2014 Act was subsequently strengthened and extended by the Immigration Act 2016:

These two Acts make a wide range of third parties – including employers, bank employees, marriage registrars, the Driver and Vehicle Licensing Agency (DVLA) and landlords – responsible for conducting immigration status checks, refusing people services/jobs/accommodation, and sharing migrants' data with the Home Office.

(Griffiths and Yeo, 2021, 6)

This is just a taste of the huge volume of legislation and responses to external events that have led us to the position we are currently in. This ambivalent position is very neatly summed up in a Scottish Refugee Council news story:

Too often the movement of people who have come to this country as refugees or asylum seekers is presented as exceptional, unprecedented, threatening and new. But the history of immigrants, refugees, asylum seekers and migrants *is* the history of Scotland, whether people stayed for a week or stayed forever. There is a parallel history of emigration running alongside this, and most of us will have experience of one, or both, within our own lives or those of our families.

Refugee history is the history of solidarity from local communities, campaigns to support newcomers and to fight against injustice. Refugee history is also the history of animosity from the settled population, histories of structural racism and discrimination, fear and loneliness.

And refugee history is not something that only belongs to the past. Every day in Scotland people arrive, leave, get their refugee status, receive refusals from the Home Office, get citizenship or decide that this is their home for good.

(Scottish Refugee Council, 2021, emphasis theirs)

Institutional racism

Since 1999, we have known – formally – that institutional racism exists in the UK. This topic deserves a book of its own but just needs to be noted here. A quick outline follows.

Stephen Lawrence was murdered on 22 April 1993 in an unprovoked racist knife attack in Eltham, South London. After some considerable delay, the then Home Secretary, Jack Straw, announced in 1997 the establishment of an inquiry into his death.

The Report of the Inquiry (MacPherson, 1999) found that there had been massive failings in the police investigations and was highly critical of the way in which Stephen Lawrence's family and friends had been treated. There were also significant findings about racism and institutional racism:

> The Macpherson report found that racism was an important factor in the failure of the Metropolitan police investigation into Stephen Lawrence's murder. It concluded that the problems it found amounted to 'institutional racism' and highlighted racism at both individual and institutional level . . .
>
> (Great Britain. Home Affairs Committee, 2021)[29]

This had a huge impact on the way that local authorities, for example, carried out their duties, and led to developments in library service provision (see below).

Issues around institutional racism continue to surface, perhaps under the additional spotlight of the Black Lives Matter movement: for example the Metropolitan Police is, at the time of writing, being highly criticised for the actions of some of its officers (see for example Dodd, 2022; Mortimer, 2022; End Violence Against Women, 2022).

Immigration and the UK – a summary of who is coming (and going)

Before looking further at some of the effects of these changes in legislation, it is worth just summarising the position (as far as we can). Clearly no country is static, and the UK has constant flows of people arriving and leaving, albeit that these have slowed with the arrival of COVID-19.

The latest published figures show that there were some 140.9 million passenger arrivals in the year ending March 2021, the majority of whom were returning UK residents. In addition to them and to people seeking sanctuary, these included people arriving for:

- **Work:** 'There were 205,528 work-related visas granted in the year ending September 2021 (including dependants). This was a 55% increase on the year ending September 2020, and 9% higher than in the year ending September 2019.' (Home Office, 2021a)
- **Study:** 'In the year ending September 2021, there were 428,428 sponsored study visas granted (to both main applicants and their dependants),

143% (252,327) more than the previous year and 55% (152,077) higher than the year ending September 2019.' (Home Office, 2021b). The majority came from China and India.

- **Family reasons:** 'There were 263,415 visas and permits granted for family reasons in the year ending September 2021, 79% more than the year ending September 2020, a period affected by the global pandemic, and 47% more than the year ending September 2019, largely due to increases in dependants of people coming on work or study visas, and the dependants of the newly introduced British Nationals (Overseas) route.' (Home Office, 2021c). This included: family-related entry clearance visas; dependants on other types of visas (excluding visitor visas); European Economic Area (EEA) family permits; and EU Settlement Scheme (EUSS) family permits.

In terms of people leaving the UK, the latest available figures at the time of writing show: 'In the year ending March 2020, emigration was 403,000.' (Sturge, 2021, 8)

The same Briefing Paper notes that, between 1991– 2020: '. . . immigration increased 117%, rising from 329,000 in 1991 to 715,000 in the year ending March 2020.' (Sturge, 2021, 8)

Immigration and the UK – growing hostility

It is clear that, although there have been political voices raised in support of migration, the overwhelming language has been of reducing, limiting, containing, controlling – from all political parties. Some have even used immigration as a cheap 'point-scorer', and some have made claims that could not possibly be achieved; for example, during the 2010 General Election campaign, the Conservative Party pledged to bring 'net migration'[30] down to the 'tens of thousands' by the end of Parliament in 2015 (see, for example: Allen and Sumption, 2015).

According to writer and researcher Maya Goodfellow:

> The left often fear that, if they don't accept people's 'concerns' about immigration, they will leave a political vacuum that the right will fill. This has been tested to death. Over Ed Miliband's five years as Labour leader, barely a conversation would pass without a front-bench politician asserting they were listening to people's concerns and accepting immigration was a problem . . . Concerns about immigration aren't 'legitimate' and practising anti-immigration politics doesn't destroy it – it strengthens it.
>
> (Goodfellow, 2020, 191)[31]

Journalist Gary Younge expressed similar views even more strongly:

> Attempts to triangulate with weasel words about the 'legitimate concerns' of 'traditional voters' are dishonest. Concerns about high class sizes and over-stretched welfare services are obviously legitimate; blaming ethnic minorities for them is obviously not. Facilitating a conflation of the two and hoping no one will notice is spineless. It also doesn't work. Those who dedicate their lives to racism are better at it, and will never be satisfied. Pandering does not steal their thunder – it gives them legitimacy.
>
> (Younge, 2019)

These wild claims and arguments do not help sort out fact from fiction. Evidence shows that the scale of immigration is often vastly over-estimated – for example, a review of existing data carried out by market research company IPSOS Mori in 2014 found that, on average, people were estimating migration at twice the level it really was (Duffy and Frere-Smith, 2014).

The 'refugee crisis'

One further major factor was the so-called 'refugee crisis' in 2015.

Much media coverage focused on numbers, without attempting to create an understanding of why people were migrating. According to the BBC, more than one million refugees and migrants entered Europe in 2015, primarily escaping conflict in Syria, ongoing violence in Afghanistan and Iraq, abuses in Eritrea, as well as poverty in Kosovo (BBC News, 2016).

More detailed analysis by Heaven Crawley and colleagues,[32] drawing on research by the IOM (International Organisation for Migration, 2016), showed that there were, in fact, two flows, one to Italy and one to Greece:

> While 90% of those arriving in Greece came from just three countries (Syria, Afghanistan and Iraq), arrivals in Italy were much more diverse: around a quarter of all arrivals were Eritrean (25.5%), followed by Nigerians (14.5%), Somalis (8.1%), Sudanese (5.8%), Gambians (5.8%) and Syrians (3.8%), with the remainder originating from 53 different countries . . .
>
> (Crawley et al., 2018, 39)[33]

We also know that there are a number of other countries from where people are fleeing – as the Refugee Council noted in 2019: 'Over the past 7 years 14 different countries have appeared in the list of the top ten asylum applicant producing countries. Eritrea, Iran, Pakistan, Afghanistan, and Bangladesh have been in the top ten in every one of the last 7 years.' (Refugee Council, 2019, 1)

32 LIBRARIES AND SANCTUARY

In addition, the research by Heaven Crawley and colleagues has suggested that, in fact, it was 'not one crisis but many' in 2015:

Our analysis leads us to conclude that it was symptomatic of, and became shorthand for, a range of economic, political, foreign policy and humanitarian crises taking place at the national, regional and global scales:

- a global financial crisis;
- a European financial and Euro-zone crisis, most notably the Greek debt crisis;
- an EU foreign policy crisis related to the rise of new and mostly illiberal powers (Russia, Turkey, Iran, Saudi Arabia);
- a political crisis in the Arab countries ('Arab Spring');
- a crisis of war and civil war, most notably in Syria, Iraq and Libya;
- a security crisis related to the rise of terrorism (especially IS[34]and Boko Haram)[35] and manifesting itself in Nigeria, Turkey, Brussels, Paris, London and different parts of Germany;
- a humanitarian crisis in war-torn countries and subsequent crisis of displacement;
- a humanitarian emergency in neighbouring countries (Turkey, Jordan, Lebanon);
- a personal crisis for refugee and migrants making the journey;
- a humanitarian crisis in the countries of first arrival, most notably Italy and especially Greece;
- a humanitarian crisis along the Balkan route;
- a crisis of the external border controls of the EU;
- a crisis of the sovereignty of EU;
- a moral crisis in relation to the search and rescue (SAR) effort;
- a crisis of identity for the EU and individual Member States manifested in public hostility towards refugees and migrants and the rise of the far right.

(Crawley et al., 2018, 115)

This series of events led, possibly inevitably, to the creation of what has been shorthanded as 'Fortress Britain' (see for example Haynes, 2019; Ryan, 2018; Winder, 2013, 439– 453), where border barriers come down, and migration is unwelcome, and, with it, the creation of an 'hostile environment'.

The hostile environment

So, what exactly is the 'hostile environment'?

In the words of the House of Lords Library:

The 'hostile environment' policy (which the Government now refers to as the 'compliant environment' policy) refers to a range of measures aimed at identifying and reducing the number of immigrants in the UK with no right to remain. Many of these were introduced by the Immigration Acts of 2014 and 2016, and include measures seeking to restrict illegal immigrants renting property in the UK, driving, having bank accounts and accessing benefits and free healthcare. Some of these measures included data-sharing between other government departments or external organisations and the Home Office, and the requirement for document checks by those providing certain services.

The Government has stated the policies are needed to deter illegal immigration. However, the Opposition has called for an end to the policy, believing it has had a negative impact on individuals' lives, including those with a right to live in the UK. For example, there have been a number of reports of Commonwealth migrants who have lived in the UK since before 1973 (often referred to as the 'Windrush generation'), who have a legal right to live in the country under the Immigration Act 1971, being denied access to services and being sent letters threatening them with deportation or detention due to their inability to provide documentation of their right to reside in the UK.

(Taylor, 2018, 1)

The House of Lords Library Briefing also refers to the comments made by the UN Special Rapporteur on Contemporary Forms of Racism, Racial Discrimination, Xenophobia and Related Intolerance, E. Tendayi Achiume, in which she outlines how the 'hostile environment' has operated, including the use of high-profile enforcement campaigns, '. . . which saw controversial vans printed with the slogan "Go Home or Face Arrest," as well as legislation restricting access to basic services for a range of categories of foreign nationals and criminalizing those who find themselves without status.' (Achiume, 2018) She went on to comment that:

. . . the hostile environment that prevails in the UK is rooted in a much larger legal and policy framework, including beyond the narrow confines of immigration law. Furthermore, this hostile environment applies not only to irregular immigrants, but to racial and ethnic minority individuals with regular status, and many who are British citizens and have been entitled to this citizenship as far back as the colonial era.

One aspect of the hostile environment that has had an impact on all our lives is the devolving of responsibility for carrying out checks on people's status to all sorts of organisations and individuals:

Although the Home Office remains responsible for operationalising the immigration system, the hostile environment 'deputises' responsibilities, devolving the spaces and agents of immigration policing across everyday society, and making an unprecedented range of agencies, services, institutions, companies, charities and private individuals responsible for checking immigration status, passing on information to the Home Office and delivering immigration-related exclusions.

(Griffiths and Yeo, 2021, 18)

Yet it would be too easy and simplistic to assume that this was a sudden policy redirection; as noted above, there had been a succession of laws and policies through the 1950s–1990s that aimed to tighten and limit immigration into the UK. For example, as journalist Nesrine Malik writes:

Much of the 'hostile environment' infrastructure of immigration controls that exists today is the legacy of Labour's last government. The tier system that sorts immigrants according to their value to the UK, the high barriers to gaining citizenship and the conversion of employers into border guards were all policies established by Labour in 2006 . . .

The presence of immigrants was now a matter of 'legitimate concern'; there was a need to look out for 'the indigenous population', in the words of Labour's immigration minister Phil Woolas.

(Malik, 2020)[36]

As noted above, one event that possibly focused most attention on the hostile environment was 'Operation Vaken'.[37] This was a one-month Home Office immigration publicity campaign in 2013, as part of which:

. . . two Go Home vans . . . were driven through six of the most ethnically diverse London boroughs (Hounslow, Barking and Dagenham, Ealing, Barnet, Brent and Redbridge). The full message carried by the vans . . . read: 'In the UK illegally? GO HOME OR FACE ARREST. Text HOME to 78070 for free advice, and help with travel documents. We can help you return home voluntarily without fear of arrest or detention.' Along with these words was a close-up of a border guard's uniform and handcuffs, a telephone number to call, and the claim: '106 ARRESTS LAST WEEK IN YOUR AREA'.

(Jones et al., 2017, 12)

The impact of the hostile environment – and the criticisms of it – were noted in a 2019 Freedom from Torture report, *Lessons Not Learned: the failures of asylum decision-making in the UK*, that examined '. . . 50 reports from 17

WHAT HAS BEEN THE RESPONSE IN THE UK? 35

different organisations, including parliamentary committees, the United Nations, nongovernmental organisations, academics, and independent inspectorates.' (Tsangarides and Williams, 2019, 6). The reports analysed found a number of causes of poor decision-making, including:

- 'flawed credibility assessments;
- the unrealistic and unlawful evidential burden placed on applicants;
- a starting point of disbelief and a broader 'refusal culture' in the ethos of the Home Office;
- an inadequate learning culture and a lack of independent oversight.'

(Tsangarides and Williams, 2019, 6)

In addition, research in 2021 by charity Pro Bono Economics (Oldfield, Siu and Sheikh, 2021) showed that '. . . overturned asylum decisions cost the government over £4 million a year in administrative costs alone.' (Pro Bono Economics, 2021)

The legacy of the 'hostile environment' lingers on, as a newspaper report indicates: 'Hundreds of thousands of migrants are much less likely to get the [COVID] vaccine due to fears of deportation stemming from the government's hostile environment policies, cross-party politicians have warned.' (Bulman, 2021d)

Finally, the perception of a wider 'hostile environment' also seems to persist: in March 2021, a member of the UK Government's LGBTQ+ advisory panel resigned from the panel, accusing ministers of creating '. . . a hostile environment for LGBT people . . . ' (Allegretti, 2021).

The Equality Act 2010

Before looking at some of the effects of the hostile environment (particularly the Windrush scandal), it is worth noting here that all this was taking place at a time when the UK had recently adopted the Equality Act 2010.

Prior to 2010, there was separate legislation covering some aspects of equality, but there were also areas that were not protected legally. The 2010 Act brought together all these aspects into one piece of legislation, and introduced the nine 'protected characteristics' (groups protected by the Act):

- age
- disability
- gender reassignment
- marriage and civil partnership
- pregnancy and maternity

36 LIBRARIES AND SANCTUARY

- race
- religion or belief
- sex
- sexual orientation.

Significantly, the Equality Act also included the Public Sector Equality Duty [PSED]:

> A public authority must, in the exercise of its functions, have due regard to the need to
>
> (a) eliminate discrimination, harassment, victimisation and any other conduct that is prohibited by or under this Act;
> (b) advance equality of opportunity between persons who share a relevant protected characteristic and persons who do not share it;
> (c) foster good relations between persons who share a relevant protected characteristic and persons who do not share it.
>
> (Pyper, 2020, 7)

and introduced Equality Impact Assessments:

> An Equality Impact Assessment ('EIA') is an analysis of a proposed organisational policy, or a change to an existing one, which assesses whether the policy has a disparate impact on persons with protected characteristics.
>
> (p. 23)

It is also worth noting that, despite attempts to remove the requirement to use the PSED and EIA (particularly via the 'Red Tape Challenge'),[38] nevertheless they are both still in force.

The Windrush scandal

The scale of the problems caused by the 'hostile environment' began to surface nationally in 2017–2018 (see particularly Gentleman, 2020) and, taken from a 2018 article:

> About 50,000 people who arrived from Caribbean countries after the second world war, at the invitation of the UK government, face eviction, NHS bills and deportation if they have not formalised their residency status or no longer have the documentation to prove it.
>
> The problems have arisen as a result of the government's 'hostile environment policy', which requires employers, NHS staff, landlords and other bodies to demand evidence of people's citizenship or immigration status.

Some of the Windrush-generation children, often travelling on their parents' passports, were not formally naturalised and, as adults, never applied for passports. The Home Office destroyed their landing cards, making it almost impossible for many people, including those below, to prove they had the right to be in the UK, and having a serious impact on their lives.

(Guardian Staff, 2018)

Setting out the scale of problems that ensued, the JCWI[39] noted:

Because many of the Windrush generation arrived as children on their parents' passports, and the Home Office destroyed thousands of landing cards and other records, many lacked the documentation to prove their right to remain in the UK. The Home Office also placed the burden of proof on individuals to prove their residency predated 1973. The Home Office demanded at least one official document from every year they had lived here. Attempting to find documents from decades ago created a huge, and in many cases, impossible burden on people who had done nothing wrong.

Falsely deemed as 'illegal immigrants'/'undocumented migrants' they began to lose their access to housing, healthcare, bank accounts and driving licenses. Many were placed in immigration detention, prevented from travelling abroad and threatened with forcible removal, while others were deported to countries they hadn't seen since they were children.

(Joint Council for the Welfare of Immigrants, n.d.)

Given the massive impact of the Windrush scandal, the Government commissioned Wendy Williams (Her Majesty's Inspectorate of Constabulary) to undertake a review, in which she confirmed that the Home Secretary in 2012 (Theresa May) had '. . . outlined the government's "hostile environment" policy, a set of measures to make living and working in the UK as difficult as possible for people without leave to remain.' (Williams, 2020, 37)

The assessment of this Review by Joe Owen (formerly Programme Director, the Institute for Government) was even harsher in its criticism of the Government:

The review is extremely successful in matching the often-horrific personal stories of individuals affected with the usually dry technocratic processes that led to them. The mistreatment of Windrush citizens stemmed from failures in every element of modern government, with the Home Office, as an institution, heavily criticised by the review.

(Owen, 2020)

He also argues that not only did the Home Office appear not to understand its own immigration legislation but there were failings by policy-makers who '. . . ignored how their policy to make life difficult for illegal immigrants – the so-called "hostile environment" – would affect people who had every right to be here but did not have easy means to prove it,' and by politicians who ignored warning signs:

> Ministers (Labour, Conservative and Liberal Democrat) refused to act when cases of hardship emerged – and did not reconsider their approach even when concerns were raised about the potential impacts on groups who were lawfully here. In 2015 for example, MPs passed the new Immigration Bill despite concerns about the impact on undocumented citizens.
>
> (Owen, 2020)

The EHRC also looked at the hostile environment policies and their impact on the Windrush generation, using the Public Sector Equality Duty (see above), and found that:

> In the documents we assessed, we found insufficient evidence of the Home Office taking the required steps to show due regard to the need to advance equality of opportunity in relation to colour. This included the documents the Home Office supplied to show compliance.
>
> (Equality and Human Rights Commission, 2020, 6)

In addition, IPPR assessed the hostile environment and its impact, and concluded that:

> We find that the hostile environment has contributed to forcing many people into destitution, has helped to foster racism and discrimination, and has erroneously affected people with the legal right to live and work in the UK. . . .
>
> We also find little evidence that the 'hostile environment' approach to immigration enforcement is working on its own terms. According to the National Audit Office, the Home Office has no way of assessing the impact of the hostile environment on individual decisions to leave the UK. . . .
>
> In our view, the impacts of the hostile environment indicate systemic flaws in the government's approach to immigration enforcement. Inherent in the design of the hostile environment is the targeting of individuals on the basis of their lack of documentation, the deterring of people from accessing public services, and the transfer of responsibilities away from immigration officials and towards untrained professionals such as landlords. It is this policy design which, when implemented in practice, pushes people into poverty, facilitates discrimination

against minority ethnic groups, erroneously affects those with legal status, and risks public health and safety. The solution therefore requires fundamental reform of current policies rather than simply more effective implementation.

(Qureshi, Morris and Mort, 2020, 3–4)

Despite all this, the Windrush issues were continuing at the time of writing. For example, although a scheme was established in 2019 '. . . to compensate thousands of Commonwealth nationals who had been wrongly classified as illegal immigrants in Britain, preventing them from working and accessing services and sometimes leading to detention and deportation', in May 2021, 500 Windrush victims had been waiting more than a year for their compensation claims to be processed (Bulman, 2021a). In addition, at the time of writing, the scheme is being applied with limitations:

> The current rules state that children who arrived as adults over the age of 18 after 1988 are excluded from the scheme. This group do not have a path to citizenship through the Windrush scheme even if they have been resident in the UK for many years.
>
> . . . Four Windrush generation descendants who took their case to the High Court are at risk of removal from the UK as they are not eligible to remain here under the Windrush scheme. They plan to submit ordinary (non-Windrush) applications for leave to remain under the immigration rules.
>
> All four have Windrush families who they came to the UK to join. The three women in the case are all grandmothers.
>
> (Taylor, 2022)

In addition, increasing numbers of stories of people affected by the Windrush scandal are appearing – for example, that of Lynda Mahabir, who was, the High Court decided, unlawfully separated from her husband and children (Gentleman, 2021a), and that of Paulette Wilson:

> In October 2017 I received an email from an immigration charity in Wolverhampton with the disturbing subject line: 'Urgent – Imminent deportation of a lady who has been in the UK for 49 years'. The email explained that Paulette Wilson, a 61-year-old grandmother who had arrived in the UK from Jamaica at the age of ten in 1968, had been wrongly classified as an illegal immigrant and detained in the notorious immigration detention centre, Yarl's Wood, ahead of removal to Jamaica – a country where she had no surviving relatives and which she had not visited for almost half a century.
>
> It was clear from the email (sent by the Refugee and Migrant Centre in Wolverhampton) that the Home Office had made a terrible mistake in handling

40 LIBRARIES AND SANCTUARY

her case. Within hours of the email being sent Paulette was driven in a prison van to another detention centre near Heathrow Airport, and she would have been deported if the charity's lawyers and her MP had not stepped in to make a last-minute intervention.

I went to visit her soon after her release at her daughter Natalie Barnes's flat. She was devastated by what had happened, unable to understand why she had been categorised as an illegal immigrant when she had attended primary and secondary school in Britain, worked and paid taxes for around 34 years and had brought up her daughter and granddaughter here, both of whom are British. For a while she worked in the House of Commons canteen, serving meals to MPs and parliamentary staff. 'I don't feel British. I am British', she told me.

(Gentleman, 2018)

Incidentally, as well as deporting people from the Windrush generation, the UK has been actively deporting other people – for example Jamaican nationals who came to the UK as children (Gentleman and Taylor, 2021); one example is the rapper, Cashief Nichols, who, with his mother, had arrived in London when he was seven:

When he received a national insurance number at 16, he thought this meant he was eligible to stay and so began the process of applying for indefinite leave to remain, which meant weekly visits to an immigration centre . . .

At one such weekly visit, Nichols learned that his application had been rejected [and he was removed to Jamaica].

(Renshaw, 2021)

The UK has also been deporting to Jamaica people with a criminal record, who had lived in the UK since they were children (de Noronha, 2020; Byron, 2020).

Brexit

Possibly heavily influenced by the hostile environment policies, Brexit ('Britain exit' – the referendum on membership of the European Union (EU) held in June 2016) was a defining moment for the UK, and one which is still playing out.

As researchers at University of Wales Trinity Saint David, Swansea, Paul B. Hutchings and Katie E. Sullivan (Hutchings and Sullivan, 2019) argue, although there was a multitude of issues which were oversimplified to '. . . a binary referendum question of whether to leave the EU or remain a member, . . . there can be no doubt that issues relating to prejudice were paramount in many of the discussions leading up to the vote in 2016 . . . '.

It has also been suggested that the reason that so many people voted to leave the EU was, to a significant degree, people feeling a lack of control in their lives over issues such as unemployment, access to welfare, and immigration (see for example Guderjan, Mackay and Stedman, 2020); although some commentators argue that the roots go much further back:

> Opposition to Britain's membership of the EU has fluctuated over the years, but has remained substantial ever since the UK joined in the mid 1970s; somewhere between ~30 and ~60 per cent of the British public has always been opposed to EU membership. Of course, the Eurosceptic fraction of the population almost certainly increased as a consequence of the rapid rise in EU immigration, which began in the late 1990s, and the Eurozone debt crises, which precipitated mass unemployment across Southern Europe. Nevertheless, the most important phenomenon to be explained vis-à-vis the referendum result in our view is that a sizable Eurosceptic faction has remained extant in Britain over the last four decades, in contrast to the other countries of Europe.
>
> (Dennison and Carl, 2016)

What is undoubtedly clear, with hindsight, is just how far from the truth many statements (from both the Leave and Remain campaigns) were (see for example Stone, 2017); some of these had a particular impact on views about migration – for example, as James Ker-Lindsay[40] wrote in 2018:

> More than a year and a half after the EU referendum, debate still rages as to what exactly led 52% of the population to vote for Brexit. While many argue that sovereignty was the issue that resonated most with Leave voters, others point to the claims about the amount of money that would supposedly be saved – and thus put into public services – if Britain left. Whatever the merits of these arguments, there can be no doubt that for a significant proportion of British voters the question of immigration was at the forefront of their decision . . .
>
> (Ker-Lindsay, 2018)

He also noted the impact of rumours – and unfounded claims – about Turkey's joining the EU. For example: 'In a video that received widespread criticism for its racist and Islamophobic undertones, UKIP claimed that Turkey would join the EU by 2020 and that as many as 15 million people would leave the country for the EU in the first ten years of its membership . . . ' (Ker-Lindsay, 2018). The end result of this was a controversial poster campaign by the Vote Leave group, claiming: 'Turkey (population 76 million) is joining the EU. Vote Leave, take back control.' (Boffey and Helm, 2016)

Whilst there had been considerable previous evidence of discrimination and racism (e.g. Fox, 2012, who looks at racism towards East European migrants) prior to 2016, in many ways the referendum brought things to a head. For example, the Institute of Race Relations described an 'explosion of racist violence' (Burnett, 2016, 3); and the Centre for Social Investigation concluded that:

- Racially or religiously motivated hate crime in Britain increased by 111.8% between 2011 and 2018.
- Racially or religiously motivated hate crime spiked following both the EU referendum and Manchester Arena bombing[41] in May 2017.
- Accounting for time trends and patterns in overall crime, the increase in hate crime after the EU referendum has been over-stated elsewhere, but there was nonetheless a clear increase.
- The increase in violent hate crime does not appear to be purely 'cosmetic' – it cannot simply be attributed to increased police efforts to pursue these offences or to changed reporting practices.

(Cavalli, 2019, 1)

Where are we now?

To start more broadly, and then focus in, Mattias Ekman (Stockholm University researcher) argues that 'Anti-immigration sentiments are permeating public discourse across the global North – particularly subsequent to the "refugee crisis" of 2015' and he links these to the '. . . upsurge of far-right, including populist, politics throughout Europe and beyond.' (Ekman, 2019, 606)

Ojeaku Nwabuzo and Georgina Siklossy (from the European Network Against Racism) argue that this has led to '. . . the criminalisation of migration. Several EU member states, politicians and other commentators have represented irregular, "Muslim" and/or African arrivals – however much in need of humanitarian protection – as "economic" or "illegal" migrants.' (Nwabuzo and Siklossy, 2020)

As humanitarian aid worker, consultant, writer and activist Mohamoud Yusuf writes:

Immigration and asylum has become one of the most politically sensitive issues within the European Union since the major influx of refugees and other migrants in 2015, when some member states refused to operate a quota system for sharing responsibility. . . .

An arc of crises across the middle east, Africa and Asia has shaped a perfect refugee storm in recent years: Libya, Syria, Iraq, Yemen, Somalia and

Afghanistan among them. There are also countries within Europe affected by conflicts, now or in the recent past, generating movements of the desperate, such as Ukraine and former Yugoslavia.

(Yusuf, 2020)

There is also growing evidence of the use of 'push-backs'[42] across Europe, with the allegation that over 2000 deaths can be attributed to these actions (Rybarczyk, 2021; Tondo and Smith, 2021; Tondo, 2021; Protecting Rights at Borders, 2021).

The borders stand-off between Belarus and Poland/the EU has left people seeking sanctuary in danger – for example:

No one knows exactly how many migrants are stranded or have died in the forests. Grupa Granica,[43] which relies on a network of local residents for information, estimates that up to 5,000 people, including children, are trapped there for days, even weeks at a time. According to Polish officials, at least nine people have been found dead. But aid workers say the unofficial death toll is much higher, based on information they have received from those who have passed through the 'emergency zone'. Last week, Polish media reported that a 14-year-old Kurdish boy froze to death overnight on the Belarusian side of the border. The Belarusian Border Commission denied the reports. . . .

The Polish government has denied multiple requests by NGOs to enter the emergency zone, meaning the only assistance migrants in that zone can hope to get is from local residents, who help at their own risk.

(Roache, 2021)

In February 2022, researcher Felix Bender[44] wrote:

Refugees are being apprehended and detained in containers or camps surrounded with barbed wire. They are being beaten, robbed, insulted, humiliated and debased, marked like cattle and forced blindly through razor-wire fences to countries where the right to claim asylum is effectively denied.

(Bender, 2022)

and argues that there are dangers that this way of dealing with new arrivals may be introduced within Europe, not just at its borders.

A long-standing monitoring project, 'Fatal Policies of Fortress Europe', co-ordinated by UNITED,[45] collects details of and maps the deaths of people trying to seek sanctuary in Europe – between 1993 and June 2021, there had been at least 44,764 deaths which could be attributed to 'Fortress Europe' (UNITED, 2021); in their view:

Europe's exclusion policies make it almost impossible to enter Europe regularly. These fatal policies have forced thousands of people to resort to irregular ways of getting to a country where they are safe and where economical survival is possible. No matter how different the circumstances of these deaths are, they can all be ultimately put down to one reason: the building of a Fortress Europe which refers to the policy of exclusion and the on-going tightening of EU asylum policies. These decisions are taken on highest political level: the Schengen Treaty, the Dublin Convention and EU border control programmes.

We face a rat race of tougher asylum policies amongst the European Member States – accompanied by common European initiatives to reduce immigration. EU migration policies are driven by targets and objectives rather than humanity.

In the face of civil war, conflict and global political and social unrest, Europe responds by adopting exclusionary practice and policies, turning a blind eye to the root causes of migration. Refugees and migrants fleeing to Europe are presented to the public opinion (and as a result perceived) as the reason of many problems in Europe. They are abused as scapegoats, thus stimulating racist ideology and offering ground to right wing populist parties. Instead of being the problem, refugees and asylum seekers are in search of a solution to the serious problems they leave behind in the countries they had to flee. Refugees are not the problem! The real problem is a general lack of vision in Europe on migration and a lack of support for the peaceful development in their home countries.

It is important to bear in mind that all these deaths are due to policies that criminalise a fundamental human right: freedom of movement. Many also violate other rights such as the right to leave and return to your country of origin, the right to seek asylum and the right to family reunification. These rights are laid out in the 1951 Geneva Convention and are not simply a set of values and principles the EU should try to uphold, but constitute international law to which each participating country is bound.

(UNITED, n.d.)

In an article for the Institute of Race Relations, Anya Edmond-Pettitt and co-writers argue that Fortress Britain (mentioned above) in fact forms part of this Fortress Europe approach:

Imposing a heavily militarised border aligns with the French objective of avoiding 'points of fixation' in the northern coastal region and UK desire to prevent irregular arrivals. The UK has financed the securitisation with the purchase of surveillance cameras, truck-scanning technology and barbed wire throughout the area, with sums exceeding £300 million in recent years thereby creating a 'Fortress Britain' within the bounds of 'Fortress Europe'.

(Edmond-Pettitt, Galisson, and Timberlake, 2021)

A Refugee Council 'Briefing' in November 2021 looked at different responses that could be taken to people trying to reach the UK across the English Channel and suggested that possible solutions could include:

a) An ambitious expansion of existing safe routes including both resettlement and refugee family reunion. . . .

b) Establishing a humanitarian visa system to allow people to apply for a visa to enter the UK for the purposes of claiming asylum, thereby reducing the need for people to make dangerous journeys across the Channel. People can only claim asylum in the UK when they are physically here, which is why they make desperate, often fatal journeys to reach the UK. It doesn't have to be this way – humanitarian visas would enable people in need of protection to travel to the UK in a safe manner.

c) A recognition that many people seeking asylum will have no other option other than making an irregular journey as recognised in the 1951 Refugee Convention, and therefore they need to be treated fairly and humanely by being granted a fair hearing on UK soil. The government need to put in place an efficient and effective asylum decision making system with timely decisions that are of high quality so people do not have to wait for months or years for an outcome on their case.

(Refugee Council, 2021a, 9)

At the same time, there is also continuing research into the effects of migration and new arrivals on communities, and one interesting piece of work (which also needs to be explored further) suggests that social mobility is a key factor in how well new arrivals are welcomed and accepted: 'The experience of social mobility allows people to adapt more easily to ethnically diverse social contexts. The socially mobile have encountered different social environments throughout their lives. This experience involves the adaption to, and navigation of, lifestyles typical of different social environments.'(Kraus and Daenekindt, 2021)[46]

Where are we now in the UK?

Despite the severe criticisms (noted above) of the Government's hostile environment and its handling of the Windrush scandal, nevertheless attitudes, policies and behaviour do not seem to have changed significantly. Here are some examples.

Asylum decision-making

- There is a large backlog of asylum cases awaiting decisions: ' . . . at the end of March 2021 there were 66,185 people awaiting an initial decision from the Home Office, the highest number for over a decade. Of this, 76% (50,084 people) had been waiting for more than six months.' (Hewett, 2021, 5)
- People have to wait a very long time to obtain a decision; for example, 'Addis was granted refugee status this year after more than a decade in poverty and unsettled housing . . . ' (Bartholomew, n.d.). According to the University of Birmingham: 'After arriving in the UK many forced migrants are trapped in the asylum system for years. The policies and practices within the system are often harmful; exacerbating existing trauma, generating new trauma, or increasing the likelihood of experiencing SGBV [sexual and gender-based violence] again. Being detained and without a secure future, many forced migrant victims of SGBV experience deteriorating mental and physical health.' (University of Birmingham, 2021)[47]

Accommodating people seeking sanctuary

- In October 2020, it was estimated that there were just over 9,500 people seeking sanctuary housed in temporary accommodation (House of Commons. Public Accounts Committee, 2020).
- In places, the level of support offered to people seeking sanctuary is poor (to say the least): 'In a rare insight into how newly arrived asylum seekers are treated by authorities, prison inspectors visited Tug Haven in Dover, where migrants are first taken from the beach or sea, and found a shortage of dry clothing and other basic supplies.' (Grierson, 2020)
- There are also currently people seeking sanctuary who are housed in former military sites[48] in Norfolk (RAF Coltishall) and at Napier Barracks in Kent, where there was a fire in early 2021, which highlighted the appalling conditions in which the people were being detained (Trilling, 2021).[49] However, an inspection[50] carried out in February 2021 found lack of preparation and linking with local stakeholders, criticism of the health provisions, concerns about safety, and the overall environment which was described as ' . . . impoverished, run-down and unsuitable for long-term accommodation.' (Independent Chief Inspector of Borders and Immigration, 2021)
- According to openDemocracy: 'The housing of asylum seekers in overcrowded and poorly-facilitated barracks and hostels by profit-making contractors is the trademark of anti-asylum, anti-migrant policies

seen across Britain and Europe. Brexit or not, Britain has a lot in common with the continent in terms of hostility to "outsiders".' (Pai, 2021). It may also be a means of warding off anticipated criticism: 'Home Office put refugees in barracks after fears better housing would "undermine confidence" in system.' (Bulman, 2021c)

Immigration enforcement

In the UK (and elsewhere), one result of this focus on borders and immigration has been a growth in immigration enforcement – as one example, Liz Fekete (the Institute of Race Relations) writes that:

> In the UK, the Home Office and other agencies engaged in immigration enforcement are amassing ever more resources and powers, with the estimated net resource cost for Home Office immigration enforcement being £392 million in 2019–20. Meanwhile, Frontex (the EU's border control agency) has gone from a budget of €6m in 2005 to €460m in 2020. The fact that budgets are expanding exponentially relies on a habitual recourse to the portrayal of migrants and refugees as a 'threat to our way of life'.
>
> (Fekete, 2020)

In addition, people trying to arrive in Europe – including the UK – are subject to '. . . restrictive laws and regulations, lengthy asylum processes, patronising integration programs, not to mention a generally unwelcoming public debate.' (Abdelhady, Joormann, and Gren, 2021)

'Overhauling' the immigration system

- At the time of writing, the Government is also in the throes of 'overhauling' the UK immigration system, including the Home Office's announcement that '. . . it will "stop illegal arrivals gaining immediate entry into the asylum system if they have travelled through a safe country – like France."' Other measures include introducing 'life sentences for people smugglers' and increasing 'the maximum sentence for illegally entering the UK' (O'Nions, 2021). There has been considerable questioning of the proposal that people seeking sanctuary should seek asylum in the first country they reach: 'The requirement for individuals to claim asylum at the first "safe" country arguably ignores all but the most basic of human needs. So, the asylum-seeker continues on, like any other rational individual in the same position, to find a place where he [*sic*] can best re-group and re-build: be safe, but also, be alive.' (Nason, 2017; see also Yeo, 2021)[51]

- In addition to this, the Government changed the rules for making asylum claims from January 2021: 'The [new] immigration rules say that your asylum claim may be considered for inadmissibility if you've made an asylum claim in another country; or you were in a "safe country" and you didn't make an asylum claim and "there were no exceptional circumstances preventing such an application being made["]; or you have a "connection" to another country, so it would be "reasonable" for you to be returned there.' (Right to Remain, 2021)
- 'The Government has introduced a new immigration rule which means someone could have their permission to stay in the UK refused or cancelled, if they've been sleeping rough' and 'The rough sleeping rule has applied to non-EEA nationals since 1 December and will apply to newly arriving EEA nationals from 1 January 2021.' (Cromarty, 2020)

People crossing the English Channel

One of the major triggers for restarting the discussions about so-called 'illegal immigrants' has been the influx of migrants who have crossed the English Channel – as The Migration Observatory notes:

Despite the closure of Sangatte[52] to prevent Eurostar stowaways, and the clearance of the Calais Jungle[53] to prevent lorry and ferry stowaways, crossings continue, having been recorded regularly since late 2018. Campaigners argue that this is because people seeking asylum have little choice but to enter the UK irregularly and via clandestine means, as there are no safe and legal alternatives. It is not possible to apply for asylum from outside the UK.

The representative to the UK of the United Nations High Commissioner for Refugees has stated that more stringent controls on road travel, and the coronavirus pandemic, have had the effect of closing off lorry and air routes to the UK, leading to more people using alternative means – such as crossing the Channel in small boats. This is supported by the fact that a rise in small boat crossings has coincided with a fall in the overall number of people seeking asylum.

As they conclude:

As an island nation, the UK has in recent years generally received fewer asylum seekers than other more accessible European states, such as Germany, France, Greece, Italy and Spain. Nevertheless, many people planning to claim asylum identify the UK as their preferred destination.

But to claim asylum in the UK, a person must first reach the UK. It is not possible to apply for asylum abroad, and there is no asylum visa, and no legal way of entering the UK for the specific purpose of seeking asylum.

(Walsh, 2020b)

Young people's access to the UK

- Gaining access to the UK has become increasingly hard for young people. Introduced in 2016: 'Section 67 of the Immigration Act 2016 (known as the "Dubs amendment") placed a requirement on the Secretary of State to "make arrangements to relocate to the United Kingdom and support a specified number of unaccompanied refugee children from other countries in Europe".' (Coram Children's Legal Centre, 2017). However, in January 2021, the Home Office announced that:
  '. . . although the Home Office took the "responsibility for the welfare of children very seriously", there would no longer be a legal route to Britain for these minors. The only children still able to seek help in the UK are those who have relatives in Britain, who Mr Philp[54] said would be able to come to Britain through the existing immigration rules.' (Bulman, 2021b)
- In addition: 'When children arrive in the UK on their own and claim asylum they don't always have identity documents with them. Instead of accepting them as a child, local authorities frequently decide to assess their age. Too often they wrongly decide the child is an adult, often after a very brief meeting. This means children can be moved to another part of the country to live in asylum accommodation with adults they have never met before. It also means their asylum claims are decided as if they were adults and they can face detention, removal or destitution.' (Greater Manchester Immigration Aid Unit, 2019, 1)
- Young people may also face barriers when applying to move into higher education if they are seen to have 'insecure immigration status': 'Our research finds that many young people, including those that have lived in the UK for the majority of their lives, are unable to access HE as they are ineligible for student finance support. This has a detrimental effect on individuals as well as a social and economic cost, as young people are prevented from fully realising their skills and talents.' (Mulcahy, Joshua, and Baars, 2021, 7)[55]
- The process for young people is gruelling, and may not always end with a happy conclusion: 'I had one meeting in Liverpool, it lasted more than 4 hours with 1 break. They did not believe my age.' (Greater Manchester Immigration Aid Unit, 2020, 7)

The impact of the EU Settled Status Scheme

Since Brexit and the launch of the EU Settled Status Scheme (EUSS),[56] there are some groups of people that were, in early 2021 at least, falling through the net. These include looked-after children and care-leavers (Barnard and Costello, 2021); care workers (Boswell and Patel, 2021); other vulnerable groups, such as '. . . elderly Italians who have been in the UK for 40 or 50 years in some cases but do not have a mobile phone or access to a computer . . .' (Kvist, 2021)

The dangers for people trying to gain access to the UK

Finally, it is worth reiterating just how difficult it is to gain access to the UK – and the terrible results for some migrants of attempting entry; in writing about the death of a stowaway who fell from a Kenya Airways plane, journalist Sirin Kale says:

> The horror of the Kenya Airways stowaway's death made for newspaper headlines, but many more migrants die, in equally horrific circumstances, every week. They are locked in the back of lorries and asphyxiate, or fall from moving freight trains, or drown in the Channel. They are shot by border patrol guards through chain link fences, or electrocuted in the Channel Tunnel, or beaten to death by racist mobs. They are held in detention centres for years, where they are subject to physical and sexual abuse. Sometimes, they burn themselves alive, out of despair. Since 2014, 10,134 people have died on global migration routes, according to the Missing Migrants project. These figures are likely only a tiny fraction of the true picture.
>
> (Kale, 2021)

Perception and representation of new arrivals

Early in 2020, as COVID-19 spread, and the UK entered its first lockdown, Migrant Voice decided to look at the representation of migrants and migration. To do this, they analysed coverage across nine online news platforms[57] between 1 March and 31 May 2020. Amongst their key findings was:

> There was a tendency across media outlets to box migrants into very specific categories and subcategories (such as 'Channel crossers', 'frontline NHS workers', 'asylum seekers') and to present these groups in simplistic ways, as 'Heroes' or 'Threats', for example. In doing so, emphasis is placed on a particular and often time-limited action, the service a group is providing or on their legal status, rather than on their existence as individual human beings. This fuelled the

existing narrative of the good or deserving migrant and the bad or undeserving migrant. In some cases, we found that the same group of migrants (e.g. agricultural workers) was presented one day as 'Threats' and the next as 'Heroes', highlighting both the pervasiveness and absurdity of these categorisations.

(Migrant Voice, 2020, 5)

These findings have been echoed by a more recent report which looked at television news coverage on the BBC, ITV and Sky News:

... migrants, refugees and asylum seekers are regularly quoted in their reporting, but are narrowly framed; stories overwhelmingly favoured hard over soft news topics; and migrants, refugees and asylum seekers are mainly talked about as victims, and to a lesser extent, as threats.

(Abraham-Hamanoiel, 2021, 2)

There are also sweeping – and often incorrect – generalisations about who new arrivals are: for example, lots of young men trying to cross the English Channel are seen as trying to get to the UK predominantly for economic reasons, whereas, in fact, there is a wide range of reasons (see for example Bulman, 2020); and:

- In terms of safe and legal routes into the UK, the current UK immigration regime divides migrants between: economic migrants, who largely enter via the UK's Points Based System; and refugees, who enter through the UK's resettlement programme, largely under criteria set by the United Nations High Commissioner for Refugees (UNHCR).
- Reality is not so neat. Many people can make a case to enter the UK on both economic and humanitarian grounds, but end up being 'stuck in the middle' and unable to enter.

(Hargrave and Thomas, 2021, 5)

In addition, research has shown that people seeking sanctuary are often depicted in large groups, and that this, combined with pictures of the means by which they arrive, has a dehumanising effect: 'This suggests that current visual representations of refugees emphasise a security issue rather than a humanitarian debate – refugees are depicted as "being a crisis" for host nations, rather than finding themselves "in a crisis".'(Tsakiris, 2021)

It is also important to move beyond a limiting stereotype of who new arrivals are; for example, Domenico Sergi argues that we need to consider a much wider migration narrative when talking about new arrivals to avoid what he has called 'the politics of pathos' creeping in and to avoid regarding new arrivals as one 'community' (Sergi, 2021).

Continuing rhetoric

As we have seen above, there was much rhetoric around Brexit – and it has continued since. For example:

- In an interview with Channel 4 preceding the 2021 COP26[58] meeting in Glasgow, the then Prime Minister, Boris Johnson, suggested that, if climate change was not tackled, then the world could return to a 'Dark Ages', and went on to claim (erroneously) – and somehow managing to drag migration into the story – that: 'When the Roman Empire fell, it was largely the result of uncontrolled immigration, people that the empire could no longer control its borders, people came in from the east and all over the place. And we went into a Dark Ages, or Europe went into a Dark Ages, that lasted a very long time.' (Parker, 2021)
- As Ian Cummins[59] suggests: 'There is a long history of regarding welfare systems as expensive and dependency-creating. Populist notions about "scroungers" and the alleged exploitation of the welfare system by the so-called "undeserving" are used to attack the overall notion of the welfare state.' (Cummins, 2021a)
- Priti Patel, then Home Secretary, referred to the asylum system as 'broken',[60] and argues that one of its problems is that it is generous; however, research by Nando Sigona[61] and Michaela Benson[62] has shown that:
  'At a first glance, the current success rate in the UK (64%) is higher than in countries like Germany (39%) and France (23%). However, this may be the result of differences in how countries managed the COVID disruption. In the case of the UK, a minority of relatively straightforward cases were decided quickly during the pandemic. And because they were straightforward cases, they were likely to result in asylum being granted. The consequence is a success rate over the past year that is significantly higher than in previous years. The flipside to this is that many cases were left undecided and an overwhelming backlog has accumulated.' (Sigona and Benson, 2021)

Increased racism and hate crime

As noted above, since the Brexit vote in 2016, there has been an increase in racist incidents, and it is noticeable that the far right in the UK have made immigration one of their platforms (see, for example: HOPE not Hate and Migration Exchange, 2021). Researcher at HOPE not Hate, Joe Mulhall, has explored this further in his book, *Drums in the Distance*, particularly in his investigations into the European far right and the 2015 'refugee crisis', and the (failed) attempts by Identitarians[63] to 'Defend Europe' against incoming people seeking sanctuary (Mulhall, 2021).

We have known for a very long time – and, officially since the MacPherson Report (MacPherson, 1999) – that racism is institutional, but it is also systemic, and there need to be ways of demystifying, understanding and dealing with this (see for example Lingayah, 2021).

Hate crimes are also on the increase. For example, 'A number of social media posts about asylum seekers being accommodated at a Carrickfergus hotel are being investigated for potential hate crimes.' (BBC News Northern Ireland, 2021)

A statement from Euro-Med Monitor[64] in August 2021 said that:

> As racist attacks on asylum seekers in the United Kingdom are witnessing a sharp increase, the UK government's pervasive anti-immigrant rhetoric is extremely dangerous and may exacerbate, ignite, or increase such condemnable violence and prevarication against already vulnerable groups. . . .
>
> The safety of asylum seekers in UK seems to have worsened this year, as the number of racist incidents recorded in state-provided accommodations has tripled, rising from 13 across all of 2020 to 40 so far in 2021.
>
> (Scoop Media, 2021)

It is also worth remembering that children and young people may have escaped one set of harmful circumstances, but then find themselves in another: 'Our children can be bullied at school for their race, culture and class – help prevent our children being bullied.' (YoungMinds Welcome, n.d.)

Health and wellbeing and COVID

In 2020, the world was hit by the coronavirus pandemic. According to Amnesty International's 2020/2021 report:

> During the COVID-19 pandemic, the government failed to adequately modify immigration policies and practices to safeguard public health. People continued to be held in immigration detention for the purposes of removal from the UK, despite the heightened risk of infection in detention and obstacles to effecting removal . . .

The government resisted widespread calls to suspend the 'no recourse to public funds' policy, which restricts access to benefits for many migrants, during the pandemic.

(Amnesty International, 2021a, 380)[65]

Apart from the obvious effects on people's health, the pandemic highlighted huge health inequalities. For example, according to Tom Vickers (Senior Lecturer in Sociology at Nottingham Trent University, and writer and researcher):[66]

The COVID-19 crisis has intensified precarity for some groups, and extended precarity to wider sections of the population. For example, in hostels like Urban House in Wakefield, people seeking asylum reported being kept in close contact with one another for months. When infections started to spread, they were dispersed, in some cases to houses totally unfit for human habitation.

(Vickers, 2020b)

The situation for many people seeking sanctuary is already difficult in terms of their accessing health and medical care. For example, in a report[67] from Doctors of the World UK (part of the Médecins du Monde international network), which audited service users:

- 44.4% (12/27) of service users had a refused asylum claim and 37% (10/27) had an outstanding human rights or asylum application, or appeal.
- In total, 44.4% (12/27) of service users could not be removed from the UK due to an outstanding legal case, for example an outstanding human rights application or appeal, an outstanding asylum claim or appeal, or an outstanding judicial review, which meant they could not be removed from the UK until their case had been closed.
- 96.3% (26/27) of service users were destitute, which meant they did not have adequate accommodation or any means of obtaining it or could not meet their other essential living needs.

(Doctors of the World, 2020, 4)

These points were reiterated in the Refugee Council's note on barriers faced by new arrivals when trying to access health services; their report outlines the following key barriers:

- accessing health services (including fears based on previous experience or that their personal details will be shared with the Home Office)

- living situation (e.g. homelessness) and immigration status (as well as the impact of the hostile environment)
- digital exclusion and lack of skills
- access to information (e.g. people not having the necessary means to engage with digital information or being afraid that they will come under surveillance by the state) and restrictions on mobility
- existing health conditions (Refugee Council, 2021c).

A further Refugee Council report, *I Sat Watching Life Go By My Window For So Long*, highlighted the impact on new arrivals' mental and physical health of spending lengthy periods in hotels (Refugee Council, 2021b).

The JCWI have researched the impact of COVID and the hostile environment on undocumented migrants: 'The Government's Hostile Environment policies have undermined public health efforts, excluded undocumented migrants from the public safety net and subjected them to the worst COVID outcomes.' (Boswell, 2022, 7)

Some people who are seeking sanctuary regard the COVID vaccines with suspicion: this is partly because of unreliable media coverage and misinformation (about other substances being injected with the vaccines, for example); partly concerns about whether the vaccines have been tested thoroughly enough; partly because of religious views about vaccination; and partly from the belief that '. . . the vaccine is "not right for them" – people are not all exactly the same and that perhaps people from their background will react differently to the injection.' (Burne, 2021)

As noted earlier, there has been a surge in anti-Chinese, anti-east and southeast Asian feelings and anti-Semitism in the wake of the coronavirus pandemic (see, for example: Dawson, 2021; Ng, 2021; Human Rights Watch, 2020; Detzler, 2020). Heaven Crawley (Research Professor, Coventry University) argues that COVID-19 has become:

> . . . an excuse to double down on border closures as well as using migration policy to demonstrate the robustness of their response to it. Although countries are entitled to close borders on health grounds, they must still provide access to asylum for those seeking protection from persecution. In practice this isn't the case – there is evidence of pushbacks from Europe, the US and other parts of the world.
>
> (Crawley, 2021)

In addition, there is evidence of a lack of support and protection for migrant women. First, regarding women who are pregnant: two pieces of research published at the end of 2020 showed that '. . . pregnant women can fall through the gaps in terms of welfare support and housing. And how, in some cases, delays in processing welfare benefits and finding accommodation can leave vulnerable women without food or anywhere to live for the duration of their pregnancy.' (Haith-Cooper, 2020); and also that '. . . migrant women who are destitute in pregnancy face many difficulties that impact their mental and physical health. These difficulties relate to having no money for food, being homeless and having to move around frequently. For the majority of their pregnancies, women could not access support they needed from the Home Office or their local authority.' (Ellul, McCarthy and Haith-Cooper, 2020)

Secondly, there is also a broader lack of protection for migrant women; for example, according to Southall Black Sisters:[68]

> On a daily basis we face challenges in supporting women with insecure immigration status who report abuse. For example, it is incredibly difficult to secure refuge accommodation for them because refuges inevitably need to know how their housing and subsistence costs will be met in the long term. Supporting migrant women is also resource-intensive and most refuges simply do not have the skilled or experienced staff to assist with complex immigration matters.
>
> A further difficulty for migrant women is the very limited specialist refuge provision for BME women across the country (with only around 30 in total). These are mainly concentrated in London but they are oversubscribed and many are threatened with closure due to lack of funding.
>
> (Southall Black Sisters, 2020b, 3)

Although policies may be in place, there are still barriers to accessing healthcare for people seeking sanctuary:

> During the pandemic, those who live in the UK, but have an uncertain immigration status, have faced major barriers to receiving the COVID-19 vaccine. The simplest route to getting vaccinated is to be registered with a GP: invitations to book an appointment are sent to the mobile number or address held by your surgery.
>
> NHS England policy is clear. It says on its website: 'Anyone in England can register with a GP surgery. It's free to register. You do not need proof of address or immigration status, ID or an NHS number.'
>
> But an investigation by the Bureau of Investigative Journalism has found that less than a quarter of GP surgeries (24%) surveyed in cities across England, Scotland and Wales would register someone without proof of address, proof of ID or legal immigration status.
>
> Almost two-thirds (62%) told us they would not register the patient, while the remaining 14% said they were unsure whether they could.
>
> (Hamada et al., 2021)

These barriers and their effects were also noted in a June 2021 Doctors of the World report (Lessard-Phillips et al., 2021), and can be summarised as:

- lack of understanding or knowledge of the healthcare system
- administrative barriers
- fear of arrest or immigration enforcement by the Home Office
- linguistic barriers
- financial barriers.

Finally, a further effect of the pandemic has been its impact on social cohesion within communities:

> The pandemic has pressed pause on opportunities and occasion for social contact between migrant and receiving communities – as the spaces in which these groups might meet had closed and the need for social distancing and lockdowns saw more people relying on established family and friend networks.
>
> (Mort, Morris and Grinuite, 2021, 4)

It has exacerbated tensions within communities; and there is also evidence that new arrivals '... faced challenges during the pandemic that were a direct result of or amplified by their immigration status and related inequalities.' These included:

- Heightened feelings of social isolation and disconnection – particularly for people seeking asylum – as a result of dispersal policies that saw them dislocated from their support networks and due to digital, technological, and language barriers that made it difficult to access services for support or home-school their children.
- Dangerous living conditions that increased their exposure to the virus, particularly for asylum seekers living in initial accommodation such as hotels or housed in former military barracks.
- Challenges finding work – even in cases where asylum seekers had been granted a work permit, they were unable to find work on the shortage occupation list that matched their skills or was available in the local area.
- Participants from the Romanian Roma community faced heightened insecurity and precariousness as they were concentrated in gig economy work and were concurrently facing uncertainties brought about by the settlement scheme deadline and concerns that their future may not be secure in the UK.
- As a result of social isolation and language barriers, some were at particular risk of exposure to COVID-19 conspiracy theories. At the same time, participants in the immigration system also faced experiences of

discrimination and prejudice over accusations that they were more likely to be spreading the virus.

(Mort, Morris, and Grinuite, 2021, 4)

Despite all this, there is hope . . .

At the same time, there has been a change in attitudes towards migration – for example: 'Immigration was perceived to be one of the "most important issues" facing the British public in 2015– 2016, but its salience declined after the Brexit referendum' (Blinder and Richards, 2020). A survey by Ipsos MORI carried out in November 2020 (Kaur-Ballagan, Gottfried and Day, 2020) had a positive message ('The proportion of those wanting to see immigration reduced is now 49%, which is the lowest we have recorded since our study that began in 2015') and also showed that: 'A majority (56%) say they have sympathy with the migrants attempting to cross the English Channel (was 53% in March) while 39% say they don't have sympathy (down from 43%).'

However:

> The public are split when it comes to having an asylum system that is either made to be fair or to deter people from seeking asylum in the UK. Overall, 42% say it's more important to have an asylum system that is fair, even if that means allowing more asylum seekers to stay and live in the UK than we do now, while 37% say it is important to have an asylum system that deters people from seeking asylum in the UK.
>
> When it comes to potential measures relating to the asylum system people are split on whether to continue the UK's commitment in the United Nations' refugee resettlement programme (40% support it while 39% oppose it).
>
> (Ipsos MORI, 2021)

This continuing move towards a more positive view of new arrivals was echoed in the most recent Ipsos MORI poll (September 2021) which concluded: 'Immigration attitudes have softened significantly over the last seven years, with public sentiment becoming more positive after the 2016 EU referendum and sustaining at that level ever since.' (Rolfe, Katwala, and Ballinger, 2021, 4)

There is also growing evidence that there is a strong link between economic growth and diversity: '. . . looking at economic and demographic changes during the 2010s . . . the places which have seen the biggest rises in prosperity since the recession have also tended to see the biggest increases in diversity. The towns that recovered post-2011 were those that attracted people from across the country and around the world.' (Clarke, 2021, 4)

There has also been a welcome for new arrivals, particularly in some parts of the UK and at a local level. For example: 'Scotland has a long history of welcoming those fleeing conflict and persecution. Those fleeing conflicts in Vietnam, Kosovo, Bosnia, and the Democratic Republic of Congo have all built new lives in Scotland in recent decades.' (Christie and Baillot, 2020, 4)

In addition, more recently:

> Since 2015, Scotland has welcomed refugees to communities across all 32 local authorities through the UK Government's Syrian Resettlement Programme and Vulnerable Children's Relocation Scheme . . . People arriving through resettlement are recognised by the UK Government as refugees and thus have refugee status on arrival and access to mainstream benefits and services. As of March 2020, 3,569 refugees had arrived in Scotland, representing 16% of the total (21,833) resettled to the UK under these schemes. The top five local authority areas resettling refugees are Glasgow (521), Edinburgh (483), North Ayrshire (201), Dundee (197), and Aberdeenshire (192).
>
> (Christie and Baillot, 2020, 6)

Across Britain, families have provided homes to people seeking sanctuary, for example:

> Denise Lepore and her partner Carol Munro are currently hosting their third guest through Housing Justice. Their first was a gay woman who fled a country that persecutes homosexuals. 'It was nice to show her a culture where it's ok to be openly gay,' said Denise.
>
> (Tanner, 2020)

Communities are working together to provide sanctuary:

> We are a little team of volunteers near Bangor in North Wales, called Croeso Menai – and we have just welcomed our first Syrian refugee family into our community. . . .
>
> It is only one family that we are helping but if one small village in a rural and relatively deprived area of Wales can do this so smoothly, it seems likely that this process could be replicated in villages throughout the UK. Each village community benefits from the opportunity to make a real difference to someone's life and if there were 20,000 villages that did this, the entire country would benefit.
>
> (Woodward, 2021)

Some local groups, such as Hastings Supports Refugees, are providing regular support and comfort to newly arrived people:

> On 11th November [2021], 53 people were rescued in the Channel from their tiny dinghy by Hastings RNLI and brought into Hastings beach, having spent 18 hours on the water. Among them were five children, all girls, and three women, one of whom was six months pregnant.
>
> Hastings Supports Refugees has recently convened an Emergency Response Team after a similarly tiny boat washed up on a nearby beach two months ago when an HSR member happened to be there and witnessed what happened then – the boat being held on the water by Border Force for more than three hours, and no official provision of food, drinks or clothing.
>
> Since then the HSR team has raced to provide food, drink, dry clothes and a warm welcome to more groups of people who have made the perilous journey across the Channel and been brought into Hastings.
>
> (Hastings Community of Sanctuary, 2021)

Some of these welcomes also led to success stories:

> A refugee who was taken to a Kent asylum seeker centre after arriving in the UK alone is set to open a restaurant in London . . .
>
> [Sohail] told KentLive: 'Kent was my first home when I came to the UK, the first step I took on UK soil was in Ashford.
>
> 'Kent social services played an incredible part in my life in terms of settling me into the country and integrating me into the system.'
>
> Sohail described his time at the Swattenden Centre as a crucial period in his life. He added: 'They had incredible programmes and routines for kids like books and libraries, and people who came to educate the kids, teaching them English, and integrating them into society.'
>
> (Heap, 2021)

and the celebration of the enrichment of Scottish culture:

> There is a long history of Scotland welcoming migrants and international artists, who have enriched its artistic production. Over the past century in particular, Scotland has attracted waves of European and international migrants, who came initially to seek refuge or to study and then chose to remain.
>
> As Scottish culture diversified, so to have definitions of 'Scottishness', which is shaped by a vibrant contemporary artistic landscape . . .
>
> (Cotrona, 2021)[69]

To finish, here are wise words from someone who knows:[70]

> The refugee crisis, the greatest global crisis since World War II, has been caused by conflict, wars, poverty, injustice and oppression. It is our moral duty to treat these fleeing human beings with dignity and respect. We cannot shy away from the fact that recent wars in Iraq, Libya, Syria or Afghanistan have exacerbated this crisis. Nor can we pretend that the Western desire to buy cheap products or possess the latest must-have items at a bargain price does not contribute to poverty and inequality.
>
> True freedom and democracy demand that people educate themselves about the world around them. That requires an honest and inquisitive mind – one that questions all opinions, yet hates none.
>
> (Passarlay and Ghouri, 2015, 357)

3

What Does Any of This Have to Do with Libraries?

I have worked in libraries long enough to remember angry responses from some library staff when it was suggested that they might go out into the community and meet people! These responses were often accompanied by comments about 'not being social workers' or something similar.[71]

Yet, at the same time, other library staff saw the immense opportunities that outreach and other community-based working offered, and grabbed them enthusiastically!

These varied views as to what a library is for can lead to healthy debates about our work – but can also lead to polarisation.

Statements of ethics by library associations

In order to start to pull the different kinds of library and information service together, CILIP agreed an Ethical Framework to define a core element of library work:

As an ethical Information Professional I make a commitment to uphold, promote and defend:

- Human rights, equalities and diversity, and the equitable treatment of users and colleagues
- The public benefit and the advancement of the wider good of our profession to society
- Preservation and continuity of access to knowledge
- Intellectual freedom, including freedom from censorship
- Impartiality and the avoidance of inappropriate bias

64 LIBRARIES AND SANCTUARY

- The confidentiality of information provided by clients or users and the right of all individuals to privacy
- The development of information skills and information literacy.

(CILIP, n.d.)

It also published a set of *Clarifying Notes*, which includes: 'Library and information professionals should stand for diversity and challenge prejudice wherever it is found in the information, knowledge and library sector. We should uphold, promote and defend the contribution of a diverse workforce across and at all levels of the profession'. (CILIP, 2018, 2)

Following on from this, in 2019, CILIP published *Libraries, Information and Knowledge Change Lives*, its: '. . . commitment on behalf of librarians, information and knowledge professionals to tackle some of society's most urgent challenges. It outlines our plan to become an 'activist' organisation, through proactive advocacy and the promotion of inclusive, participatory and socially-engaged knowledge and information services'. (CILIP, 2019b)

This document sets out CILIP's priorities, which are:

1. True equality and equity for groups that are marginalised in our society
2. Equality of opportunity for all, irrespective of class or socio-economic status
3. Overcoming the debilitating impact of all forms of poverty on people's lives
4. Opposing all forms of prejudice, conscious or unconscious bias, discrimination or hate speech
5. Supporting our members to rebalance structural inequality in their collections and services
6. Environmental and climate change and their social and ecological impact

(CILIP, 2019a, 4)

Each priority is then expanded in the report. Of particular relevance are:

Priority 1: Equality and equity for marginalised groups

CILIP will be an ally to individuals and groups that are under-represented both in society and in our profession. This means ensuring that these groups are actively included in our work, that we do more to listen to and amplify their voices and that we think critically about and take action to address our own role in perpetuating exclusion and inequality.

(CILIP, 2019a, 5)

Priority 2: Equality of opportunity for all, irrespective of class or socio-economic status

CILIP believes that in order for our society and economy to flourish, we must actively campaign for equality of opportunity for all, irrespective of class or socio-economic status.

In modern Britain, class still acts as a fundamental factor in determining your opportunities in life. We believe this is unfair and that we should do everything we can to improve working class representation in the library and information sector.

At the same time, we want to work with libraries and information services to target support for social mobility and opportunities for all.

(p. 7)

Priority 4: Opposing prejudice, conscious and unconscious bias, discrimination and hate speech

Achieving a fair and just society depends on everyone coming together actively to oppose prejudice, discrimination and hate speech and calling out both conscious and unconscious bias. In light of the rise of nationalist populism, extreme political opinion and polarised public rhetoric, we must stand firm in our opposition to the language of hate and division.

As ethical librarians, information and knowledge management professionals, we must reflect critically on our own conscious and unconscious biases and how they impact on the services we provide.

CILIP will make a clear declaration on behalf of the library, information and knowledge profession that we will not tolerate discrimination or hate-speech and will actively challenge rhetoric that directs hatred toward specific groups or characteristics.

(p. 9)

Librarians in the UK are not alone in doing this. The American Library Association has also published 'Core Values of Librarianship', which include:

Access
All information resources that are provided directly or indirectly by the library, regardless of technology, format, or methods of delivery, should be readily, equally, and equitably accessible to all library users. . . .

Diversity
We value our nation's diversity and strive to reflect that diversity by providing a full spectrum of resources and services to the communities we serve. . . .

Social Responsibility
ALA recognizes its broad social responsibilities. The broad social responsibilities of the American Library Association are defined in terms of the contribution that librarianship can make in ameliorating or solving the critical problems of society; support for efforts to help inform and educate the people of the United States on

66 LIBRARIES AND SANCTUARY

these problems and to encourage them to examine the many views on and the facts regarding each problem; and the willingness of ALA to take a position on current critical issues with the relationship to libraries and library service set forth in the position statement.

(American Library Association, 2019)

In addition, as we will see in Chapter 7, individual library services across the world are developing approaches to welcoming new arrivals.

As the examples that follow will show, both historically and currently, libraries see the provision of services for new arrivals as a key part of their core offer.

Library workers – journeys to the UK

It is also important to challenge the assumption that new arrivals are always 'them' as opposed to 'us' – there are huge dangers of othering people we work with on a daily basis.[72] To help demonstrate this, I am including accounts of their journeys to the UK from three library workers.

Ayub Khan
I asked Ayub what brought him to the UK:

2022 is the 50th anniversary of the Ugandan Exodus, as it came to be known. In 1972, my family was expelled from Uganda – at short notice, and with little more than they could carry. We have few family photos from the time so an early picture of me on my ID card has real sentimental value. It is strangely ironic that it appears on an ID card – and I now head up a registration service dealing in formal family documents.

I was only two when we left but this was a key point in my life. I was the youngest of four children. My family had lived in Uganda, East Africa, for generations.

They were wealthy business people when Idi Amin, Uganda's third President, came to power in 1971. He was determined to wage economic war on the country's Asian population who were disproportionately successful in manufacturing, trade and the Ugandan civil service at that time.

We were amongst around 70,000 Ugandan Asians with British passports forced to leave the country. Many came here – in my family's case, to Birmingham. On arrival we were placed in refugee camps at Stansted. We were not always welcome.

The story is now part of this country's heritage, too. The Ugandan Asians left their homes, careers and businesses behind but brought their entrepreneurial skills with them. My mother, for example, went from a large house with domestic staff to working in a factory making spectacles. My father worked in factories, too, but eventually opened his own secondhand car business. Their struggle, strength and determination undoubtedly shaped my early life.

I still remember what it felt like to be a refugee, and the difficulties I experienced growing up in the 1980s and 1990s, when the National Front was active, and racism was more overt.

I also remember widespread prejudice against Muslims like me following the 9/11 World Trade Centre attacks in New York.

My heart goes out to more recent migrants – fleeing conflicts or persecution in Afghanistan, Ukraine and other dangerous places around the world.

English was my second language, as we say today, so inevitably I was behind with my reading when I started school. Despite my early struggles I did catch up. I later became the first black Muslim President of CILIP – the Library and Information Association, in its 125-year history. I was awarded an MBE, for my services to libraries and culture, in 2013.

I have recently taken on a wider remit which includes managing the Council's Communities and Partnership division. I am now involved with supporting new refugees to the UK settling in the county and have recently been working with Afghan and Ukrainian families. It's strange how things turn out!

Deborah Varenna

What brought you to the UK?
I've wanted to 'try out' living in the UK since I was 15; I loved the language and the impression I got of the culture from fiction (not everything was quite how I thought it'd be, but I still love it nonetheless). In 2017, I got the chance to study abroad for one semester (~5 months) in Liverpool. I ended up meeting my current partner at the university and proceeded to move back in early 2018 after finishing my undergrad. I was planning to gain some experience in libraries at the time to start an MA in Librarianship in fall 2018 – and I did!

Were you here before the Brexit vote in 2016? And have you found that attitudes have changed since then?
I wasn't in the UK before the Brexit vote. In 2016 I was studying English Literature at a German university and vividly remember sitting with course-mates worrying about studying abroad (for example via the Erasmus programme)[73] and our chances of moving to the UK after Brexit. Thankfully for me, I was able to take advantage of the Erasmus programme, which is now no longer the case for many students in the UK – and students from Germany will have a much harder time being able to study in the UK as part of their course.

Have you faced any problems because of your country of origin? And have these had any impact on your work?

Mostly not, thankfully. Overwhelmingly, the response is 'Where in Germany are you from?' and 'Oh I've been to Cologne!' or, less often 'My grandpa was stationed in Germany during World War 2.' All of those I would class as positive and friendly (yes, even the last one!) I met the grandpa in question, who was delighted to practise some of his German with me. I am also fluent in English, and I've lost a lot of my accent in the last few years, so the majority of people I meet don't realise I grew up in Germany – I'm certain this has made my life here easier.

A singular experience was working at a library and meeting a volunteer with learning difficulties, who gave a Hitler salute upon hearing where I was from. While I don't blame them for thinking of that gesture as the identifying feature relating to my country, it was shocking, and somewhat intimidating. I did not know them, and for a split second I did think 'Oh sh*t, is this a neo-nazi?'. Another member of staff told them that that's not okay, and told me the volunteer 'didn't mean it that way'. It did impact the way I behaved around the volunteer from then on, I have to admit. I was cautious and less friendly than I could have been. It does make me wonder about Germany's portrayal in fiction and history lessons in the UK. I had heard similar things happening to a friend who studied abroad in the US when we were 16 – classmates doing the Hitler salute and then being surprised when my friend was shocked.

I should clarify that the Hitler salute is incredibly taboo in Germany, and not in a 'haha – oh, stop it!' sort of way. I've never had it directed at me by someone who wasn't an edgy teenager trying to provoke a reaction from the teacher, and it was an unpleasant experience. In Germany, it's used as a signal to say 'I am a neo-nazi, I defer to Hitler, and I think you share my views.'

What do you think that library workers need to do to make sure that 'new arrivals' feel welcome here?

I think a lot of it seems common sense to me (and maybe it does to you, too) but here goes:

- Be friendly and welcoming.
- Don't get annoyed if you have to repeat yourself.
- Think of your standard sentences used within your library (e.g. 'You need something with your name and address to join the library') and render them into very plain English.
- If you can, have a translation of those sentences into different languages available as a handout.

- Don't get annoyed if the person you're speaking to has a thick accent, and you have to ask them to repeat themselves (if you can't understand them at all, Google translate and similar things are free and helpful!).
- If it is possible within your budget, have bilingual books (both aimed at children and adults), as well as books for people who are learning English as a foreign language.
- Don't talk negatively about them just because you think they can't hear or understand you.
- Let new arrivals complain about the ridiculous immigration policies – nod and smile sympathetically. If you knew the immigration policies, you'd never stop complaining (let's not even address the cost of Visa applications).

Anything else to add?
I often get asked if I've noticed any cultural differences between Germany and England (I'm in Liverpool, apologies to the Welsh, Northern Irish and Scottish). While there are many fun answers – people using everyone's first name right off the bat (wild!), no 'formal' you (slightly uncomfortable), the bread[74] . . . there are also a few less neutral ones – the most obvious and stark one being attitudes to World War 2. A few things are the same though; the weather most obviously, some of the socio-economic issues . . . also, as people keep telling me, the monarchs are actually German, but I have to say that we Germans don't claim them.

Toni Velikova

What brought you to the UK?
I moved to the UK in 2013 to begin my undergraduate degree in Media and Communications. Studying and living in the UK had been my dream since I was 16 years old. 2013 was the year Bulgaria (where I'm from) officially joined the EU and even back then, there was already a sort of moral panic regarding immigration from Eastern Europe. I remember clearly, in December 2012, watching Nigel Farage on national television, saying there would be an influx of 'Romanians and Bulgarians' at the national borders. That television appearance haunted me more or less every day until I actually arrived in the country in September 2013. I was fully aware that, being part of a very international university community, I was very lucky with the acceptance I saw everywhere. Sometimes I would get slightly micro-aggressive comments, mainly from managers at the part-time jobs I was working at the time. 'Your English is pretty good for a foreigner' was the most common one, I think. Other than that, I hadn't really felt ostracised in any way because of where I'm from. On the contrary, my first few years in the UK were liberating to me – as a gay person, who had grown up closeted in an institutionally homophobic place, I was enjoying the

opportunity to explore my sexuality and to finally be myself. I remember attending my first Pride parade in the UK (Durham in 2014) and breaking down crying afterwards because of the stark contrast with my experiences back home.

Were you here before the Brexit vote in 2016? And have you found that attitudes have changed since then?

When the Brexit vote happened in 2016, I was working as a freelance journalist. I was following the referendum from its very beginning and reported live on the results. It was a very distressing time for me as I watched the progression of the vote. Especially because the North East of England (which is where I was living at the time) had a very strong 'Leave' contingent. On the morning after the referendum, I experienced perhaps my first incident of outright xenophobia ever since I've lived in the UK – three different people I had on Facebook, who I had worked with in the past, messaged me to say that they were glad I would be leaving their country for good. I don't know what prompted them to send these messages, and I don't know why they chose me, specifically. But to me, this was the sign that something had changed in this country, and I knew there was more to come. Before then, I really hadn't given much thought on where I was from, or how it impacted my work. I guess that this was a bit of a reality check for me, and it really made me feel quite desolate and hopeless.

Have you faced any problems because of your country of origin? And have these had any impact on your work?

Apart from the aforementioned Facebook messages, the odd argument online (mostly born out of ignorance) – not really. It helps that I am one of what the government and society sees to be 'the good immigrants' – I'm white and I have a full-time paying job. I recognise the privilege in this position and the fact that despite this I still face the odd incident every now and again is very telling.

What do you think that library workers need to do to make sure that 'new arrivals' feel welcome here?

I think education and knowledge of new experiences is key. Before I started work in the library profession (specifically in special collections and archives), a lot of colleagues had no experiences of meeting someone from Eastern Europe and I think educating them on my experiences really helped. So a general broadening of horizons, an understanding of the prejudice that still exists would really help. Another thing that fellow Eastern Europeans need in these times is hope. Many need help and resources to navigate the settled status schemes and are terrified about its implications on their life in a country they've made their home. Perhaps some reassurance, directions and guides on how to dispel this may be helpful. Reaching out to Eastern European communities, discussing their fears with them and reassuring them they're welcome and wanted would go a long, long way.

Library workers – offering support

In September 2021, SCONUL[75] issued a 'Statement of Solidarity with Librarians and Archivists in Afghanistan' which includes:

> Librarians and archivists at CILIP, Research Libraries UK, and SCONUL stand in solidarity with fellow librarians and archivists in Afghanistan.
>
> We are gravely concerned at the threat to the safety and security of librarians and archivists resulting from the change of regime in Afghanistan. They have dedicated their professional lives to serving the people and institutions of Afghanistan and we call on the new regime to guarantee their ability to carry out their professional duties without threat or coercion.
>
> Of particular concern is the place of women librarians and archivists. They are a key part of the profession in Afghanistan, and are vital to encourage women to make use of library and archival services and to ensure that they feel safe to do so. They must be allowed to return to their institutions, and continue to work without any barriers. . . .
>
> The library and archive community in the UK will work together with colleagues internationally to offer whatever support we can to our colleagues in Afghanistan.
>
> (SCONUL, 2021b)

This was followed in 2022 by a similar Statement in support of library professionals in Ukraine:

> We the undersigned, representing the UK community of librarians, archivists and information professionals, wish to extend our solidarity and support for our professional colleagues in Ukraine during the current military action by Russia.
>
> We are gravely concerned at the threat posed by this action to the safety of the Ukrainian people, their heritage and identity, as well as to the security of our professional colleagues. . . .
>
> The library, archive and information professional community in the UK will work with our colleagues around the world to offer whatever support and solidarity we can to our professional colleagues in Ukraine.
>
> (SCONUL, 2022)

At a wider level, the City of Sanctuary Local Authority Network issued a statement of solidarity, including: 'We stand in solidarity and share compassion with all our Afghan community members living in the UK and with the people in Afghanistan. We believe that Local Authorities need to stand ready and willing to support the Government in resettling those who desperately need sanctuary.' (City of Sanctuary Local Authority Network, 2021)

Universities of Sanctuary have also made statements in support of people fleeing Afghanistan (Universities of Sanctuary, 2021) and the war in Ukraine (University of East Anglia, 2022).

4

Libraries' Responses in the UK – Historical Background

This introduction to the background to libraries' relationship with sanctuary has been written by Molly Newcomb (at the time of writing, Molly was a PhD student at the Information School, University of Sheffield, supervised by Dr Briony Birdi and Dr Anna Barton).

Introduction

The discussion about the relationship between public libraries and the concept of 'sanctuary' has spanned almost the entirety of public library provision in UK. Having its roots in the height of the public library legislative debates of the 1850s but also continuing into the present day, this discussion has involved academics, historians, public figures and local communities. Although rarely explicitly using the word 'sanctuary' to describe public libraries and the services they provide to users, nevertheless historical conversations consistently equate public libraries with a place that, in a time when conflict and societal norms controlled daily life, '. . . encapsulates the aspirations of the modern self: a liberal desire for progress, self-realisation, social emancipation, freedom of thought, the questioning of "things established" and, although respectful of tradition and history, for release from the chains of custom.' (Black, 2000a, 169)

Primary source periodicals and journals of the late 19th and early 20th centuries often included arguments, from the public and from members of Parliament, that both praised and criticised the diversity of communities of public libraries (*Chambers's Journal*, 1875; Lubbock, 1891; Leigh, 1906). John Lubbock articulated that users of the public library should not be discriminated against because of their economic background or social standing, that 'all are welcome in the house of knowledge' of the free library (Lubbock, 1891, 60). This was particularly relevant for working class people of the 19th and 20th centuries, who, hemmed in by strict Victorian class standards and the start of the largest conflict the world had seen, needed to give their life meaning beyond their poor living and health conditions, poverty, and less than pleasant working environments (McColvin, 1942; Black, 2000b).

The public library provided the opportunity for people to choose what to read, a place where they could socialise, a place that kept them sheltered from the elements and a place where they had the freedom to think. Paul Sykes sums this up by explaining that 'The pursuit of reading, therefore, was firmly rooted in the pursuit of pleasure; in particular, it was a means of escape from the grim reality.' (Sykes, 1979, 20). Ann Robson states that public libraries could provide '. . . books available with facts, which allowed those accessing texts to interpret their own understanding' – this in turn would help users 'shape their own destinies'. (Robson, 1976, 198)

While Robson refers to everyone who used the public library, Margaret Marshall takes this a step further by promoting the importance of 'self' for the working population. 'At a time when industry was loud, dirty and often all-encapsulating, recreational reading [in the library] allows those working in factories and workhouses the ability to distance their minds from the toll of their everyday work. Effectively, by frequenting the public library, people could have control over one aspect of their life: the definition of their own self.' (Marshall, 1969)

Michael Cart develops this even further by arguing that, by creating self-identity in the public library, one creates a personal refuge, both in one's mind and in the library. He states that '. . . in this increasingly fragmented, factionalised, fractionalised and decaying society of ours, the library is . . . one centre which can hold.' (Cart, 1992, 22). Brendan Howley sums up the importance of this stating that the public library '. . . helps us have the tools to grow our interior lives so they can be part of something bigger. Libraries are the living, breathing toolkits for one of the most basic human instincts: to understand the self.' (Howley, 2018, 16)

All this emphasised the urgent need for a quiet intellectual sanctuary; one that could pull a person away from the hardships they, and their country, faced on a daily basis. These elements fostered a new outlook from the public on the uses of the free public library (Black, 1996). Peter Cowell stated that the essentials of a popular library service include its ability to provide a quiet, well stocked, and centrally located library building (Cowell, 1893). All this had an impact on the services the public library provides, by attempting to establish a space where all can come to enjoy the act of reading and are given the ability to choose their reading material, thereby giving patrons access to a location that could pull them away from the hardships they, and their country, faced on a daily basis (Jast, 1915; Whyte, 1967).[76]

These primary and secondary sources engage with the idea of public library users taking refuge from their different social and personal situations, and, although most do not use the term 'sanctuary', by simply drawing connections between notions of refuge and escape to the idea of sanctuary, clear connections can be made between those who used the library and the need for sanctuary. 'Then came the Great War, and from its grievous effects the libraries of this country have not yet recovered. The altered economic conditions will deeply affect them for many years.'(Pacy, 1926, 222)

There was a steady increase in free public library provision, starting from Queen Victoria's Jubilee in 1887 up until the start of the World War 1. Austerity measures, death tolls, population reactions and the change of focus to other economic trials halted the progress that lasted for over 30 years. As the war brought heightened turmoil to the people of England, the public library remained to be seen as a '. . . source of both useful knowledge and rational recreation' (Black, 2000a, 4). These uses, in addition to the need to maintain the social structure of the day, drove the direction of the public library during the 1910s, when almost 556 adoptions of the Public Library Act of 1850 were passed (Pacy, 1926).

Whereas before the war there was a focus on the establishment of the public library, during the war years there was a focus on maintaining libraries rather than producing new library buildings (Black, 2000a). As the World War 1 progressed, this need to maintain rather than create library provision was critical. As more men went, greater austerity measures were put in place and this, plus a lack of library materials available to each location, forced library committees to adjust their hours of operation (see for example Sheffield. Libraries Art Galleries and Museums Committee, 1956, 3).

The Great War halted the progress of public libraries in England. Even into the 1920s, projects and plans to bring public libraries into the 20th century were halted. A key argument that Lionel R. McColvin makes in his report *The Public Library System of Great Britain*, published in 1942, is that the importance of public libraries did not dwindle during World War 1, and in fact it was at this time when library users needed the service most – but also that libraries needed 'better, more leisurely times' to productively and progressively provide service to patrons. He goes further to say that if '. . . libraries are not themselves speedily put upon a sound basis they will fail in their duty to a reconstructing society.' (McColvin, 1942, v)

Even into modern times, social, economic and political influences are constantly changing the way public libraries can be seen and used as sanctuary. For example, the interwar years between 1920 and the 1940s shifted the focus of public libraries from being primarily on working class people to trying to be inclusive for all people (Black, 2000a). This ideological shift from the 'improvement' of working class people to the inclusion of all people within the community promoted the adoption and implementation of open access stacks, as well as increased usage numbers and in many cases the development of new library premises.

76 LIBRARIES AND SANCTUARY

While the idea of sanctuary never truly goes away, even during major international and domestic conflicts, the crossover between sanctuary and public libraries ebbs and flows and is never confined to one interpretation or strict parameters. Sanctuary can be both an internal and an external experience, one that has been, can be and is, experienced through the historical and modern public library.

The 1940s and 1950s

The Polish Library in London was established in 1942 and since 1947 has supported public libraries by sending batches of Polish books as part of their circulating loans services (see for example Sen and Listwon, 2009). According to Ewa Lipniacka:[77]

> The Polish community, which arrived during the Second World War, also went in for self-catering,[78] initially via the armed forces, then after being demobbed, through the Polish Library in London, and the Sikorski Polish Research Centre, and other collections in Scotland and Northern industrial towns, and other smaller libraries centring on the community immigrant hostels and parish centres. The Central Circulating Library Service supplied boxes of books up and down the country, including many public libraries, but although there was a charge, this was token. Government financing was infinitesimal, and finally stopped in the Sixties, when there was also an attempt to take over the stock and disperse it amongst public libraries. Bitterly fought by the Polish community, this move accounts for the wary attitude which still persists towards central funding, and most of the funds still come from voluntary contributions.
>
> (Lipniacka, 1994b, 164–5)

The 1960s and 1970s

From the late 1960s onwards some public library services were making real attempts to provide services for newly arrived communities in their area, albeit tending to concentrate on 'Indian and Pakistani' communities.[79]

Claire M. Lambert's groundbreaking article of 1969 summarised work at that time, and showed that more than 30 library services were developing book provision, concentrated in the following areas (Lambert, 1969, 44–5):[80]

- The Midlands: 'There are at least ten library authorities involved and between them they have nearly 2,000 Indian language books in their libraries, and several librarians also reported that they had further books on order.' Birmingham had the largest collection with about 600 books;

there were smaller collections at Wolverhampton, West Bromwich, and Nottingham; there were also smaller but growing collections at Dudley, Walsall and Warley, Derby and Burton-on-Trent. 'Urdu readers also have access to a privately run subscription library of about 2,000 books in Nottingham' (p. 44)

- Yorkshire: 'There are seven library authorities in Yorkshire providing Urdu books, with about 1,500 books in all.' The largest collection was at Bradford, with smaller collections at Halifax, Dewsbury, Huddersfield, Middlesbrough, Keighley and Sheffield. Lambert noted that 'No provision is made at Wakefield, Batley, Rotherham, Doncaster or Leeds . . . ' (Lambert, 1969, 44)
- Lancashire: 'There are six library authorities in Lancashire providing some Indian language books. Rochdale has the largest collection (600 books) and there are small collections at Colne, Ashton, Blackburn, Preston and Bolton. Manchester makes no provision.'
- The South, excluding the London Boroughs: 'Outside the London area there are growing collections at Luton, Gravesend and High Wycombe. A smaller collection exists at Dartford and the librarian at Bedford has also expressed an interest in possible sources of supply. Slough makes no provision but would probably subscribe to a loan collection if one were started.'
- The South, London Boroughs: 'There are no large collections in London and there has not been any sustained demand for books in Indian languages comparable to the demand for other language books in some of the Boroughs.' However, there were some signs that provision may increase in the future, with the beginnings of services in the London Boroughs of Ealing and Waltham Forest, and small collections in Hillingdon and at Hammersmith library (which formed part of the Metropolitan Special Collection set up in 1948). However, Lambert noted that: 'The Association of London Chief Librarians is unlikely to make any policy decision on the provision of books in Indian languages until they know what action is to be taken by the Department of Education and Science, to whom the problem was referred in 1966.'
- The North of England and Scotland: there was a small collection of about 200 books in Urdu in the City Library at Newcastle; and Lambert also noted that: 'One of the largest and best used of all the Indian language collections is at the Foreign Language Library in the Gorbals district of Glasgow (645 vols.). The Glasgow City Librarian commented in the 1966/67 annual report that this collection of Indian language books, mostly Urdu, but including some Hindi books, accounts for the significant increase in the use made of the library over the past few years:

78 LIBRARIES AND SANCTUARY

> 15,378 books were issued from the 8,616 volume library; of these issues, 10,828 were oriental books.'

Some library services had started to develop links with local communities (working with volunteers, for example); some were organising exhibitions (e.g. Luton)[81] and other 'extension activities'[82] – as outreach and community-based work was called at that time (e.g. the London Borough of Newham's programmes of activities for children);[83] and some were using promotional methods, for example: 'At Dewsbury the librarian has used the local Pakistani cinema to advertise the Urdu collection' (Lambert, 1969, 47).

However, at the same time, the article raised a number of key issues which still run through discussion of provision today: for example – whether such provision should be seen as a 'special' service or mainstream (even a 'duty'); whether new arrivals should have their language needs met or be encouraged to learn English in order to 'integrate' (interestingly, the article suggests – based on the experience of the Polish community in Britain – that '. . . the desire for books in the mother tongue is not likely to weaken as the time spent in contact with the host society increases.' (Lambert, 1969, 43)); how to find and select suitable library materials and sources of supply – which, in the 1960s and early 1970s, were very few and far between; how to develop and maintain healthy contacts with communities; and how to promote library services more widely.

In addition: 'Some librarians offered little information or few comments, and when this was the case in library authorities with large immigrant communities, it can be indicative only of an almost total lack of communication between the librarians and the immigrants themselves.' (Lambert, 1969, 42)

These themes of developing meaningful communications with communities themselves, together with reassessing existing provision, gathered pace in the 1970s.

As one example (as Geoff Mills outlines):

> In Birmingham Public Libraries in 1974, the 'Inner Ring Zone' was set up to address falling visitor numbers in some inner-city libraries, acknowledging a perception in some new communities that the local library service had little to offer, if they even knew it existed. The institutional image was a barrier, as was the traditional passive role of librarians waiting for people to find the service.
>
> There was a need to adopt outgoing promotion/activities to reach 'disadvantaged communities', which in the mid-1970s meant largely 'multicultural' (to use the term at the time). This 'outreach' approach required staff with different skills, outgoing people who were prepared to leave the

library for storytelling activities and with the confidence, empathy and communication skills to promote the service and take part in activities in the community. Fortunately there was a rich source of local people with these skills, who understood the issues, reflected the multiracial mix of the inner-city, and could welcome all-comers and develop a rapport. Recruiting staff with these skills was by far the most important and influential way of reaching new communities. We found some fantastic people.

(Interview with Geoff Mills, 2022)[84]

As we shall see in a moment, issues such as racism started to be discussed; however, there was also recognition of the potentially positive role that public libraries could play: 'Libraries as one of the media of communication can be used to extend the literary and visual appreciation of the immigrants' cultural background, and to encourage among the host community an attitude that welcomes a pluralistic society in which each of us is willing to "permit others to be different".' (Croker, 1975, 129)

There was also growing interest in publishing lists of books and other materials that reflected the lives, needs and demands of new arrivals; the early 1970s saw, for example:

- Janet Hill (ed.), *Books for Children: the homelands of immigrants in Britain* (Hill, 1971) – and see more on this groundbreaking title below
- Judith Elkin, *Books for the Multi Racial Classroom* . . . (Elkin, 1971)
- Alison Day, *The Library in the Multi-Racial Secondary School* . . . (Day, 1971)
- John Buchanan, *Black Britons* (Buchanan, 1972), produced by the library service in Lambeth
- Merseyside Community Relations Council, *Sowing the Dragon's Teeth* . . . (Kuya, 1973).

It is also interesting to note that these developments were influenced by (and influenced) similar activities abroad, especially the pioneering work of the *Interracial Books for Children Bulletin*, '. . . a groundbreaking social justice oriented reviewing source that was published between 1966–1989.' (IBCB, n.d.).[85] A collection of significant articles published in the *Bulletin* between 1968 and 1974 was republished in the UK in 1975 (Writers and Readers Publishing Cooperative, 1975).

Many library services were providing books that tried to reflect for children and young people something of their life in the UK as well as their 'homelands', yet many of these titles were still extraordinarily old-fashioned, irrelevant, patronising – and, in some cases, inaccurate (and bordering on racist

80 LIBRARIES AND SANCTUARY

– see below). In 1971, a group of London children's librarians produced the first critical assessment of all children's books then in print (excluding textbooks) on selected countries, which was published by the Institute of Race Relations (Hill, 1971). As Janet Hill pointed out in a newspaper interview: '. . . you could hardly work in Brixton library for nine years and not realise that virtually the entire book stock was white while the customers clearly were not.' (Tuft, 1972)

The racism theme was picked up very strongly in a critical and hard-hitting article in the *Library Association Record*:

> The following article takes a critical look at the public library service and its failure to cater to the needs of the black community. It examines some of the traditional responses and attitudes of professional librarianship which effectively debar the service from achieving greater relevance, and demonstrates how librarians, in refusing to come to terms with issues of racism and prejudice, simply provide a climate in which racist attitudes can flourish unchecked . . .
> Racism is a fact of the public library service.
>
> (Waters and Wilkinson, 1974, 3)[86]

According to Alistair Black and Dave Muddiman, this article '. . . provoked a furious response in the correspondence columns of the *Library Association Record* of the time . . . ' but also led to '. . . the widespread adoption of multiculturalism as a service philosophy in public libraries.' (Black and Muddiman, 1997, 82)

Around the same time, there were also a growing number of groups and individuals who commented critically on and worked to change the ways that books for children and young people were produced (written, illustrated, published, sold), including, for example, the Children's Rights Workshop (which went on to establish the annual 'Other Award', which ran from 1975 to 1987);[87] David Milner,[88] Bob Dixon[89] and CISSY.[90] (Despite this, many of the issues around racism were not really explored thoroughly until some 20 years later. . .)

Responses at the policy level included a key report, published in 1976, of a working party set up by the then Library Advisory Council[91] and Community Relations Commission;[92] although now obviously dated, nevertheless many of its findings and recommendations are still pertinent: '. . . the existence of a multi-cultural society in Britain requires two broad types of response from librarians. The first is a recognition of the implications of the changed nature of our society as a whole; the second, the need to identify and meet altering requirements in multi-racial areas.' (Library Advisory Council and Community Relations Commission, 1976, 2)

The report urged libraries to reflect society, in areas where there are few or no new arrivals, as well as in areas of high concentration: 'This involves both initiating an active policy to project positive images of our multi-cultural society, and also facing up to the admittedly difficult issues of prejudice and bias.' It recommended:

- continued reassessment of existing library stock
- the withdrawal of dated or inaccurate items, and
- examination of new materials.

'Each library authority and its staff must evolve their own methods of assessing needs and devise programmes to meet them.' (p. 3)

The report noted the vital need for formal and informal contact at all levels with a wide range of agencies: '. . . there can be no real alternative to exhaustive local fieldwork by library staff direct with the "grass roots".' (p. 3)

The report recommended engaging with local communities via 'extension' and outreach activities, such as talks; loans to playgroups, childminders, hostels, prisons, community centres, play-sites, parks, swimming pools; provision for housebound readers.

Finally, the report urged that: 'There should be a multi-cultural component in the training of all new staff. Specialist in-service courses should also be provided.' (p. 9)

As an example of loans of library materials and outreach activities, in Birmingham Public Libraries:

> The loan scheme to school classes and playgroups, following storytelling
> sessions in and out of the library, was the most likely way of introducing the
> availability of reading and information materials to refugees and asylum seekers.
>
> Apart from liaising with schools, the next most likely way of successfully
> promoting access to library services was through talking to community advice
> centres and offering them bulk loans of materials which they could then use with
> local people. Generally this was community information materials, key
> handbooks (they rarely had much funding), specific legal books in Urdu, and
> citizen advice resources that were effectively on permanent loan.
>
> (Interview with Geoff Mills, 2022)

As public libraries increased their contacts with their local communities, there was growing recognition of the demand (just as Claire Lambert had identified) for books in community languages. For example, Vera Jacques (then Children's Librarian, Bradford Libraries) contributed to a 1979 practical storytelling guide a piece on 'Storytelling in a multi-racial society', in which she said: 'We cater for children from Asia, the West Indies, Greece, China, Yugoslavia, children whose parents come from Poland or the Ukraine and local children from the British Isles, including an occasional gypsy family. Most speak English – though for some it is a second language.' (Jacques, 1979, 18); and, in Nottinghamshire, provision of books for people reading Bengali, Gujarati, Hindi, Punjabi and Urdu developed from 1974 onwards from just being at the Central Library to becoming almost county-wide, assisted by the appointment in 1978 of an Ethnic Minorities Librarian (funded via an Urban Aid grant) (Brahmbhat, 1990).

Patricia Coleman recalled that, when she was appointed to head the East Manchester group of libraries in 1974:

One of the developments was to introduce books in languages of the Indian Sub-Continent into the old Longsight Library. First of all I had to seek permission from the Library Committee . . . I had to prepare a report for the committee and then go to answer questions when it was discussed. The only question I can remember being asked was about whether it was better to let recent immigrants sink or learn to swim, that is, to learn English. I am sure I said something to the effect that I considered they were more likely to settle and integrate if they were also able to retain some of their own language and culture. The committee allowed me to proceed.

(Interview with Patricia Coleman, 2022).

This illustrates the difference then in terms of decision-making about library stock! The approach was obviously successful, as Pat notes:

When the new Longsight Library opened it was, from the outset, welcomed by local people of all ages and was really well used. I was particularly pleased that many of the users were from the Asian community and other black and minority ethnic groups too. Many of the new staff we had appointed, particularly library assistants and security staff, were from these groups and I am sure that helped. We now had proper arrangements for purchasing books in Asian Languages from recognised library suppliers. We also had a much expanded collection of Black Literature and non-fiction relevant to Africa and the Caribbean. We also had music collections with tape cassettes and records for loan and a picture/framed print loan collection. In both music and picture collections we aimed to reflect the interests and backgrounds of the local community.

and the library quickly became a community hub.

A running theme throughout this period – and later! – was where to obtain library materials, how to afford them, and how to ensure that there was a

LIBRARIES' RESPONSES IN THE UK – HISTORICAL BACKGROUND   83

regularly changing selection available, and I have included a brief look at this in Appendix 4.

In 1977, the Library Association issued a policy statement *Public Libraries in a Multi-cultural Britain* (Library Association, 1977) to encourage the improvement of services to minority ethnic groups, and this in turn led to a research project carried out by Eric Clough and Jacqueline Quarmby, published in 1978 as *A Public Library Service for Ethnic Minorities in Great Britain* (Clough and Quarmby, 1978). This included the results of surveys together with commentary and recommendations, and looked at, for example: the make-up of the population in the UK; a survey of public library provision (plus a larger case study looking at the Midlands); a survey of co-operative purchasing arrangements; research into methods of stock selection (which included 'blanket' orders; using booksellers in the UK; using booksellers in India, Pakistan and Bangladesh; book-buying visits to the Indian subcontinent).

The commentary included the authors' dissatisfaction with the overall level of provision by public libraries and a criticism of the tendency to look for 'standards' as being the solution, which they saw as being: '. . . either pitched at an average level designed to encourage the below-average . . . or fixed at a level of best . . . ' (Clough and Quarmby, 1978, 283)

Many of the recommendations in the report strike a chord today. For example, they identified the need for staff to reflect the local community (and focused on better recruitment and stronger in-service training). There needed to be signage in community languages. Public libraries needed to find out what should be done by working with other library authorities and other agencies, and particularly by finding out what the community needed and wanted.

The report also has some powerful messages about the public library's role:

> The public library has an important rôle to play in countering prejudice and in helping to develop a racially just society, and this can best be done by enabling all communities to learn something of the background of the many and various minorities that go to make up the British people.
>
> Secondly, the public library service must face up to the need to counter racial prejudice by the care it shows in the book provision it makes.

(p. 87)

and:

> . . . books in the children's library should reflect the society of which they form a part and avoid the ethnocentricity of a white British culture.

(p. 300)

84 LIBRARIES AND SANCTUARY

In 1979, the British National Bibliography Research Fund[93] funded a piece of research by Madeleine Cooke[94] into public library provision for ethnic minorities in the UK, and its findings neatly highlight key issues at the end of this decade:

> The survey returns suggest that many libraries provide an inadequate choice of materials and that the collections available in individual languages are often both too small and too static. An uneconomic service is provided at a disproportionately high cost in staff time. Those libraries without specialist staff with the relevant language skills and knowledge of the local community usually find selection very difficult. The bookstock provided may be irrelevant to the real needs of the community, both in content and, occasionally, in language.
>
> (Cooke, 1979, 2)

These themes were re-emphasised by Patricia Coleman in her report *Whose Problem?* (which was written in 1980), along with criticisms of seeking external funding rather than '. . . directing some portion of normal expenditure . . . ', and the absence of any written policies except in a few authorities, which she said showed a lack of commitment to provision (Coleman, 1981, 25).

The 1980s

Up until now, there had been an emphasis on providing library materials in Bengali, Gujarati, Hindi, Punjabi and Urdu; however, there was growing recognition, drawing on research, of the need to provide material in other languages and for other communities. The late 1970s and early 1980s saw the publication of a number of research reports, including several into the literacy, library and information needs of:

- Cypriot people in Haringey (Leeuwenberg, 1979)
- Armenian people in London (Sabbagh, 1980)
- Indian women in the UK (Gundara, 1981)
- Black children attending West Indian Supplementary Education Schemes in London (Wellum, 1981)[95]
- African Caribbean communities (Alexander, 1982)
- Vietnamese people in the UK (Simsova, 1982)
- Chinese people in London (Simsova and Chin, 1982) and, later in the decade, Chinese people across the UK (Ng, 1989).

Sylva Simsova's work on the library needs of Vietnamese people was particularly noteworthy. Her research included a survey of public libraries' provision: surveys were sent to 168 library authorities, of which 117 replied. She concluded from this that: 'It seems that library service to the Vietnamese is beset with problems.' (Simsova, 1982, 22)

These problems included:

- making contact with Vietnamese communities
- the supply of library stock – where to get it from, and what titles?[96] The survey also threw up the possible need for some sort of 'back-up' service from where titles could be borrowed.

Many of her recommendations and observations are just as relevant today, for example: 'Support groups should as part of the general induction to the "British way of life" introduce them to the public library, and at the same time the public library itself should address some publicity to the refugees resettled in its catchment area.' (p. 11)

She went on to recommend that public libraries can offer support by:

- making accommodation available for classes and individual tuition
- providing reading materials both in the library and the education centres where English is taught as a second language
- making a room available for holding meetings
- providing accommodation and books for Saturday schools
- holding Vietnamese storytelling sessions.

She also recommended that public libraries make formal links to Social Services and Housing and establish further links to the community via the 'grapevine'.

Also in 1982, Ziggi Alexander's *Library Services and Afro-Caribbean Communities* was published. This looked at a number of major – and recurring – themes, including: the need for greater awareness of Black history and Black lives; the need for more positive images; the importance of representative staffing and of staff training; the need to tackle racism. She called particularly for assessments of community needs; the greater use of volunteers to engage the community; activities and exhibitions that reflected Black lives – '. . . positive material concerned with cultures other than the dominant Anglo-Saxon one, should be housed in all service points.' (Alexander, 1982, 14)

She was also critical of existing provision, describing an '. . . atmosphere of increasing complacency' and argued that: 'It is time that the library profession addressed itself to the attitudes and assumptions prevalent within its ranks and in society as a whole; the one cannot be isolated from the other.' (p. 51)

Ziggi Alexander also argued strongly that appropriate funding should be found: 'Section 11 funds and Urban Aid Grants should be viewed only as expedients in an economic climate when growth is almost impossible. There should be a willingness to divert and reallocate existing resources on a priority basis in order to meet the demands of a racially diverse society.' (pp. 13–14)

There is some further information about sources of funding in Appendix 3.

In 1986, the Library Association's Association of Assistant Librarians published my introductory pamphlet on community librarianship (Vincent, 1986), which included a chapter on 'Serving the Black community'. This included recommendations of ways in which provision for the Black community could be developed (and the majority of these are still relevant today):

- develop contact with Black library users and with local groups which are either predominantly for the Black community, or which have a high proportion of Black users
- examine the library's stock of materials directly relevant to the Black community: 'There are arguments for and against setting up 'black literature' collections as separate areas in the library, but, certainly, in a library which has not had a history of serving the black community, this can be a useful feature. The aim, of course, should not be a form of 'stock apartheid' but to highlight the stock periodically, and to ensure that all areas of stock include materials giving a black perspective.' (Vincent, 1986, 18)
- remember that the Black community needs access to the widest range of materials, not just materials by Black writers
- 'at the same time, build up collections of materials of particular interest, for example history and geography of India, Pakistan, Bangladesh, Africa, the Caribbean; black people's history in Britain; books on race issues; materials on black art, music, fashion; literature by black writers. Remember to include materials in translation and published outside the UK, not just mainstream UK-published books' (p. 18)
- re-assess your collections of Black music
- promote services via displays and booklists, as well as by taking materials out to community groups
- look at the library building as a whole: 'Does it put over a positive black image, through displays (either by the library itself or by local organisations), posters, and feature collections of materials?' (p. 18)
- 'be prepared to deal firmly with issues of racism that occur, for example comments from members of the public to black staff' (p. 19)

- begin to develop a strategy for assessing library materials – and also for dealing with items which could be racially offensive.

By the mid-1980s, 'multicultural' provision was spreading; Madeleine Cooke reported that there were multicultural bookfairs and events in a number of public library authorities, including Brent, Cambridgeshire, Derbyshire, Edinburgh, Enfield, Glasgow, Hounslow, Kirklees, Merton, Newcastle, Northamptonshire and Walsall (Cooke, 1988).

There was also a greater focus on 'community librarianship' by a number of public library authorities, including Manchester and Derbyshire (Astbury, 1989b), and, from my own experience, Lambeth and a number of inner-London library services.

At the same time, the increasing impact of cuts to library services was being felt; these had started in the 1970s, and, as a report from the Centre for the Public Library In the Information Society, Department of Information Studies, The University of Sheffield noted: 'The new Conservative government, elected to power in 1979, placed a more explicit emphasis on reducing public sector spending, and the next eighteen years saw increasing restrictions on local authority expenditure.' (Proctor, Lee and Reilly, 1998, 12)

The last half of the 1980s was also rather dominated by discussions about the future funding of public libraries (see for example Prichard, 1991), including discussions about the possibility of charging for – or even privatising – library services:

> Proposals for income-generation by public libraries and, in certain circumstances, for the levying of direct charges on clients for the borrowing of books and for the provision of information services, would seem to herald the end of the free library service as established since the Victorian period.
>
> Potentially even more damaging to the role of the free and genuinely freely accessible public library service, were it to be implemented, is the suggestion in the Green Paper[97] that some of its current services, such as those to local old people's homes, the lending of video tapes, or, eventually, even all the services being provided by branch libraries, might be privatised, that is contracted out to commercial interests.
>
> (Astbury, 1989a)

The 1990s

Despite a considerable number of developments during the previous 20 years, nevertheless, by the early 1990s, there was growing dissatisfaction with levels of provision for new arrivals (as well as many other communities).

88 LIBRARIES AND SANCTUARY

For example, despite the provision of Birmingham's 'Library of Asian Languages' since the 1970s, by 1990–1991 John Dolan described it as under-resourced and marginalised; and he also cited discussions at the Public Library Authorities Conference in Autumn 1990, which he said that, under the surface, demonstrated: '. . . confessing yet again, the failure of British librarianship to understand the multi-racial character of the UK and to restructure their services accordingly.' (Dolan, 1992, 16)

Research undertaken in 1990 (Cooke, Feather and Malley, 1991) showed the extent of provision of books in 'minority languages' and also identified the number of library authorities per region making or needing provision in these languages, referring to 27 languages, of which the most common were Urdu, Bengali, Punjabi, Gujarati, Hindi, Polish and Chinese. There was reliance placed on a number of co-operative purchasing schemes, although:

> Many respondents drew our attention to their view that responsibility for the control of materials in Indic and other languages ought to be integrated into mainstream collection management policies and procedures. This view appears to be growing in currency among those most involved in such work, despite the obvious difficulties which it is acknowledged to present.
>
> (Cooke, Feather and Malley, 1993, 82)

The authors also made a strong, critical recommendation for future action:

> Library authorities have their own priorities, and it is within these that the future planning of provision for minority languages will take place. At present, however, there is a clear lack of a national vision. This was noted by several respondents, and we endorse the observation. There was, in general, a view that the right direction for future developments was towards the development of a strategic approach, rather than the traditional pattern of co-operative arrangements between authorities or service providers . . . A national infrastructure is needed which would bring together all the parties involved, and all the potential service providers. Such a body could not ignore the existence of both stock and linguistic expertise in the academic libraries, and would have to explore the possibility of their involvement.
>
> (p. 83)

Many of these points were echoed by research by librarian S.K. Raitt, which showed just how isolated older Punjabi people were, and which highlighted their need for access to information (Raitt, 1993).

Despite the lack of such a body, there was, however, still some good practice, for example as noted in a social audit report on Newcastle Library Service:

It was also pointed out, by staff, that libraries were often seen as safe place for formal meetings of groups recruited from Newcastle's ethnic minority communities. One example of this, from the case study area, was the weekly meetings of a Bosnian refugees' group at Heaton Library. There were other similar examples from elsewhere in the City.

(Linley and Usherwood, 1998, 36)

and in a news report on shortlisted entries for the UK Library Association Community Initiative Awards, which included a reading scheme for ethnic minority children in Enfield, involving storytelling, crafts, learning about the library and introductions to books and targeting 3–8-year-olds from the borough's Turkish, Bangladeshi, African-Caribbean and refugee communities (Raven, 1998; Vincent, 1999, 172).

In 1996, Anthony Olden,[98] Ching-Ping Tseng and Alli A. S. Mcharazo published *Service for All?*, which was subtitled 'a review of the published literature on black and ethnic minority/multicultural provision by public libraries in the United Kingdom'. This report made some key points about library provision at the time, including the following:

- There were continuing discussions about providing collections of books in languages other than English; for example, Westminster public libraries established a Chinese collection at Charing Cross Library in the 1980s and early 1990s – which is still thriving in 2021 (City of Westminster, 2021). However, they also cited work by Sylva Simsova on 'linguistic minorities' (of which they said that '. . . once a linguistic minority reaches the fifth generation it is extremely unlikely that members would retain the original language of their forefathers.' (Olden, Tseng and Mcharazo, 1996, 7)) and suggested that this was having an impact, for example on the Polish Central Circulating Library which, they said, was overstocked with children's books
- Public libraries could also serve as social venues, for example the Wandsworth Multicultural Library at Tooting Library (see for example Lipniacka, 1994b, 169)

In 1999, Anthony Olden published key research into how Somali refugees found information, which concluded and recommended:

A Western information environment is a new experience for the majority of Somalis. Apart from those attending college they do not make use of libraries: 'they are not reading a lot – but they're talking a lot'. One drawback to oral communication is that the person passing on information might not be

90 LIBRARIES AND SANCTUARY

sufficiently well informed and might mislead without intending to do so . . .

Statutory providers of information such as public libraries need to do more to link with the community and find out how to help.

(Olden, 1999, 222–3)

Public Libraries, Ethnic Diversity and Citizenship

In April 1996 the University of Warwick began a major 18-month study, looking at how public libraries had engaged with 'ethnic diversity'; the research report, *Public Libraries, Ethnic Diversity and Citizenship*, was published in 1998 (Roach and Morrison, 1998a). The key findings were critical of provision to date, and included:

1 'The public library has not yet managed to engage fully with ethnically diverse communities;
2 A social distance exists between the public library and ethnic minority communities which tends to exclude ethnic minority citizens whilst preserving professional autonomy;
3 There is a lack of clear vision and leadership on ethnic diversity and racial equality matters within the public library service;
4 Across the public library service there is a lack of coherence in strategies to identify and track the changing library needs of ethnic minority communities and in those strategies which seek to engage ethnic minorities in debate on the future of public library provision;
5 The public library is not yet central to or sufficiently supportive of the social and community networks established by ethnic minorities;
6 The structure, culture and ethnic profile of the public library service is restrictive in terms of service access and denies ethnic minorities a stake in the public library system;
7 The public library service has failed to account fully for its progress in respect of race equality whilst current performance systems are largely colour-blind;
8 The resource pressures on the public library service coupled with current uncertainty regarding the loss of special funds may present further challenges to ethnic minority engagement and inclusion.' (Roach and Morrison, 1998a, 7)

Interestingly (as this issue has recently moved centre stage again), the report also argued that libraries needed to consider an anti-racist stance, rather than focusing on multiculturalism, drawing on work that had been carried out in the education sector to indicate that there are '. . . fundamental theoretical differences between multiculturalism and anti-racism' (Roach and Morrison, 1998a, 16) and that we need to differentiate between seeing racism as an individual 'attitude' problem, and seeing it as institutional.[99]

The report (known subsequently as the 'Warwick Report') had considerable impact on public libraries: for example, Enfield Libraries (as one example) used it as the basis for overhauling their provision to local communities, setting up a Warwick Report Steering Group to implement the recommendations (Vincent and Hill, 1999). The Network – see below – also organised a subsequent training course in 2001, 'Roach & Morrison 3 years on', to highlight what developments had taken place (Durrani, 2001).

Information needs of refugee groups

1998 also saw the publication of a research report which still has considerable relevance today. Librarians Rosemary Raddon and Christine Smith looked at the provision of services to refugees and asylum seekers in voluntary organisations[100] and local authorities throughout the UK; as part of this, they carried out a survey of local authorities, to which they had 109 responses: 99 had completed all or part, 10 had been unable or unwilling to complete (or wrote to say that refugees were not an issue in their area).

Their findings were critical of existing provision, noting: 'It was felt that systems were frequently dense and unhelpful' and noted what they perceived as: '. . . general unhelpfulness of the local library service and the lack of sensitivity on the part of staff.' (Raddon and Smith, 1998, 26)

In London, the boroughs of Barnet, Brent, Camden, Enfield, Greenwich, Harrow, Hounslow, Islington and Redbridge were addressing the information needs of refugees, although not always through the library service; Islington were running a 'Service to Refugees' project, funded by Section 11 and set up by their Race Equality Unit involving the library service. However, at the same time: '. . . several boroughs known to have large refugee populations made no direct service provision' (p. 35) and 'Two claimed to have no refugees in their boroughs although it was rather alarming to find in one of these responses the assumption that refugees are *de facto* black . . . ' (p. 36)

Responses from library services outside London were: '. . . very patchy. The majority offered no service at all to refugee communities, and whilst some of these authorities undoubtedly do not have any need to provide such services, some surprising negative responses were received from areas where returns from the voluntary sector would indicate that refugee populations existed.' (p. 36)

Generally, responses from the Midlands and North were more positive; for example provision for Vietnamese new arrivals in Coventry and

Northamptonshire; for Vietnamese and Somali new arrivals in Manchester; and they also noted Warwickshire's work with an ESOL co-ordinator to provide information about interpreting services through library enquiry points.

One significant recommendation from the report was the need to investigate the lack of communication between libraries and other services, something that was echoed in succeeding reports.

Open to All?

Between 1998 and 2000 the research project 'Public Library Policy and Social Exclusion'[101, 102] carried out an assessment of public libraries in the UK and their capacity to tackle social exclusion. The project's findings were published in 2000 in three volumes – *Overview and Conclusions* (Muddiman et al., 2000a); *Survey, Case Studies and Methods* (Muddiman et al., 2000b); and *Working Papers* (Muddiman et al., 2000c). The project outputs included:

- 16 working papers which explored the historical and international context of social exclusion itself, and of public library responses to it;
- a survey of all UK public library authorities, which assessed the nature and extent of current UK public library activity and initiatives relating to social exclusion;
- detailed case studies of eight UK public library authorities and their social exclusion strategies and initiatives;
- recommendations and guidelines which suggest how public library exclusion strategies might be enhanced and strengthened through both innovation in practice and new models of local provision.

(Muddiman et al., 2000a, 2)

The survey found that, overall, 129 out of 208 library authorities responded to the survey (a response rate of 62%). The final project report noted that the survey:

. . . provides evidence that many of the UK's most marginal/excluded people are not widely considered in library strategy, service delivery or staffing. [A table in the report] suggests that a majority of PLAs [public library authorities] have developed some level of prioritisation of children and young people, the elderly and housebound, and people with disabilities. However, the same cannot be said of marginal groups such as travellers, refugees, and homeless people who have been considered by under 20% of PLAs.

(Muddiman et al., 2000a, 27–8)

The specific figures from the survey are set out in Table 4.1.

Table 4.1 *Provision by local authorities for refugees* (from Muddiman et al., 2000a)

Excluded social group	% of authorities identified as service priority	% of authorities with permanent service	% of authorities with staff specifically responsible	% of authorities with time-limited projects	% with materials selection guidelines
Refugees	16%	8%	9%	9%	2%

In addition, even 'racial and ethnic minorities' were a service priority in only 54% of public library authorities – and only 49% of library services said they had permanent service provision. There were over 50 recommendations, which are nearly all relevant today.

In 1999, the MacPherson Inquiry Report (MacPherson, 1999) was published and, from then onwards, there was a gradually increasing focus on both racism and the position of Black workers within libraries and information services (Durrani, 1999; Pateman, 1999).

2000 onwards

In 2001 Gloucestershire County Council created a website for people seeking sanctuary; this article is quoted at some length, as it is a very early and important example of this kind of tailored provision:

> We are in the process of piloting a website in partnership with GARAS, the Gloucestershire Association for Refugees and Asylum Seekers, GlosCat (the local FE College) and the Barton and Tredworth Community Development Centre. (BTCDC). The GARAS drop-in centre is in the Barton & Tredworth area of Gloucester and this is the area where most of the asylum seekers are presently living. We had identified a need for quality information both for asylum seekers themselves and for those advice workers working with them. The web offers the opportunity to provide easy access across a wide area to one authoritative and up-to-date version of the necessary resources.
>
> The project is in 4 stages:
>
> - Research – what is needed? Identify and collect text or links to existing pages
> - Construction – build and test the site and act on feedback from the users
> - Market – familiarity sessions and/or ICT training for users, advice workers, library staff
> - Consider future developments/partnerships

94   LIBRARIES AND SANCTUARY

and has a budget of £900 from the Gloucestershire ACET,[103] as part of their Ethnic Minority Achievement Project, and matched funding of £1200 plus contributions in kind from the partners. We employed a young person from the community to research the information needs of asylum seekers by a series of interviews, using the facilities at the BTCDC and at GARAS. The GlosNet team then built the web pages and a 'stand-alone' version was tested by asylum seekers at the GARAS centre with the assistance of community workers.

The pages got a favourable response, but also the expected comment – *what about those who don't read English?* Asylum seekers have come to Gloucester from places as diverse as Syria, the Czech Republic, Algeria, Somalia, Sudan, Poland and Eritrea and we have identified 13 relevant languages. Many but not most have English or French as a second language. Funds and time have been very restricted, but our plan now is to build a home page which has HELP buttons labelled in the appropriate languages linking to pages advising users, also in the appropriate languages, that help is available at GARAS. We see this as an interim stage in the progress towards being able to provide information in whatever language is required.

Some asylum seekers already have internet skills but most do not and an important part of this project is to offer ICT training using the facilities at the college and the mobile IT unit and to link them up with suitable ESOL courses e.g. medical English, English for job searches. GlosCat – the local FE college – is organising familiarity sessions for those asylum seekers who have no previous experience of ICT.

The web pages are hosted on the county council server and can be seen . . . free of charge in all public libraries in the county and on the internet. The libraries in Gloucester have direct links to it from their computers' home pages, and the staff will help users find what they need. Many of the topics covered relate to the information needs of asylum seekers wherever they are in the UK but the contacts given are local contacts. The information will be regularly reviewed with the assistance of GARAS, the community librarians and the GlosNet team.

Links are made to national sites such as the Immigration & Nationality Directorate and the Benefits Agency. We hope to build a relationship with other information providers, including the London Boroughs . . . I am sure that a large proportion of information needs are independent of local conditions, and it doesn't make sense for us all to be providing versions of this. Our efforts should go into making local information accessible. We are also very interested in providing links to 'recreational' sites – and to talking to anyone who has experience of providing leisure reading for these groups.

(Frodin, 2001)

LIBRARIES' RESPONSES IN THE UK – HISTORICAL BACKGROUND   95

In June 2001, The Network held a conference, 'Libraries, Museums, Galleries and Archives for All – Tackling Social Exclusion across the Sectors' (Vincent, 2001), at which there were presentations by Di Reynolds (then Manager, Outreach/BME, London Borough of Merton) on Merton's work with refugees and asylum seekers; and by Diane Chilmaid (then Access Services Manager, Kent Arts & Libraries), who outlined some of the work that Kent was doing to reach refugees and asylum seekers and drew attention to a forthcoming partnership bid for DCMS/Wolfson[104] funding for reader development work with refugees and asylum seekers . . .

. . . and, in 2001– 2002, Kent Arts & Libraries (in partnership with South East Arts, Kent County Council Asylum Seekers Support Unit, NW Kent Racial Equality Council, Migrant Helpline, Folkestone Asylum Seekers Forum, Kent County Council Adult Education, and The Network) were awarded the grant via the DCMS/Wolfson Challenge Fund to develop a piece of work, 'Words without Frontiers', which assessed provision by public libraries for refugees and asylum seekers, and produced guidance. For the assessment, they carried out a survey of every public library authority in England, Scotland, Northern Ireland and Wales – 108 (52%) authorities responded. The results were published (Ryder and Vincent, 2002) and give a snapshot of provision at that time. As we said in our introduction: 'From the results, it is clear that some public libraries are providing excellent levels of service (although none felt that they were really on top of this area of work), some are beginning to find out what was needed in their communities, and some are barely providing a service at all.'

We also hoped that: '. . . this work will now kick-start an urgent review of provision, and will lead to exploration of ways of raising additional funding and the development of services for refugees and asylum-seekers.' (Ryder and Vincent, 2002, 3)

'Welcome To Your Library'

In 2003–4 the Paul Hamlyn Foundation (PHF) launched its Reading and Libraries Challenge Fund.[105] As part of this, it funded the pilot phase of 'Welcome To Your Library' in five London library authorities (Brent, Camden, Enfield, Merton and Newham). This project was designed to build on previous initiatives, and, in particular, Merton Libraries' work with refugees and asylum seekers, for which they won the CILIP Libraries Change Lives Award 2001.[106] This pilot project was evaluated (Advice Development Project, 2004), and Helen Carpenter (the Project Co-ordinator) produced a final report – this noted that, despite the project's running for just 12 months, and with part-time staffing, its key achievements included:

96 LIBRARIES AND SANCTUARY

- Detailed mapping of the location, identity and needs of emerging communities and the organisations that support them in every participating borough
- Development of new local partnerships with RCOs [Refugee Community Organisations] and others across the project
- Relevant training for over 200 library staff with more at planning stage at the time of writing
- Enhanced management information for service planning for and with refugee communities
- Simplified library joining procedures and proposals to capture better data on number of refugees who are public library members
- Introductory tours of public libraries for refugee communities leading to over 300 new users
- ICT and other taster sessions
- Purchase of relevant stock with active involvement of refugee communities
- Celebratory cultural events bringing different communities together.

(Carpenter, 2004, 40)

As noted above, the pilot project was evaluated and then, with further PHF funding, developed from 2005 to 2007 into a national project. This involved working with library services (and partners) in Leicester City Council; Liverpool City Council; London Borough of Hillingdon (in partnership with Healthy Hillingdon and HOPE, the Healthy Living Centre for Hillingdon); London Borough of Southwark; and a consortium of library authorities in Tyne & Wear (Gateshead, Newcastle, North Tyneside, South Tyneside and Sunderland). The national project was also evaluated, and found that:

WTYL contributed highly relevant learning to public library service planning and delivery and provides good practice examples in relation to:

- mapping need
- developing project management skills
- reaching refugee communities
- building effective and sustainable partnerships
- enhancing access
- providing a range of effective projects that support community cohesion
- enhancing non-project staff awareness of relevant issues.

(ADP Consultancy, 2007, vii)

The Welcome To Your Library project won the 2007 CILIP Libraries Change Lives Award (specifically for the work in Camden and Leicester around volunteering and employment) and also gained a positive write-up in *The Guardian* (Pati, 2007).

Although the project finished in 2007, some of the resources are still available, and have provided valuable background information for more recent work. These resources include:

- a paper exploring the role of libraries as promoters of health literacy and community cohesion (Knight et al., 2008)
- a paper by Helen Carpenter looking at the role of public libraries in multicultural relationships (Carpenter, 2007)
- Welcome to Your Library project final reports:
  – Gateshead (McKinlay, 2007)
  – Hillingdon (Welcome To Your Library Steering Group, 2008)
  – Leicester (Leicester Libraries, 2007)
  – Liverpool (Jones, 2007)
  – Newcastle upon Tyne (Merritt, 2007)
  – North Tyneside (North Tyneside Libraries, n.d.)
  – South Tyneside (South Tyneside Council, 2007)
  – Southwark (Prendergast, 2007)
  – Sunderland (Sunderland Libraries, 2007)

In addition, as part of the Reading and Libraries Challenge Fund, PHF funded an extension to a project run by Leeds Library and Information Service, 'A Sense of Belonging', focusing on meeting the needs of people seeking sanctuary and also helping work towards community cohesion in the city. The aims of this one-year extension were:

- To bring together information and leisure opportunities for refugees and asylum seekers and to be a one stop shop of information
- To raise awareness of our services to other organisations working with refugees and asylum seekers and bring together information in this field
- To be the first step to integration in the local community through learning support and citizenship
- To continue to promote libraries and literacy

(Ahmed, 2007, taken from pp. 1–3)

The project report includes examples of the publicity used and results from consultations with community organisations.

Other developments

At the same time, there were also developments elsewhere – for example, library services providing staff training around working with new arrivals (e.g. Nottingham in 2004).[107]

Although, sadly, not all the work continued beyond the project funding, nevertheless there was enough of a legacy for this project to form part of the background to the successful bid by Thimblemill Library, Sandwell, to become the UK's first Library of Sanctuary in 2017 (see p. 99).

In 2010 PHF published an evaluation (Carpenter, 2010) of all the pieces of work funded as part of their Reading and Libraries Challenge Fund initiative. Looking back, probably the most significant finding of this evaluation was:

> In order to contribute to sustained local and national change, projects must identify social needs, audiences and latent demand, and place what they plan to achieve within policy context. Projects also need to follow funding with strong leadership, workforce development and community participation and partnerships.
>
> (Carpenter, 2010, 4)

Significantly, the PHF then went on to fund another piece of research (Lynch, 2012) which identified significant issues with the constant focus on project-based – as opposed to mainstream – funding.[108]

In 2008, we saw the worldwide 'banking crisis' and, a little later, the adoption in the UK by the coalition government of the strategy of 'austerity' (which included a massive programme of cuts), leading to increasing levels of poverty and inequality (see, for example: Poinasamy, 2013). This had a huge impact on public service provision in the UK: for example, to take libraries in England, Wales and Scotland alone: 'As at 31 March 2005 there were a total of 4,367 service points that were open 10 hours or more per week across England, Wales and Scotland. At the same date in 2019 this figure stood at 3,583 – a reduction of 784 (18%).' (Woodhouse and Zayed, 2020, 17)

As part of this, staffing levels were also cut – often affecting those people who worked in the community and led on work with newly arrived people – and many library services also reduced their staff training budgets drastically.

Despite this grim setting, many library services did manage to continue to develop their provision for new arrivals (and other socially excluded groups too). Several 'snapshots' captured some of this, for example Helena Leeper in her MA Librarianship thesis (Leeper, 2017); and Arts Council England in their survey of diversity and inclusion in English public libraries (Vincent, 2018, 30–4).

Libraries of Sanctuary

As noted previously, Thimblemill Library in Sandwell became the UK's first Library of Sanctuary in 2017.

Libraries of Sanctuary is one of the 'Streams' supported by the City of Sanctuary movement:

> Launched in October 2005 in Sheffield, City of Sanctuary started with the vision that the UK should be a welcoming place of safety for all and proud to offer sanctuary to people fleeing violence and persecution. From this start in a single location, the idea of celebrating and promoting welcome to those seeking sanctuary has spread into a grass-roots network of over 100 local groups across villages, towns, cities and regions in the UK.
>
> (Schools of Sanctuary, 2022)

There is a very full published case study (Clark, n.d.) showing how Thimblemill Library achieved their Award; as Barry Clark[109] says:

> [The local community organisation] Bearwood Action for Refugees were aware of the work of City of Sanctuary (there is no group operating in Sandwell, the nearest being Birmingham), and had read about the award of Theatre of Sanctuary status to Leeds Playhouse (now West Yorkshire Playhouse) in 2014. They reasoned that if there was a Theatre of Sanctuary, there could be a Library of Sanctuary, and proposed that Thimblemill apply in recognition of the range of services provided to refugees and asylum seekers.
>
> (Clark, n.d., 2)

To understand more about the circumstances that led to Thimblemill Library's being awarded the status of the UK's first Library of Sanctuary, I interviewed Julie Mckirdy, the Library Supervisor.

The most striking feature was the importance of a long-term connection to the local community – Julie had grown up in the area and had worked at Thimblemill Library for over 40 years. This meant that she had an in-depth personal knowledge and understanding of the community and its needs and was also very aware of any changes to it.

Julie said that the work that led up to becoming a Library of Sanctuary started properly in 2015–16 with Bearwood Action for Refugees;[110] they were collecting books to send to the Calais Jungle[111] and were looking for a collection point, and Julie agreed that the Library could be used for this. The work at Bearwood Action for Refugees and the Library started to take off, and they also started working with Brushstrokes Community Project.[112] Developments included:

- A local church network group was running ESOL classes and started running these in the Library too.
- Bearwood Action for Refugees put together packs for Afghan refugees who had been placed in local hotels, and included information about the Library Service, encouraging the new arrivals to visit, to use the public computers, and to take part in English lessons.
- Together, Bearwood Action for Refugees, Brushstrokes and the Library organised craft sessions for children at the hotels.
- More recently, the local foodbank has evolved into the Pantry (a local food-store to support people who need access to food), and Julie can refer people from the Library to the Pantry.

Sandwell Library Service has a long history of championing developments in the local community, and the Council has been right behind the development of Thimblemill Library as a Library of Sanctuary. (Interview with Julie Mckirdy, Oct 2021)

Following this successful accreditation, public library services in the West Midlands began an initiative to develop a national approach to and promotion of libraries becoming Libraries of Sanctuary, drawing on the Thimblemill Library experience. A small working group from the West Midlands (including library contacts, Birmingham City of Sanctuary and Bearwood Action for Refugees) put together a proposal for a UK-wide approach to developing Libraries of Sanctuary, and, with support from Arts Council England and Libraries Connected, the group commissioned me to develop a resource pack to support libraries considering applying to become Libraries of Sanctuary. The resource pack was first published in May 2020, with a revised edition published in October 2021 (Vincent, 2021b).[113]

Since then, a number of other libraries have been awarded Libraries of Sanctuary status, including Bolton (Vincent, 2021a); Brighton & Hove (Brighton & Hove City Council, 2020); Kirklees Libraries (Sanctuary Kirklees, 2021); Manchester Libraries (Vincent, 2021a); Newcastle Libraries (Newcastle City Council, 2021); Oldham Libraries (Vincent, 2021a); Southampton (Southampton City Council, 2020); and The Kittiwake Trust Multilingual Library (Kittiwake Trust, 2021) – and, at the time of writing, we know that there are more in the pipeline.

5

What Barriers are There to the Take-Up of Library Services by New Arrivals? And How Can We Begin to Dismantle These?

Introduction

Before looking in detail at examples of some of the work that different types of library and information services are currently undertaking and developing, it is important to understand the barriers that may stand in the way of new arrivals actually taking up these services.[114]

These barriers can be seen as falling into four main areas:

- personal and social
- perception and awareness
- environmental
- institutional.

This chapter outlines what some of these barriers are – brief practical examples of how to overcome them are included here and then fleshed out in the following chapter.

Overcoming barriers: personal and social

- New arrivals' previous experiences may make them fear institutions (or, indeed, anything official). Libraries can go some way to overcoming these fears by making the building welcoming and ensuring that all library staff are aware of the issues that new arrivals may have faced and can respond positively to them.
- New arrivals may not have used a library before, and may also not understand what its purpose is.

- Cultural barriers, such as the attitudes of men in some cultures towards women in public places; attitudes to queuing.
- Lack of literacy: all libraries can help new arrivals find literacy classes – and some may have organisations running classes in the library.
- Lack of IT literacy and experience.
- Digital exclusion.[115]
- Lack of spoken English: all libraries can also help new arrivals find ESOL classes.
- Health/mental health issues: all libraries can signpost people to organisations where they can get health and mental health support.
- Feelings of not belonging, social isolation and lack of social integration: by being community hubs, libraries are creating places where people have an opportunity to meet others and begin to integrate.
- Low income/poverty: libraries are places which new arrivals can visit without, in general, having to pay (although there may still be issues about the cost of travel needed to reach a library – bus passes to allow people to attend activities may go a long way to help).[116]
- Feelings of shame/embarrassment about having to ask for money and help.

Overcoming barriers: perception and awareness

- A common perception – and not just by new arrivals – is that libraries are 'not for us' or that libraries 'do not have anything that we need'; new arrivals may also be unsure exactly how to ask for what they need.
- You have to pay to join or use the service: it is surprising to lots of people (not just new arrivals) that public libraries are free. Via outreach visits and talks, tours, meeting new arrivals to outline what libraries offer, publicity, word of mouth and other community initiatives, libraries can promote the message that they are free to join and you do not need to pay to use most of the services.
- Lack of confidence to use a library, especially if the person's status is not settled: when libraries welcome people and offer real support to new arrivals, this can go a long way to starting to overcome lack of confidence.

Overcoming barriers: environmental

- The largest barriers are not knowing where library buildings are, not being able to reach one easily and then not understanding how the library is laid out: simple, visual plans showing the layout – where different types of library materials and other facilities are – make finding your way around the library much easier, as will special guided tours.

- Lack of visible welcome: many libraries have overcome this by, for example, prominently displaying welcome posters (perhaps in a range of community languages) and making sure that the entrance to the library is as bright and welcoming as possible; staff also greet visitors to the library and help make them feel comfortable there. There is more on this below.
- Attitudes of other library users: this is one of the most difficult barriers to overcome, but many libraries organise events and activities where people can meet and begin to mix socially (and library staff are also clear about their role should something unpleasant be said). Book displays and collections telling the stories of people seeking sanctuary and other new arrivals help to raise awareness and empathy.

Overcoming barriers: institutional

- Joining procedures, including the need for proof of ID and the terminology used on forms.
- Lack of staff awareness and training.
- Staffing capacity and library opening hours: as we know, many public libraries have had their funding reduced, so it is difficult to recruit and employ as many staff as they need – as a result, opening hours are sometimes reduced (and, in some cases, libraries have been closed). Within often very limited resources, however, libraries are still finding ways of extending their staffing capacity and their opening hours, often by reaching out into the community.
- Using jargon: as in all fields, this can be hard to overcome, but libraries are working hard to make the language they use as jargon-free as possible.
- Lack of networking by library staff with organisations supporting new arrivals: it is vital to make and maintain these contacts in order to keep up to date with changes in the community such as nationalities of new arrivals, languages spoken and so on.
- Problems with identifying the language of newly arrived people, as these can be very diverse and populations can change: liaison and partnership-working with local organisations that support new arrivals can help to overcome this barrier – and it is important to make contact regularly in order to keep up to date with changes in the area.
- Inappropriate staff attitudes and behaviour: many libraries have organised training courses looking at the needs of new arrivals, in which

the importance of appropriate responses by library staff is stressed. All libraries also have codes of conduct and Equal Opportunity Policies and are undertaking work around equality, equity, diversity and inclusion, which guide their staff.

- Not purchasing material suitable for new arrivals: once libraries have built up a picture of the needs of their local new arrivals (especially language needs), they can then plan to purchase material that is available. Many also focus on providing good collections of books and other materials to support ESOL and literacy students, as well as materials that help show how things work in the UK (e.g. job seeking).
- There not being appropriate material available to buy for new arrivals: this is a difficult issue to resolve, but the developing network via Libraries of Sanctuary will mean that libraries can share information about sources and also, if required, put joint pressure on publishers to produce more relevant material.

6

How Are Libraries Responding Today? And What More Can We Do? Some Practical Ideas . . .

Introduction

This section draws together examples of the work that different types of library and information service are currently providing, together with some ideas about what more could be developed.[117] We are looking at library work as broadly as possible, including examples of provision by public libraries, information about which is also still available in the *Libraries of Sanctuary Resource Pack* (Vincent, 2021b).

There is a danger that this – as with any area of library and information work – is seen as too large, too new, too political or too complex. This section breaks down the key areas of work involved so that it is clear that most can be built on existing frameworks, especially with the involvement of new arrivals themselves, people from the wider community and from across your organisation and other partners.

City of Sanctuary have outlined the key components that are at the heart of this work, summarised as Learn, Embed and Share; we will use this as a framework for this next practical section of the book.

Learn

Learning about what it means to be a 'new arrival', seeking sanctuary, facing racism, etc.

Before starting work in this area, it is vital that library staff learn what it really means to be a 'new arrival' (and particularly a person seeking sanctuary) – in general (especially the political issues behind and meanings of the different terms used for new arrivals); in the context of overall health and mental wellbeing; and specifically in terms of information and support needs and how a library might help. This can involve:

- Organising training and learning activities: for example, Birmingham and Newcastle public library services have organised short courses for their staff, looking at who new arrivals are; what we know about new arrivals in the local area; the response of libraries (and the cultural sector) in the past and currently; barriers to the take-up of services; and practical ways in which we can improve library provision (a possible course outline is included in Appendix 5). Other library services have organised training provided by their local City of Sanctuary (e.g. Greater Manchester) or local refugee organisations (e.g. Southampton).[118]
- Giving a sense of what it is like to be a new arrival, for example by having people with lived experience talking about their own lives; thinking through what the impact of a lack of welcome or the 'hostile environment' is likely to be on people (and, even though the participants may not have had this experience directly, are there things from their own lives that they can draw on, for example when they have not felt welcome somewhere? Or have been verbally abused and/or discriminated against?).
- Ensuring staff and volunteers develop an empathetic approach to their work, for example by meeting and talking to people who have lived experience of seeking sanctuary; and by reading.[119, 120]
- Ensuring that staff and volunteers understand and practise effective communication with library users, especially new arrivals (and there is a guide to effective communication produced by Leicester Museums & Galleries, included in Appendix 7).
- Ensuring that staff are taking an anti-racist position in their work (as opposed to a non-racist one which can lead to people becoming bystanders to racism). [121, 122]
- Equipping staff to recognise some of the background issues – for example, where the hostile environment came from and the impact it has had; developing an understanding that much media coverage of new arrivals focuses on supposed rivalry between different groups and their needs, whereas, as Kate Pickett[123] argues: 'Instead of trying to prioritise different kinds of inequalities to be addressed, trying to understand the connections between them might help us tackle them' (Pickett, 2021). As noted above, it is also important that staff understand why new arrivals may mistrust 'authority' – people who appear to be in authority, imposing buildings and so on.

Finding out about new arrivals in your area

- Ensuring that information about local communities is collected and kept up to date:

    Available government statistics will only give you a snapshot of part of the local picture. Precise figures may be difficult to obtain because of high levels of mobility and rapidly changing world politics. The important thing is not to be put off by this. Even if there seem to be enormous research gaps, you should:
    – make intelligent management use of whatever information is available
    – gather information to find out whether people in other council departments and relevant external agencies find lack of data in this field a problem for planning purposes
    – if so, share this evidence with senior managers in your own service. You may be able to take the lead to set up a local network/use existing networks to explore better ways of collecting and sharing information to underpin service improvement and development.

    (Vincent, 2015)

- Providing staff with up-to-date knowledge about local communities, with particular reference to people seeking sanctuary and other new arrivals. This can include:
    – countries of origin
    – languages spoken and language skills
    – religious/non-religious affiliations
    – other cultural characteristics
    – meeting places (e.g. community centres, churches, mosques) – and can also include key local shops
    – accommodation, e.g. are any of them living in hostels? hotels?
    – any political affiliations and/or tensions (this might influence who speaks on their behalf, for example)
    It is also important to equip staff with the knowledge to be able to find out and keep current with this information themselves. For example, Southampton City Libraries created an internal staff information portal that contains the following:
    – Library of Sanctuary leaflet
    – a list of websites of local and national support organisations
    – a copy of the staff awareness presentation from CLEAR
    – a list of organisations that offer English learning/conversation classes.
    They also used the staff information bulletin (Cascade) to provide facts and figures about people seeking sanctuary in the City (summary of Southampton initiatives and e-mail exchange with Allison Kirby, 2020).

- As part of this, providing staff with contacts in and introductions to local community organisations and other groups: there may be a City of Sanctuary group nearby, your local authority may be part of the growing City of Sanctuary Local Authority Network, or local schools may be Schools of Sanctuary.[124] For example, the Library at NUI Galway has been involved with the local University of Sanctuary steering committee 'since we started on the path to becoming a designated UoS. The library has provided access to the library's books and online journals for international protection applicants and refugees who have wished to study in advance of returning to college/university' (e-mail exchange with Aidan Harte, 2022).
- There may also be local welcome groups, self-help and support groups, faith groups – all of these can provide an introduction to local new arrival communities.[125]
- As noted above, working with other parts of the local authority/organisation to pool information about new arrivals in the area: in Birmingham, for example, the Library Service works very closely with their LAASLO,[126] who was able to introduce library staff to key organisations and individuals in the community and who also facilitated visits to the Library. Birmingham's LAASLO, Geoff Mitchell, has outlined some of his day-to-day work: 'Before the lockdown, I visited people seeking asylum in their accommodation. These days my work is done by phone calls, texts, WhatsApp and emails. I am thinking about how I evidence these changes in the report. The report is loading on the computer, I check the phone; there are two voicemails and a text message, which simply says, "Thank you". The message is from the father of an asylum-seeking family whose child had been attending school for some time and not receiving school meals. A couple of phone calls to Dad and the school had quickly resolved the situation. There had been a communication misunderstanding. I phone dad just to confirm everything is OK. I practise my Spanish and dad practises his English. On balance, he does better. Dad recalls how difficult it had been for his daughter to sit in class with no lunch. "She is happy now", he tells me. We finish the conversation with Dad inviting me to have coffee and meet the family. We agree that when things are better, we will meet up.' (Mitchell, n.d.)
- Ensuring that staff are aware of the possible sensitivities and fears of people seeking sanctuary, especially those who have experienced persecution, torture or violence. For example, in relation to LGBTQ+ people: 'Same-sex sexual activity is a crime in 70 countries, and can get you a death sentence in nine countries, including Iran, Saudi Arabia, Sudan and Yemen. And even where these restrictive laws are not actually

enforced, their very existence reinforces prejudice against LGBTI people, leaving them feeling like they have no protection against harassment, blackmail and violence.' (Amnesty International, 2021b)

- Ensuring all staff are mindful of possible threats to the safety of users and staff, especially from those who are hostile to people seeking sanctuary and other migrants; for example, Norfolk Library and Information Service are reporting points for hate incidents and hate crimes in support of the 'Stop Hate in Norfolk' protocol.[127]
- Giving staff encouragement and time to explore key background resources (and other reading materials): for example, is there any research into new arrival communities locally or regionally? Some examples of possible sources of information are listed in Appendix 6.
- 'Inviting organisations that support people seeking sanctuary to share their learning and provide awareness-raising sessions in the library, and, where possible, arranging for library staff to visit support projects. This will include consultation with and involvement of people seeking sanctuary in staff training, identifying barriers and action-planning for embedding welcome and appropriate resources . . . ' (Vincent, 2021b, 6)
- When attending meetings of organisations/networks that support new arrivals, listen to what is important to them and build trust by delivering on any promises you make.

Starting with people's needs

As a wise observer put it: 'Much of the literature on immigrant library use is based upon a service model that focuses on what the library is doing or not doing to attract patrons.' (Burke, 2008)

Yes, of course the library's role is significant, but it is also vital that we start by looking at the needs of the people we are intending to support. As Susan Burke continues: 'By addressing barriers to public library use and targeting patron communities accurately, libraries may appeal to wider potential patron audiences.' (p. 166)

So, here we are going to start looking very broadly at the needs of people who have experienced global migration, mobility and crossing borders and racism.

As a very useful starting point, John Pateman (Pateman, 2003) – and later with Ken Williment (Pateman and Williment, 2013) and with Joe Pateman (Pateman and Pateman, 2019; Pateman and Pateman, 2021) – has outlined how Maslow's hierarchy of needs can be applied to library provision, and, rather than reinventing this, I am drawing on their work in Table 6.1 on the next page.

Table 6.1 *Maslow's hierarchy of needs applied to library provision* (based on Pateman and Williment, 2013, 43)

Maslow's hierarchy of needs	Needs-based library services
Self-actualisation – realising a person's full potential	Co-producing library services by combining the skills, knowledge and experience of local communities and library staff
Esteem – recognition, acceptance, self-respect	Sharing power and resources with local communities to give them a genuine stake in library service planning, design, delivery and evaluation
Love/belonging – friendship, intimacy, family	Building relationships with local communities; creating an inclusive public library environment where people feel welcome and a sense of belonging
Safety – personal and financial security, health and wellbeing	Working with partners and/or signposting to agencies which can provide financial advice and assistance and meet health and education needs
Physiological – food, clothing, shelter	Working with partners and/or signposting to agencies which can meet food, clothing and housing needs

John and Ken's work shows, first and in outline, what the needs of people who have experienced global migration and mobility are; and, second, that libraries can play a role at all the levels of Maslow's hierarchy, even at the most fundamental.

Drawing both on this work and on a factsheet produced by Refugee Action (Refugee Action, n.d.), we can identify some of the most immediate and urgent needs. These include:

- food
- clothing
- shelter
- personal security
- financial security
- health and wellbeing.

In addition, in their review *The Impact of COVID-19 on Refugees and Refugee-assisting Organisations in Scotland*, Gary Christie and Helen Baillot identify the following:

- isolation and loneliness
- mental health issues
- digital poverty and need for education
- poverty and food poverty (Christie and Baillot, 2020, 29–30).

Finding out what needs new arrivals in your area have

This should include:

- Regular consultation with new arrivals to ensure that they are aware of the basic 'library offer'.
- Encouraging new arrivals to have their say about the services the library offers them.
- Consulting with refugee and other community organisations to find out what they identify as new arrivals' needs – and also what they identify as gaps in the library's provision.
- This becomes even more important in an area where, for example, there may be only a couple of families arriving in a district from a particular country (or they may be the first new arrivals in an area altogether), and also where people are from very different cultural backgrounds.
- Meeting new arrivals, both in libraries and also in the community, for example via some form of outreach provision. This is vital, particularly to help get away from the idea that new arrivals are some kind of homogeneous group – they are all individuals, with their own experiences and needs – and may not otherwise engage with a library.
- Monitoring and evaluating what new arrivals think about the library service – for example, is it welcoming? How accessible is it? Is it well promoted? And are there independent evaluators who can help assess this?

Embed

In this next section, we look further at what libraries can offer. City of Sanctuary describe 'Embed' as: '. . . take positive action to make welcome and inclusion part of the values of your organisation or community, to support people who are seeking asylum and people who are refugees, and to include them in your activities.' (City of Sanctuary UK, 2022)

A need for welcome

The need for welcome is vitally important. As Refugee Action say: 'Having experienced the worst forms of hostility, many refugees will be nervous about how their new communities will behave towards them. A friendly smile and "Hello" can go a long way to relieving this fear and making people feel wanted.' (Refugee Action, n.d, 1)

This welcome could include:

- As noted previously, ensuring that all library staff are welcoming.
- Making sustained efforts to bring people from new arrival communities into libraries: Kirklees Council, for example, opened a new library in August 2021, which '. . . will serve as a hub for the community and will also provide a safe and welcome space for migrants' (Lavigueur, 2021).
- Displaying welcome posters and signs in multiple languages and/or City of Sanctuary welcome stickers (for example, Kirklees Libraries have created a multi-language 'Welcome' poster for each library, with large pull-up banners created for larger libraries).
- Ensuring that the library service website includes a welcome message – for example:

Supporting refugees in Surrey libraries
We welcome refugees and support Surrey residents wishing to do the same by providing books, online resources and more.
  In terms of books, we have drawn together a collection of adult fiction and non-fiction. This includes personal accounts, photography and graphic novels . . .[128]
(Surrey County Council, 2021)

- Creating a dual-language library guide.
- Ensuring that resources relevant to individual needs, cultures, age and experience are available in the library.
- Ensuring that joining the library is made as straightforward as possible – for example, in consultation with local organisation CLEAR (City Life Education and Action for Refugees), Southampton created a new 'welcome' library membership and simplified the joining process. This took into consideration the transient nature of many new arrivals' lives, and the Library Service accepted ID such as the biometric residence permit and application registration card or immigration/asylum letters, and this also means no fines or charges would be charged if items are lost or returned late (summary of Southampton initiatives and e-mail exchange with Allison Kirby, 2020).[129]
- Organising tours of the library and help with joining – for example, at Exeter Library, Libraries Unlimited organise tours of the library for new arrivals, including one for a group of young people who had been in the country for less than two years and who are at Exeter College – as Karen Huxtable (Senior Supervisor – Development) says: 'We had a great time looking at books in their languages and also locating books to improve their English and just using the library as a safe space for study etc.' (e-mail exchange with Karen Huxtable, 2021). Glasgow Women's Library have run building tours in a range of different languages, including

Urdu, Farsi and Mandarin (e-mail exchange with Wendy Kirk, 2021). Southampton secured funding from Southampton Family Learning to offer a three-day course on using the library. This was in response to learners who received a library card, visited the library as part of a group, but were not confident using the library on their own. Although numbers were low, those that took part gained a better understanding of borrowing books, using computers and asking for help (summary of Southampton initiatives and e-mail exchange with Allison Kirby, 2020).

- Ensuring that access to the library is as easy as possible – for example, in many university libraries, entry to the library is controlled, so there is a physical barrier, and a registration process is required. However, at Warwick University Library, the requirements are relaxed for people seeking sanctuary (e-mail exchange with Robin Green, 2021).
- At the University of Glasgow, the 'Reach Out' Library, IT support and Student Services teams work to provide access to library spaces, resources and support for summer school and other Widening Participation students who come to the university ahead of their courses starting. This also involves in-person or virtual support for new students, including people seeking sanctuary (University of Glasgow, n.d.) (e-mail exchange with Catriona MacIsaac, 2021).
- Targeted activities: at Glasgow Women's Library, they have run a number of bilingual Story Cafés in English and Urdu, to make it accessible to women from South Asian communities, and have also run a bilingual Story Café with Ricefield Arts and Cultural Centre (an organisation which celebrates Chinese arts and culture in Scotland), and a bilingual Story Café in English and Georgian, in partnership with the Poetry Translation Centre (e-mail exchange with Wendy Kirk, 2021).
- Working with local communities to collect and share their histories: for example, in 2011 Glasgow Women's Library (e-mail exchange with Wendy Kirk, 2021) co-ordinated an oral history project with women from South East Asia who migrated to Glasgow, which led to a touring exhibition, celebratory event and publication, *She Settles in the Shields* (Morrison, 2011): 'The story of Pollokshields' migrant women is one of hope and despair, challenge and success. It is the story of the women who have created and raised a whole generation of "new" Scots.' (Glasgow Women's Library, 2011)
- Outreach work to welcome new arrivals: Sandwell MBC welcomed 25 families that were initially housed in a local hotel, and two families that were housed in the local community. Sandwell Libraries and Archives worked with Brushstrokes,[130] and gifted 52 craft packs to the families in the hotel at a Christmas event. These packs contained a toy bear, books,

craft materials, folders, colouring sheets and quizzes. The children receiving the packs were aged from 0 to 18 years of age. Feedback received from Brushstrokes was that the children loved the packs, so they have followed this up with a further delivery of craft materials. Sandwell Libraries and Archives also facilitated a visit from one of the families housed in the local community to Smethwick Library. The family were accompanied by an interpreter. During the visit the children all received a pack, and the family were given a tour of the library, a storytime, and they became members of the library. Staff have seen the family using the library since the visit. Comment from Brushstrokes: 'The proactive approach taken by the service to look at ways to increase access to new communities has been wonderful and the thought that has gone in to developing new resources and materials for individuals from refugee and asylum seeker backgrounds has been of benefit to some of the families we work with. They regularly look for new ways to engage and respond to the needs of new communities and have played a key role in helping develop Borough of Sanctuary Sandwell with other community organisations.' (e-mail exchange with Dawn Winter, 2022)

- There is a case study at the end of this chapter showing how the Wirral Schools Library Service has embedded their Sanctuary approach into all their work.

Finally, just to emphasise how important this welcome can be, at a Libraries of Sanctuary event held online on 11 March 2022 and organised by CILIP Scotland, Dylan Fotoohi (Refugees for Justice) described just how welcoming Springburn Library and, later, the Mitchell Library (both in Glasgow) had been to him; he said: 'Day 3 of my arrival saw me settled in the library already, that was my daily hub from that point onwards. It was the gateway into a new society, allowing me to access information, communicate with my family and friends, and get to know a new community I was about to join.'

He talked of the library as being the place where he could really sit down and plan for his new life . . . and carried that idea of welcome through to his work with the Scottish Refugee Council where, when they were looking for venues that would be open, friendly, welcoming and accessible for running peer-support groups for new arrivals, he immediately thought of holding them in libraries (e-mail exchange with Dylan Fotoohi, March 2022).

A need for information

New arrivals will need a wide range of information to enable them to survive and thrive in their new home. For example, research has shown that:

One [research participant] expanded on this: since they had been a teacher back home, they were presumed to know how to access information, but this was not the case in a setting so culturally and technologically different from that from which they had come. Another person said how much they wished they had had someone designated to tell them which support to access, and what they need to do at each stage of the application process. Most of the discussion of information as a support need involved wanting to know where to go for legal support, or wanting to know more about what is involved in the asylum application process from start to finish, or wishing that from the start they had had a leaflet or booklet listing the charities they could go to for help.

(Dyck, 2019, 49)

The majority of Syrian refugees reported that their priority information need was to be aware of the situation in their home country, followed by issues related to their states of the diaspora that they are passing through, such as services provided to their children, shelter and aid in general, as well as rights and obligations related to their refugee status. They also showed that they need information to help get the right or any appropriate work in the host country (Egypt). The study showed that many Syrian refugees were seeking information that meets their basic daily needs.

(Mansour, 2018, taken from article abstract)

A need for sympathetic advice and signposting

Some of the fundamental needs noted above (for example for food, clothing, shelter, health information and wellbeing) may not all be directly met by libraries, although, at the time of writing with the COVID-19 pandemic raging, some libraries have become foodbank donation or distribution points – for more on this topic, please see below. However, we can provide support in terms of signposting and advice, assisting people to find their way around and discover other sources of support. According to Refugee Action:

Like all of us when we arrive in a new town or city, it can be really difficult to learn how to get around. A newly arrived refugee might not yet know the key places they need to go to and it can be really hard to learn to use a public transport system. Do you buy the ticket on the bus [or] in a shop? Do you get a day ticket or a return? And that's before you get to timetables or planning more complex journeys. Learning how to get around can be really difficult.

(Refugee Action, n.d., 1)

A need for work experience and work

Libraries can provide volunteering and training opportunities for new arrivals. For example:

- Several new arrivals have volunteered within Manchester Libraries, particularly to help with events, such as International Mother Language Day and Refugee Week (Manchester Libraries, 2021).
- In Southampton, a Syrian family who were seeking sanctuary and were granted leave to live in the City volunteered at the library and undertook roles such as shelf-tidier and digital champion (successfully helping others with IT problems) (summary of Southampton initiatives and e-mail exchange with Allison Kirby, 2020).

Library services for new arrivals

This section looks at the range of services that library and information services provide, which are – or could be – relevant to new arrivals. However, rather than assuming that we need to set up new services, it is also important to reassess existing provision – which is available to any library user – to look at how it can also be targeted towards new arrivals.

Examples of services which libraries offer include:

- Stock of library materials to support ESOL (for example, Swansea Prison Library have a collection of books for emerging readers – this is a new collection of abridged books aimed at ESOL students and those improving their literacy) (e-mail from Valerie Samuel, Library Manager, HMPS/YOI Swansea, December 2021).
- Stock of library materials to support children and young people learning and maintaining English as a spoken and/or written language (often called English as an Additional Language – EAL):[131] for example, researcher Nathaniel Dziura commented that: 'I was born in the UK (London), and my family immigrated to England from Poland. My family speak Polish at home and are very much involved with Polish culture, so I had a multicultural upbringing. Given that I didn't speak much English at home, my mum always ensured we visited the library often, and we used library resources to encourage my literacy skills. Before internet access was widespread, we used to go to the library on weekends to use their computer resources. I also remember taking part in a lot of library events during the summer holidays, such as reading challenges and book-themed activity days . . . we didn't have much money when I was growing up, so we would often borrow library books

instead of buying books, as well as buying ex-library books at our library's book sales.' (e-mail exchange with Nathaniel Dziura, Oct 2020)
- Stock of materials to give more information about life in the UK.
- Ensuring that works by new arrivals are included.
- Provision of materials in community languages: for example, Portlaoise Library provides reading materials in 13 languages besides English and Irish (material taken from a presentation at the Library Association of Ireland Career Development Group event, 29 November 2021, and an e-mail exchange with Suzanne Carroll, 2022); Southampton provides books in community languages including Pashto, Hindi, Bengali, Polish, mostly at Central Library, with a selection at Burgess Road, Shirley and Portswood. They also have dual-language books for children with English text and a wide range of languages (summary of Southampton initiatives and e-mail exchange with Allison Kirby, 2020).
- Promotion of library materials, ensuring that new arrivals are included – many libraries do this, for example Inspire[132] have a range of equality and diversity web pages, including 'Refugee stories' (Inspire, 2021a), which link to further information about recommended books on Pinterest; the University of York produced a reading list, 'Migration and Refugees' (University of York Library, 2020), as part of the promotion of the recognition of the University's becoming a University of Sanctuary.
- Cultural activities – invite and welcome new arrivals. For example, in October and November 2021, the Bodleian Library hosted 'Syria and Silence' which included Maktabah, a pop-up library with books about Syria in Arabic, Kurdish and English;[133] and events/workshops involving the local Syrian community, including toddler storytimes, craft activities, poetry events, and a range of film-screenings and talks. This work is part of a wider collaborative project the University of Oxford has organised called 'Syria and Silence' (Oxford Research Centre in the Humanities, 2021). At the beginning of 2022, Portlaoise Library Service posted six videos on its YouTube channel, introducing a group of new arrivals and letting them tell us more about their countries and why they had come to Ireland (Laois County Library Service, 2022). There is a case study at the end of this chapter looking at how Bolton and Birmingham Libraries have welcomed people via music, and also one looking in more depth at the work that Lambeth Libraries have been carrying out for some time with the local Polish community.
- Free public-access computers – essential for new arrivals to find information and to maintain contact with families and friends and with their countries of origin.

- IT taster sessions and support – some new arrivals will not have had much, if any, previous computer experience.
- Foreign-language newspapers provided online.
- Job clubs – part of the help libraries can offer to signpost new arrivals towards work opportunities. For example, at the Barnstaple and Bideford Job Clubs in Devon, between August and October 2021, the Libraries supported a number of new arrivals, including two Spanish people; two Arabic people (one from Iran); one from the Dominican Republic; one from Poland; one Chinese person and one from Pakistan. The support has included helping them access employment and relevant courses; helping one person find accommodation; and helping one person access affordable dental treatment (e-mail exchange with Iain Harris, 2022).
- After-school clubs and homework support – offering support as young people start to find their way into the UK education system.
- Young people's clubs and activities.
- Supporting community projects working with new arrivals. For example, Northamptonshire's LibraryPlus provided resources at short notice, including picture books, materials on good nutrition and wellbeing and historical artefacts, to support a summer camp run by a youth club for asylum-seeking children in Northampton (Duggan, 2021). Portlaoise Library contributed to the 2016 Social Inclusion Week as part of the area's welcome to new arrivals via the Syrian Resettlement Programme (Doras, 2016) (material taken from a presentation at the Library Association of Ireland Career Development Group event, 29 November 2021, and an e-mail exchange with Suzanne Carroll, 2022).
- Children's storytimes – for example, pre-COVID, Bristol Libraries held storytimes in languages other than English at some of their libraries, and, during the pandemic, they organised some one-off sessions that were prerecorded by library assistants at home with the books they had to hand. They e-mailed the videos to the Library Service, and they were uploaded to their Facebook page, scheduled them as 'premieres' and people were able to watch at home and share. As Katharine Seymour (Bristol Libraries' Reader Development Librarian) says: 'I think they were popular because they were a bit different – there were lots and lots of online story times being shared at that time during lockdown but not so many in different languages. Staff were able to send us stories in French, Spanish, Italian and Bulgarian.' (e-mail exchange with Katharine Seymour, 2021)
- Health-related activities: for example, yoga sessions; health walks (Oldham Libraries have organised dual-language Story Walks); gentle exercise classes and exercise sessions for children; adult colouring

sessions; keep-fit classes; a slimming group; regular health monitoring sessions; story trails and story walks. The City of Sanctuary mental health resource pack (Burghgraef et al., 2017) is a good starting point for library staff and volunteers in developing an awareness of the likely impacts of the asylum journey.

In addition, some libraries offer specific community support, which will also be of benefit to new arrivals, such as:

- Organising a foodbank donation point in the library, for example at Thimblemill Library, Sandwell (Clark, n.d.); Ivybridge Library in Devon (Ivybridge Foodbank, n.d.) and Waltham Forest Libraries in east London (Waltham Forest Community Help Network, 2021).
- Organising collections of other items, e.g. baby clothes, pushchairs, cribs, blankets and nappies, also at Thimblemill Library, Sandwell.
- Provision of free sanitary products to support the community in combating period poverty, for example Norfolk Libraries' 'Tricky Period & Toiletries to Go' (Norfolk County Council, 2021); East Renfrewshire's free sanitary products (East Renfrewshire Council, 2021).

At a broader level, work is going on across the cultural heritage sector to reassess how well we work with our communities and really meet their needs. For example, a recent report (Baring Foundation, 2021) has identified some areas of good practice, which include:

- Co-production and participant-led: this will help guard against '. . . an often unintentional downfall that participatory projects are at risk of falling into: assuming what it is that a particular group (outside of our own culture and experiences) may want to engage in.' (Baring Foundation, 2021, 4–5)
- Being aware of cultural sensitivities: 'This could be considering the time of sessions (for example not coinciding with the Muslim call to prayer), the venue in which an activity takes place, or whether particular groups of people usually and can comfortably congregate together. There may be gender divides or childcare difficulties that could prohibit people from taking part.' (p. 5)
- Locality: '. . . the importance of place and the work that goes into making places and venues accessible.' (p. 5)
- Employing artists with lived experience.
- Safe spaces: 'Not all spaces are naturally welcoming and inviting spaces. In the same way that spaces can become gendered, they can feel

unwelcoming or uninviting for particular communities. From the food that is on the menu to the décor, we need to carefully consider the venues we use, and the reasonable adjustments that can be made, when working with particular groups.' (p. 6)

- The importance of recognising the needs of new arrivals (for example, finding ways of improving wellbeing through volunteering).
- Challenges to hierarchies, for example: '. . . creating an environment where it feels safe to question and call out bad practices (whether intentional or not) in order to truly highlight diversity deficits.' (p. 6)

Use and promotion of library spaces

- Providing/promoting space in the library for ESOL and other classes (e.g. Glasgow Women's Library host ESOL classes for women – they are run by City of Glasgow College, but having them in their space, and women only, works really well for women. In addition, their Adult Literacy and Numeracy team work one-to-one with women who have English as a second language, and also run 'Conversations Cafés' to give women a safe, supportive space to practise their conversational English (e-mail exchange with Wendy Kirk, 2021). Please also see the case study at the end of this chapter about a Conversation Café at Bridgwater & Taunton College.
- Providing space for events and activities of relevance to new arrivals and to the wider community: for example, Portlaoise Library provided a venue for promoting information about voting (material taken from a presentation at the Library Association of Ireland Career Development Group event, 29 November 2021, and an e-mail exchange with Suzanne Carroll, 2022).
- Providing meeting space for voluntary refugee support organisations and groups offering support and friendship to people seeking sanctuary and other new arrivals.

Celebrating the contributions of new arrivals

Promoting and celebrating contributions by new arrivals can form a bridge between them and local communities.

Celebrating/taking part in activities such as Refugee Week

In 2021, for example, libraries organised or took part in a range of activities to mark Refugee Week and to celebrate its theme, 'We Cannot Walk Alone'.

This included:

- Bath & North East Somerset Libraries promoted some of their stock on social media (Bath & North East Somerset Libraries, 2021).
- Birmingham Central Library was illuminated in orange (Refugee Week, 2021).
- Bradford College Library Services included information on its website, e.g. an introduction to who refugees and asylum seekers are; a description of Refugee Week; a list of key organisations, documents and teaching resources; promoting a short reading list on its website (Bradford College Library Online, 2021b). It also includes books about new arrivals in its Black History Month celebration (Bradford College Library Online, 2021a).
- Brighton & Hove Libraries organised a series of events, including a 'flash fiction writing competition'; an exhibition in their window area, 'Sexual Orientation and Gender Identity Claims of Asylum: A European Human Rights Challenge' which highlights some of the materials, findings, and recommendations of the SOGICA (Sexual Orientation and Gender Identity Claims of Asylum) research project, funded by the European Research Council and based at the University of Sussex; online storytimes; plus highlighting recommended reading (Brighton & Hove City Council, 2021).
- Kirklees Libraries joined with other partners across the area to organise a series of events (Kirklees Welcomes, 2021).
- As well as promoting University-wide events, the University of Salford Library created a reading list (University of Salford Library, 2021), building on the Refugee Week's 'Simple Acts'.[134]

As well as marking Refugee Week, it is also important to include new arrivals in other activities, for example:

- In 2019, Goldsmiths, University of London, Library focused on new arrivals as part of their Black History Month events, e.g. creating a digital poster exhibition, 'Enigma of Arrival: the politics and poetics of Caribbean migration to Britain' (Goldsmiths University of London Library, 2019).
- Bolton Library has provided a safe chill-out space for Bolton Pride, where people can come into the library without needing to identify as LGBTQ+ and then can access the space quietly at the back of the library where there are drinks, bean bags, tables and chairs and books and information available. Last time, a group of young people, some of

whom were neurodiverse, spent a lot of the Pride weekend in there away from the crowds and noise but able to feel involved in Pride (e-mail exchange with Pierrette Squires, 2021).

Creating awareness for the wider community

Through their promotions, exhibitions, displays, activities and so on, libraries can also help raise the wider community's awareness of the contribution, experiences and needs of new arrivals. Some examples can include:

- Creating reading lists to draw attention to key resources that might help broaden understanding of new arrivals' experiences[135]
- Recommending books that introduce themes such as migration
- During 2020, libraries in Ireland showed the travelling exhibition, 50 Countries, 50 Stories.[136]

Targeted provision

The Bodleian Libraries have offered an Afghan Scholars Programme: 'Applicants must be citizens of Afghanistan and normally should have been resident in Afghanistan until a maximum of 8 months ago, or have refugee status, or have only a temporary visa.' (Bodleian Libraries, 2021a)

Ensuring that this work becomes embedded in the Library

Southampton organised a series of staff briefings at all libraries to talk about their application to become a Library of Sanctuary, what it means to be a person seeking sanctuary and have identified a 'sanctuary seeker champion' in each library – an advocate for the community who will champion the cause with colleagues and the public (summary of Southampton initiatives and e-mail exchange with Allison Kirby, 2020).

Benefits of this work

The benefits of developing our work with new arrivals are enormous. Most obviously, it supports new arrivals and helps make them feel welcome, but it also helps to ensure that libraries are contributing to broader organisational strategies and goals.[137] Here are two key examples:

- Community cohesion: through activities, such as those outlined above, libraries can provide opportunities for interaction between different communities and parts of communities, bringing diverse groups together, and supporting their getting to know and understand each other. Examples include: hosting ESOL groups, conversation cafés and groups; and putting on exhibitions/displays that bring people together and help to foster understanding. Also, by engaging local library users with books and other library materials about sanctuary, you can broaden understanding and advocate for new arrivals, as well as promoting the message of cohesion and inclusion. There is further information about community cohesion in Appendix 8, and also please see the case study about a conversation café at the end of this chapter.

- Community engagement: 'In its simplest form, community engagement is the process of involving people in the decisions that affect them. It can mean involving communities in the planning, development and management of services or be about tackling specific issues in an area, such as crime, substance misuse, or lack of facilities.' (ADP Consultancy, 2007, 6). At the British Library, for example, their community engagement work '. . . falls into two main areas: ongoing community engagement and community liaison, and developing collaborative community projects led by community interest.' (British Library, 2021)

Share

'Sharing' includes promoting the benefits of welcoming new arrivals: for example, at the launch of Portlaoise Library as the first Irish Library of Sanctuary, County Librarian Bernie Foran said: 'Places of Sanctuary is a movement that seeks to promote a culture of welcome in every sphere of society, a network of places of sanctuary where refugees and migrants are welcomed and included. We know that newcomers have a lot to offer, and we believe that as barriers come down and connections are made, the whole of society benefits.' (Cooke-Escapil, 2021; Kiernan, 2020)

A good example of both sharing and learning was the CILIP Working Internationally Conference held online in June 2021, part of the 'Working Internationally for Libraries' initiative; the aim of this work is:

> . . . to promote collaboration and partnership between libraries in England and their international counterparts.
>
> The project is funded by Arts Council England and delivered in partnership with the British Library, Libraries Connected, British Council, Carnegie UK Trust, CILIP Public and Mobile Libraries Group and CILIP International Libraries and Information Professionals Group. In its first phase, the project focused on English public libraries to develop a programme of activities

124 LIBRARIES AND SANCTUARY

including grants for international collaboration projects and an international conference that featured ideas and inspiration from across the world.

(CILIP, n.d.-a [2021]-a)

There were grants to support four international collaborative 'Building Bridges' projects, and these featured at the Conference and demonstrated ways in which we can both share what we are doing and learn from experiences at other library services. The projects were:

- Coding collaboration: Redbridge Libraries, UK together with PKV Library and The Quilon Library, Kerala, India, in which 'Libraries in the London Borough of Redbridge set out to build long-lasting partnerships with public libraries in Kerala, India by collaborating to create innovative makerspaces for children and young people in Kerala.' (CILIP, n.d.-b [2021]-b, 14)
- Oldham Libraries together with Cologne, Hamburg & Bremen libraries, Germany:

'Oldham Libraries, in the north of England, had been looking at ways to enhance their services to migrants and were aiming to achieve Library of Sanctuary status. Research revealed the borough of Oldham had similar patterns of immigration to some German cities. CILIP put them in touch with libraries in Bremen and Hamburg and, following a successful application for Building Bridges funding, the collaboration began.

The partners decided on a Climate Connections theme which would resonate with refugees. Climate change was likely to be a driver of migration in the future, and disaster displacement, as a result of climate change, was a growing problem . . .

A series of Climate Connections workshops, aimed at refugees and asylum seekers, gave participants opportunities to learn about climate change – and how to create short social media clips on the subject. Competitions were held, in Oldham and Germany, to find the best creations, followed by celebratory events for entrants in both countries.' (p. 18)

- Barnet Libraries together with Copenhagen & Allerød Libraries, Denmark, looking at self-service best practice:

'The online collaborators focused on four key areas: safeguarding and security, building maintenance and design, customer training, and partnerships. The Barnet team soon realised Danish libraries had considerably more spending power, and their use of SSO [self-service opening] was comparatively advanced. Copenhagen, for example, offered live video links to customer service staff from self-service kiosks . . .

Despite the disparities, there was much to learn, particularly around Danish 'behavioural design' – using open spaces, inventive and inspirational displays, good lighting and low shelving to minimise disruptive behaviour, and making unstaffed libraries look welcoming from the outside. The Barnet team was also impressed by the Danes' use of partnerships – working with local charities and community groups to run events during unstaffed opening hours. The learning will inform the design of two new libraries in Barnet.' (pp. 12–13)

- Oxfordshire Libraries together with Bergen Libraries, Norway:

'Oxfordshire Libraries collaborated with Bergen Public Library – the second largest in Norway – to develop and test a web application and workshop model for creating virtual reality (VR) interactive stories. The new app and toolkit, aimed initially at young adults, would be a free, open-source resource produced with co-creative practices, designed for ease of use and rapid results, with the option to publish stories produced . . .

The pandemic postponed plans for a roll-out programme of sessions with Oxfordshire schools, rescheduled for September 2021. Similarly Bergen's plans to use VSAT [the Virtual Storytelling Application and Toolkit] to help immigrants tell their stories and improve their language skills were delayed.

Despite these setbacks, the ongoing project has successfully developed a working app and workshop model with potential for other library services, and will almost certainly lead to further international collaborations.' (p. 16)

The sharing and learning themes were clear, and encapsulated in the comments by Vickie Varley from Oldham Libraries: 'Bringing an international perspective to the project was brilliant; we shared so many ideas and experiences, got the confidence to try new things and share skills.' (p. 22); and from one of the Conference participants: 'Then it was on to the *Building Bridges* Projects. Listening to the presenters talk about these projects and what they had achieved was truly inspiring. I had never considered that a library in the United Kingdom (UK) could team up with another library across the globe to create something new, innovative and exciting.' (Winterbottom, 2021, 14)

126   LIBRARIES AND SANCTUARY

CASE STUDIES

Case study 1: Wirral Schools' Library Service Library of Sanctuary Scheme

Catherine McNally and Louise Rice (Schools' Librarians, Wirral Schools' Library Service)

Introduction

The Schools' Library Service (SLS) is a library and learning resource centre for all the local maintained primary schools (90+) and any special schools, primary academies and high schools that opt to buy into the service.

Provision for new arrivals

The SLS is open to teachers to use as a library (although not as visitors at the time of writing – because of COVID, they are just running a click-and-collect service). School staff order for delivery termly but can also visit any time to borrow books for themselves or their pupils – and occasionally some staff may bring in a couple of pupils to help them select books. There is a nice welcome poster in lots of languages at the front door!

The SLS welcomes the Wirral Minority Ethnic Achievement Service (MEAS) team to visit and to borrow any books they need from their shelves, and they welcome opportunities to work with the MEAS manager and her team.[138]

The SLS has put together School of Sanctuary boxes which they offer to any local primary schools that are Schools of Sanctuary or working towards becoming one (of which there are some 25 on the Wirral at the time of writing); the plan is to contact them all in the autumn term to offer a touring display of books that the SLS hopes to put together. In addition, they have made some contacts from meetings that MEAS set up about Refugee Week, which they hope to follow up on when they have time, to see how SLS might be able to support work with refugee and asylum families in the wider community, perhaps through loaning family book boxes.

They hold a collection of dual-language books in a range of languages – mostly picture books – available for schools to borrow. To encourage schools to use these this term, they have added a new page to the order forms that the schools receive each term. This now enables individual teachers to request books in particular languages if they feel they would be useful for any children in their class, and they have already had a number of forms back requesting books in Arabic, Kurdish, Mandarin and Tamil for the autumn term.

The SLS has included offers of other books to aid inclusion here too, such as wordless picture books and books in braille. They have also considered adding LGBTQ+ books here too but the number of books published for primary level is still very small, so they do not really have enough books to make this offer as yet to all schools, although they will usually be able to supply a small selection to any teacher requesting them.

They offer artefact loans, including boxes on all the world faiths and different cultures. These are boxes of items the children can handle and look at, maybe try on or try out, or just for staff to have in classrooms on display for interest and discussion points.

The SLS has social media accounts for Twitter, Facebook (and, recently, Instagram), and they have been using these to highlight the items they offer to do with Schools of Sanctuary, recommending books and authors, re-posting relevant items from other groups. They were very active on Twitter in Summer 2021, highlighting as much as possible to do with Refugee Week.

Case study 2: Music and new arrivals
Donal Brennan (Bolton Libraries) and John Vincent

The impact of music

There is a large volume of evidence of the beneficial impact of music – and, increasingly, in terms of new arrivals too. For example, research with an integrated music group in Wales showed that participation in structured musical activities and improvisation sessions, as well as public performances, had the following outcomes:

i. ... encouraged individual unscripted performances, instilling confidence in solo performance,
ii. gave individuals who had experienced displacement and marginalisation a chance to lead in a safe, performative space,
iii. gave other participants a chance to follow and accompany this piece instrumentally or vocally, drawing on their own cultural traditions and thus creating innovative cross-cultural pieces; and
iv. provided participants and audience members with a unique and unrepeated, uplifting experience that triggered their imaginations, and prompted questions and further discussion between participants.

(Vougioukalou et al., 2019, taken from abstract)

A project in Scotland:

... brought together traditional Scottish musicians with musicians who are refugees or asylum seekers from Syria, Iran and El Salvador ...

Together they ran a series of six workshop sessions where the musicians could share music with each other and get to know each other as individuals and musicians.

(Live Music Now, 2020)

and, in England:

A co-creative composition and performance project, Displaced Voices (2019) amplified the voices and experiences of young refugees and migrants in the UK, breaking down barriers to orchestral music and building cultural bridges in our communities.

Displaced Voices built on the Oxford Spires Academy award-winning poetry programme developed by writer Kate Clanchy, which over the past decade has supported young migrants and refugees as they develop English-language skills and process their extraordinary journeys.

(Orchestra of St John's, 2022)

Music, new arrivals and libraries

Public libraries have played and performed music as part of their activities for a long time (for example as part of library sessions for young children and their parents/carers), but, until recently, much less frequently with new arrivals. Here are a couple of examples.

Donal Brennan

In **Bolton**, music events were put on at High Street Library as part of the 'Fun Palaces' initiative[139] and they demonstrated how effective music is for engaging people. These events involved discussion about and performance of a range of musical instruments. At the end of the sessions, attendees were invited to try out any of the instruments that they wished to – they expressed great interest and excitement at this.

Subsequently, at the High Street Library, Bolton Libraries decided to introduce music activities as part of their growing Library of Sanctuary programme, building on the idea that music can be a universal language to help build bridges between different communities. They provide a keyboard and drum machine for walk-up use by anyone in the library. Headphones are provided with a five-way splitter so that several people can listen or join in and play together. Acoustic and electric guitars are offered and provided on request (a headphone amp being used with the electric guitar). Staff give basic instruction and guidance to users; further beginners' tuition is offered by staff to those expressing a desire to advance their skills. All the instruments are very popular and in near-continuous use at weekends and holidays.

What we noticed was how easy it was to have something like this running – people were joining in, meeting and making new friends, and, above all, having fun!

Post-COVID, the aim is to encourage even more integration by supporting new arrivals to take their music further, for example by encouraging the formation of music bands – initial roles on offer being vocals, keys, drums, guitars and sound engineer. It is envisioned that existing staff with musical knowledge are to continue to provide mentoring in instruments and equipment whilst keeping the fun and social aspect of the music.

Bolton had also organised drumming and dancing workshops which were enjoyed by all attendees young and old from a range of diverse backgrounds, and there are hopes that more activities like this will develop.

During 2021, CAN (Community Arts North West) also took their music programme to libraries in Bolton, Oldham and Manchester, with:

> . . . family-friendly workshops in Northmoor, Chadderton (Oldham), on Bolton High Street, and Beswick, Wythenshawe, and Longsight (Manchester).
> Children and adults enjoyed Persian percussion with Arian Sadr, African and Caribbean dance with Imani Jendai, African drumming with Serge Tebu, singing with Emmanuela Yogolelo, doll-making with Gloria Saya, protest art with Mei Yuk Wong, Bangladeshi storytelling with Apu Chowdhury, Ethiopian dance and circus skills with Masresha Wondmu, and eco-art and poetry with Rabia Begum.
>
> (CAN, 2021)

John Vincent

In **Birmingham**, plans to develop a music project as part of the Library of Birmingham's welcome for new arrivals stalled because of the pandemic.

However, in March 2020, the Library organised a welcome session (again, this was going to be part of a regular programme of welcomes, which was temporarily halted by COVID). On this occasion, we worked with Geoff Mitchell (the Local Authority Asylum Support Liaison Officer) who drew on his contacts in the community.

Unfortunately, the day turned out to be wet and windy, so just four adults and three children visited. However, they joined the Library, and also had the opportunity to discuss issues with Geoff. Really to see what would happen, the library contact put out some drums, and two of the mothers started drumming, then singing (an interesting mix of songs from Angola and the latest internet sensation!) – through this, they started to form a link, and the children also joined in (this was significant, in that one of the children had been very withdrawn up to this point). The adults started to smile . . .

130 LIBRARIES AND SANCTUARY

At the end of the session, the two mothers – plus a third, whom they did not know before this – all set off together to explore the shops. After they had all left, Geoff said that we shouldn't underestimate the value of such a session. The adults had met (whereas he had to be careful introducing people, this interaction happened naturally) and gone off to do something together; they had joined the Library; they had enjoyed singing and drumming; and, in the end, these activities were not about the numbers, or about us, but about helping the families settle in Birmingham.

We are looking forward to more sessions!

Case study 3: Lambeth Libraries and the Polish community
Tim O'Dell (Development Librarian, Lambeth Libraries)

Introduction
Lambeth Libraries community development and cultural literacy work with local Polish community organisations has been gaining attention both in Poland and from Polish cultural and governmental organisations in the UK.

In 2013, Lambeth-based Stockwell Partnership was commissioned by Lambeth Council to identify the needs and strengths of the 7,000+ Lambeth Polish community. The key findings were that:

- Poles were seeking their own place in Lambeth.
- Polish residents strongly perceived the need to set up activities run in their home language.
- More activities were needed for families with younger children .
- Poles wanted to be accepted and welcomed by the local community.

The research also raised concerns within the Polish community that many respondents felt they didn't belong to, nor formed positive relationships within, their own and the wider community.

In December 2014, Lambeth Council funded Stockwell Partnership to deliver a project called *Poles Connect*. Lambeth Libraries has been working with the project to address the lack of take-up of local services that the *Polish Insight* report (Sordyl and Janus, 2013) identified and to improve the library offer to the community.

Impact of the project
As a result of the partnership, a weekly Polish story and rhyme time and playgroup was facilitated by the Polish Community Development Worker every Friday at Streatham Library, giving space to Polish families to meet up.

During the following years, over 1,600 Polish families attended the playgroup each year. The group has been visited by a number of Lambeth services and professionals, which has significantly increased parents' knowledge of available services. The group has become a platform for Polish families to meet, learn Polish songs and rhymes, celebrate culture and traditions through arts and crafts activities.

More initiatives have linked Lambeth Libraries with Polish organisations and created more space for Poles to explore their potential as a community, empowering the community and increasing confidence. A large collection of Polish books was donated by 100 Polish authors to Streatham Library and each year Lambeth Libraries puts on events with the Polish Community, many involving the Polish Cultural Institute and Polish Embassy.

In the last eight years we have seen 17 Polish community leaders trained and Libraries have run events each year with the community – from a 'Friendship Community Event' at the library with the Polish, Ghanaian, Somalian, Spanish and Brazilian communities, aiming to highlight the contribution of ethnic minorities in Lambeth, to a fantastically well attended 'Culture without Borders' festival at Clapham Library celebrating Polish culture and literature. Projects have included local Polish businesses at community markets in Libraries to Easter egg painting and decorating workshops.

Poles Connect now participates annually in the Lambeth Libraries Readers & Writers Festival each May with Polish Poetry nights and authors, often flown over to the UK with the support of the Embassy. These have included well known authors such as Jacek Dehnel and Wojciech Orliński, greatly widening local knowledge of Polish literature.

Over the last few years Lambeth Libraries and Poles Connect have partnered to run Holocaust Memorial Day events celebrating the life of Polish Holocaust survivor Lili Pohlmann and hosting the Pilecki Institute exhibition of the Ładoś list (a group of Polish diplomats who forged documents to save many Jewish lives). Lambeth Libraries now also hosts the annual 'Night in the Library' (Noc Bibliotek), run in 1,874 public libraries in Poland; Lambeth is the first UK Library to run the night, when children get to spend the night in the library.

The partnership has delivered – and continues to deliver – huge benefits to the library service and Polish community: book borrowing by Polish readers is the highest of any language group in the borough and collections of Polish books have now been extended to most libraries; Polish library users have increased substantially; and the Polish community has become part of the mainstream development of libraries' reader development programmes and activities. Over 50% of all events and initiatives delivered within the Poles Connect project were placed at libraries.

Since the project started, visibility of the Polish community in the borough has improved substantially. The scale of the achievements and delivered activities to date is testament to the unleashed energy and community spirit from the project, as well as the hard work of the community workers and volunteers organised by Poles Connect. Throughout, the project and partnership have delivered community development and collaboration, building stronger community cohesion in Lambeth.

Looking to the future

After the settlement of post-war Polish communities in Lambeth, libraries organised book collections in Polish community venues, but this community was dying out and with them the community infrastructure. The post-2004 community have brought a new energy to our library services. Poles Connect has identified libraries as innovative and creative spaces taking an active role in the community capacity-building in Lambeth. This has been of massive benefit to our service and enabled us to be relevant to the local Polish community. As a by-product it has also led to financial contributions from the Polish Embassy towards activities delivered from Lambeth Libraries.

Key learning points

- **Co-operation** The Polish community involvement in planning, designing and running activities with the library has led to a far greater integration of the local Polish community.
- **Inclusion** Services open to all: the provision of Polish language books and events has helped the community to see the library as their own and opened other available services to them.
- **Empowerment** Engaging volunteers and hosting life- and work-skills workshops has meant that the community has worked with the library to design the service it receives.
- **Visibility** Signs and information in Polish and open community events have given a proud visibility to a section of our community previously so often marginalised.

Case study 4: Promoting diversity and multicultural blending through the Conversation Café initiative

Jolanta Peters (Research & Library Services Manager (HE), Bridgwater & Taunton College)

What is a Conversation Café?

The Conversation Café is a library initiative which brings together foreign speakers to practise speaking English in a social yet educational setting. It operates as an hourly drop-in session on a weekly basis at a local College and public library and is offered to members for free. The Conversation Café attendees are also encouraged to improve their literacy by registering with the library and taking part in literacy initiatives, learning about British and other cultures, and meeting new friends. Although the Conversation Café's target audience is primarily foreign-language speakers, native English speakers are also welcome to attend because this promotes multicultural blending, equality and diversity and informal peer-to-peer learning. It helps attendees feel less isolated, integrate better into the local community and College, and make new friends. The Café increases the confidence of participants and enables them to be more effective when applying for work or enrolling on educational courses.

The roots of the Conversation Café

The roots of the Conversation Café stem from Seattle, USA, when in early 2001 three friends – Susan Partnow, Habib Rose and Vicki Robin – decided to run an experiment (Robin, n.d.). It involved inviting people to various public places, such as cafés, to come together and talk about subjects that matter to American people. They believed that such conversations can serve democracy, encourage critical thinking, expressiveness and bring people together. Each of the friends sat in different cafés every week and invited people to get engaged in an open community dialogue. This is how the global Conversation Café concept was born.

At the end of 2012, Somerset College (now Bridgwater and Taunton College) library team[140] read an article in *CILIP Update* about how this concept was adapted in North London, at the London Borough of Barnet public libraries (Bukhari and LaTulip, 2012). The article outlined how the public libraries at Barnet were inviting foreign-language speakers to come along to the Conversation Café to practise speaking English within the public library setting.

A proposal was therefore made to establish the Conversation Café in an academic library sector, in this case at the College, based on the principle of the Café at Barnet public libraries. Since 2004 the College has seen a growing number of foreign nationals coming through its doors to enrol on ESOL courses and other vocational courses, and it was therefore assumed that these students would benefit from additional initiatives that support the development of their English skills. After operational preparations were made, the Conversation Café opened its doors at the College for the first time on 22 February 2013 and has been running up until the COVID-19 pandemic in 2020. Once the lockdown restrictions ease, the College is considering reopening this popular initiative once again.

In 2016 the College expanded the initiative into the public library in Taunton, which meant that the Café could run at different days and times in other venues, enabling more attendees to benefit from this initiative. The initiative was supported through a grant from the South Western Regional Library Service (SWRLS).

In the 2017/2018 academic year, the Café welcomed a number of Syrian refugees studying an ESOL course at the College. On the same day, after their ESOL class, they would attend the Conversation Café initiative. Refugees were able to practise their conversational English and support their mental health and wellbeing through social interaction with others; reducing isolation by meeting new people and gradually rebuilding their war-torn lives and integrating into the local community. The College and the LRC have been a sanctuary for the refugees in gaining valuable lifelong skills.

Conversation Café promotion

The Conversation Café was promoted through a range of channels to ensure its success at both the College and the public library. It was marketed via social media, posters, leaflets and word of mouth. Promotional materials were distributed at the JobCentre Plus, local community centres and churches, foreign food shops, local public libraries and ESOL classes at the College. To increase the visibility of this initiative, leaflets and posters were translated into a number of foreign languages and displayed at a variety of venues frequently visited by speakers of other languages.

How does the Conversation Café work?

To encourage a conversation, a new topic is chosen each week with a vocabulary sheet and simple grammatical structures or questions to help initiate a conversation and equip the Café members with everyday language skills. A diverse range of topics is covered at the Café, with members signposting each other to local community services and helping each other understand 'how things work' in the UK. Topics range from talking about food and festivals, to accessing health and educational services, finding jobs and passing 'Life in the UK' tests.[141]

Attendees also learn about diverse cultures, religions, traditions, folklore and ways of life in other countries. They embrace and appreciate cultural differences, share their experiences, which broaden and enrich their respect for the world's diversity. The use of iPads, bilingual dictionaries and atlases at the Café help the attendees converse with each other more easily through the use of visual or audiovisual resources.

The Conversation Café additionally supports the development of English-language skills by engaging members in the library reading initiatives. For example, members are able to gain prizes for each book they finish reading. The College library has been collaborating with the Reading Agency to promote the Reading Ahead programme – this '. . . challenges participants to pick six reads and record, rate and review them in a personal reading diary – printed or digital. After completing their diary they receive a certificate' (The Reading Agency, 2021). This adds encouragement and motivation to advance Conversation Café participants' literacy skills and empowers them to read for life.

Assessing the success of the Conversation Café

Feedback from the Conversation Café attendees was gathered via questionnaires and focus groups. Attendees have highlighted the importance of the Conversation Café, as it helps them improve their English-language skills, such as speaking, reading, writing and listening. They also specified various aspirations that they can aim to achieve by having more effective English skills – mainly associated with better employability skills (increase in confidence, better CV writing and job interview techniques) and aspirations to study at the university. All of them highlighted the importance of being an active member of the library and engaging in reading as these activities additionally support the development of their English skills.

The social aspect has also been a common theme amongst the attendees, as they stated that the Conversation Café helps them meet new friends. Some of these friendships extended beyond the Conversation Café doors. Positive comments were made about the library staff who run the Café initiative with enthusiasm, professionalism and dedication. Recommendations included requests to run the Conversation Café either more than one hour a week (1½ or 2 hours) or even twice a week at each venue.

The following anonymous accounts have been collated from the College Café members:

> I am studying at the College GCSE English and also an accountancy course at Huish [another college]. I don't work at the moment, but I am looking for work. I have lived here for four years now. My family are here and I would like soon to start a new job. I started attending the Café in March 2016 at the public library and then at the College in April. I now regularly, every week, attend the Café at both places. I am also registered with the College library and, every time I come

136 LIBRARIES AND SANCTUARY

here, I borrow books. Reading books can also help improve vocabulary and reading skills. I come here to converse with other people, meet new friends and this is my discovery of the English language. I have noticed that since coming to the Café, my English has improved and I now speak more confidently with other people. Improving my English is important to me because I like to make a conversation, speak very well, read and write correctly in English. I will also recommend the Café to my Bulgarian friends because at the Café we speak about different topics every time and meet new people. (Bulgarian attendee).

I have been in the UK for 2 years now and I come from Iraq. I once was a student at Somerset College [now Bridgwater and Taunton College]. I started attending the Café in March 2016. I like to come here to meet nice people and improve my English. I already feel that my English has improved, and I know it will help me find a job in the future if I understand English and speak better. In the future I would also like to study at a university. I would definitely recommend the Café to other people because I know they will enjoy it and meet the wonderful staff who run it. It would be good if the Café at the College could run twice a week. (Iraqi attendee).

I am French and I am a student at the College studying ESOL level 2. I lived in the UK for two years now. I do not work, but I would like to find a job. I started attending the Conversation Café at the College two years ago and attend it regularly. Unfortunately I can't attend the Café at the public library as it is in the evenings. I am also registered with the College library and sometimes borrow books as I think reading books and other materials can also help people improve their English. I like attending the Conversation Café because I can practise speaking English and meet new friends. I feel that my English has already improved since I started attending the Café. I think it is important for me to improve my English because I can understand people and speak correctly with them. I would recommend the Café to other people, but maybe it could run longer than one hour, or maybe even twice a week? (French attendee).

I am very happy to come here. I meet other people; I like the history of other countries, traditional things and their language. It is nice to speak with other people and improve my language. I always learn something new here. I am interested a lot in other countries' politics, books and history.

(Polish attendee)

The initiative is run by library staff and volunteers, some of whom are speakers of other foreign languages. Positive feedback about the Conversation Café was received from the College ESOL tutor, who supported the Café by encouraging Syrian refugees-ESOL students to attend the Conversation Café after their ESOL class:

Thanks so much for having us at Conversation Café yesterday – I thought it went really well! We had had a brief look at 'Internet/social media' vocabulary in the class before we came, so that helped too! . . . Some were keen, and some were a bit worried about it, although I think they all felt they were able to participate yesterday. You [the facilitator] are so good at speaking to them at their level, but I imagine that's because you know what it's like to have English as a second language!

The Conversation Café stands for education, empowerment, inclusiveness, diversity, collaboration and literacy. The initiative has proved to work between two libraries in different sectors and, through expansion, offered more opportunities for people to attend the Café at different times and venues. The initiative is also changing people's lives, as it supports them with English skills development, which can lead to better chances of employment and enrolment onto formal English classes or vocational further or higher education courses. It supports members' mental health and wellbeing, raises their confidence levels in written and spoken English through discussing a variety of topics and using visual resources and technology to supplement the topics. The attendees' English skills are further supported by empowering them to register with the library and engage in literacy initiatives already available through the libraries.

7

And What Can We Learn From Elsewhere?

The main focus of this book has been on practice and experience in the UK, but, of course, that does not mean that we should become insular.

It is vital that we all keep up to date with world news, especially events that are likely to have an impact on people seeking sanctuary and other new arrivals. It is also vital that we find out as much as possible about what libraries outside the UK are developing – there will be things we can learn!

In preparing this book, I have regularly asked libraries other than public libraries for examples, case studies, lessons learned, but with very little in the way of response (except the terrific examples included elsewhere), so have decided to fill in some of those gaps with some examples from outside the UK. (There will be more about this lack of response in the Conclusions chapter.)

Academic libraries: 'Project Welcome'

With funding from the US Institute of Museum and Library Services, 'Project Welcome' began as a one-year planning grant (May 2016–April 2017) that was extended an additional year until April 2018. The project: '. . . aims to learn about and articulate ways libraries can address the information needs of refugees and asylum seekers in order to support and empower them in their resettlement and integration process.' (Project Welcome, n.d.)

An article published in 2017 (Bowdoin et al., 2017) summarised some of what the project achieved:

> Refugees and asylum seekers are very much in the news today, and libraries
> work to identify information resources, services, skills, training and/or research

140 LIBRARIES AND SANCTUARY

in order to support the resettlement and integration of these groups. ALA has passed resolutions and gathered information about how libraries respond to and empower immigrants, refugees, and asylum seekers. Public libraries have often been leaders in these activities providing library cards; computers with Internet access; free wifi; books, movies, and materials in a number of languages; English classes; electronic resources; programs on topics, such as job searching; and library staff to assist with questions.

Academic libraries also support research and the teaching of refugees forced into migration as well as library users who are refugees and asylum seekers. Project Welcome . . . is a planning grant funded by the Institute of Museum and Library Services to support the Mortenson Center for International Library Programs at the University of Illinois (in partnership with ALA) to learn about how libraries can address information needs of refugees and asylum seekers, and develop recommendations and an action plan to serve this community.

There are some key lessons to be learned from this work:

- In looking at the information needs of refugees arriving in the USA from the Central African Republic: '. . . one thing that became very obvious was that libraries have a long way to go in reaching this, and similar, populations. Only 3 of the 39 interviewees mentioned a local (public or academic) library at all.'
- Research into the information needs and barriers of Southeast Asian refugee undergraduates – whilst not completed at the time the article was written – highlighted some issues as being: issues of cultural identity; academic aspirations; influences involved in the decision to attend university; knowledge about college; difficulties with studies; and self-motivation in choosing and succeeding as a student.
- An assessment of the one piece of work by the Standby Task Force,[142] which involved information studies students: '. . . identified information gaps that were negatively impacting refugees traveling along the route with the aim of setting up information centers along the route and to create better information systems and help refugees arriving in Europe access services, understand their rights, and stay safe.'
- Recognising the importance of documenting the history of refugees, which looks, as an example, at the work of The 1947 Partition Archive, which has been preserving oral histories of the Partition of India witnesses since 2010.[143] As the author of this section, Trishanjit Kaur, noted: 'Libraries can play a significant role in preserving the memories of refugees, which I discovered while interviewing refugee women. There should be collaboration between nongovernmental organizations

(NGOs) and libraries. Basic information about volunteers, housing, education, medical care, job opportunities, and NGOs can be compiled and made accessible by the libraries. LIS educators can teach memory practices and play a vital role in sensitizing future library and information professionals to plan and provide library services to refugees and asylum seekers.'

- Finally, '[a further piece of] research seeks to establish how refugees from Eastern and Central parts of Africa, who have been resettled in a small town in Missouri, access information they need and make use of libraries. It also explores how libraries have tried to help them.'

The article concluded that:

Academic libraries can play an important role in supporting research about refugees and asylum seekers by acquiring relevant collections and collecting primary materials when possible. The teaching about and study of these groups can also be supported by libraries as they provide guides to library resources and information literacy instruction about how to identify and evaluate sources.

Engagement with students and faculty about these timely issues can also be important outreach activities. Book talks including international students from the country that a book discusses can be helpful in expanding awareness. The library could invite international students to suggest a book about their country and then participate in a discussion about the book. The same approach could work with international movies. Exhibits highlighting resources on these topics can be educational and hopefully lead students to learn more about these topics. Librarians can work with faculty to collect original materials about refugees and asylum seekers by collecting digital stories that can then be archived and available for research and education.

Academic librarians could also invite public librarians to share with library staff and others in the university community the work they are doing and see if there are ways to collaborate and provide support. Where appropriate, they might provide refugees access to needed information that the public library does not have available, such as books in a variety of languages. Academic libraries might also collaborate with community organizations to be certain that relevant information about local activities is being preserved and archived for future researchers.

ECHO Mobile Library

'ECHO Mobile Library is a multilingual lending library that operates from the back of an adapted Ford Transit van. The library was founded in northern

142 LIBRARIES AND SANCTUARY

Greece in 2016 and is today run by three coordinators with a team of part-time volunteers.' (ECHO, n.d.-a)

The library:

> ... is a shared, accessible common space where people from different places can come together without fear of discrimination. We have books in appropriate languages, with librarians able to communicate within cultural and linguistic differences. We advocate for full access to educational and recreational activities as well as communal spaces which allow people to engage with their own and others' cultures through reading and self-study.
>
> (ECHO, n.d.-a)

It includes:

- a collection of several thousand books in Arabic, Farsi, Kurmanji, Sorani, Turkish, Urdu, Pashto, Bangla, English, French and German
- high-quality fiction promoting the best in mother-tongue literature and translation
- up-to-date non-fiction covering subjects including politics, history, philosophy, science and sociology.

> (ECHO, n.d.-b)

It also supports language learning; operates a community space where people can meet friends, study and/or relax; offers structured learning sessions for children; and supports people wishing to study:

> Last year [2021] ECHO visited 8 sites per week. This year we are starting with 9 and are looking at a 10th shortly. Many of these sites host teenagers and people doing their best in challenging circumstances to learn or improve their English.
>
> Our library users want interesting, age-appropriate, inspirational books in English for beginners with support and structure to help them improve their English level. Mostly people need A1 through to B2 level English, with a focus on A2 and B1.
>
> Reading is also a way for many of our library users to discover the world, especially when so many of them have not had a chance to complete their formal education. For those hoping to go to university, English is absolutely essential.
>
> (ECHO, 2022)

In an article for *Information Professional*, Simon Cloudesley and Justine Humphrey discuss volunteering at the ECHO Library, and its impact:

You never know what to expect visiting a place like this. The children can present the biggest practical challenge; and yet their spirit, resilience and excitement captures what the library is about and the positive impact it is having. At the end of the day there is exhaustion and the need to process some powerful moments, sometimes moving, sometimes painful. But it is a privilege to be a small part of the refugees' world and to see the value books hold for those in desperate need.

(Cloudesley and Humphrey, 2018)

Toronto Public Library

Canada has one of the highest immigration rates per capita in the world: 'As of 2019, Canada has the eighth largest immigrant population in the world, while foreign-born people make up about one-fifth (21% in 2019) of Canada's population – one of the highest ratios for industrialized Western countries.' (Wikipedia, 2021b). 'From November 2015 to December 2016, the Canadian Government's #WelcomeRefugees[144] initiatives resettled over 39,600 Syrian refugees in communities across Canada. Approximately 6,000 Syrians have settled in Toronto . . .'(International Federation of Library Associations and Institutions, 2020). New arrivals make up 49% of Toronto's population (Bowles, 2021), and the city is recognised as: '. . . one of the most diverse cities in the world reflected in the City of Toronto's motto "Diversity, Our Strength".' (City of Toronto, 2021)

According to IFLA: 'Toronto Public Library (TPL)'s active involvement added to the city's mobilisation efforts to welcome and support Syrian refugee families, by providing pre-arrival and on-going, post-settlement support services.' (International Federation of Library Associations and Institutions, 2020)

As well as the 'traditional' range of library services, TPL offers support for settlement;[145] language acquisition; education; employment and skills upgrading; and belonging and engagement – these are backed by the federally funded Library Settlement Partnerships, which support settlement workers in 14 library branches serving a high concentration of newcomers. In addition, TPL provides materials in a wide range of languages (with increased provision in Arabic and Armenian). As Vickery Bowles emphasised:

Finding books, music, movies and news in a home language
- helps newcomers integrate into Canadian society
- makes them feel more at home in Canada.

Literacy in any language supports overall literacy
- Important for children to see reading modeled at home regardless of the language being read.

(Bowles, 2021)

They run book groups; book clubs in other languages; programmes targeted towards new arrivals (e.g. digital literacy, public health); citizenship classes and practice tests; and a 'new to Canada' blog.[146] They also stress the importance of access to technology, with e-mail, Wi-Fi, high-speed internet access and training and support to use these facilities.

In terms of the welcome that Toronto and TPL had given to Syrian refugees, Vickery Bowles said: 'Our goal was to support the Syrian refugees in their quest for *access* to information, *opportunities* to make a new life and *connections* to people and institutions they can trust.' (Bowles, 2021, emphases hers)

Joining TPL was made as easy as possible: '... because they didn't have a home address yet, the address of the local library branch was used to facilitate getting cards into the hands of the refugees ... ' (Bowles, 2021)

For the Syrian refugees, and in keeping with the City of Toronto's Refugee Resettlement Program, TPL provided additional pre-arrival support for private sponsors, with orientation sessions provided for private sponsors in library branches (11 sessions were delivered, with over 300 private sponsors attending).

Key documents – such as the 'Welcome to Your Library' guide – were translated into Arabic and Armenian, and outreach and other activities were used to reach new arrivals ('Many were temporarily located in hotels so we used our bookmobile to connect with refugees and distribute the books, and deliver programs such as story times in English and Arabic as well as get people registered with library cards' (Bowles, 2021)); and the new arrivals were encouraged to get to know the city and visit cultural venues:

> One night we hosted a night of music and celebration, where we introduced our popular museum pass lending program to help Syrian refugees discover and experience Toronto's many arts and culture venues and attractions. We wanted to encourage these newcomers to explore their City and the destinations that many Torontonians enjoy with their families. Participating cultural venues included the Toronto Zoo, the Ontario Science Centre, Royal Ontario Museum, the Art Gallery of Ontario and the Aga Khan Museum.
>
> Over 1000 passes were distributed to families.
>
> (Bowles, 2021)

8
Conclusions

Introduction

The world continues to change rapidly – for example, just in the relatively brief time that I have been writing this book we have had the withdrawal of troops from – and subsequent disasters in – Afghanistan, and the invasion of Ukraine by Russia, which, at the time of writing, had led to possibly more than 12 million Ukrainian people fleeing their homes (BBC News, 2022). Such events, combined with an increasing number of economic and environmental disasters, mean that the likelihood of people having to move around the world increases almost daily – an estimate by Zurich Insurance, for example, suggests that there could be 1.2 billion climate refugees by 2050 (Zurich, 2022).

Responses to people seeking sanctuary and other new arrivals

Responses by different countries to different groups of people seeking sanctuary vary considerably. As we have noted throughout the book, responses are shaped by a range of factors (including poverty, racism, perceptions of 'others'): this means that some refugees are perceived as 'good' refugees and some as 'bad'. The UK's response to Ukrainian refugees in 2022, for example, is noticeably different to that towards Syrian or Afghan refugees, for reasons outlined in a blogpost by LSE (Pettrachin and Abdou, 2022). There is considerable contrast between the welcome (in theory, at least) being offered by the UK government to Ukrainian refugees and the real welcome on the ground, which has been described as 'underwhelming and out of step with the rest of Europe', with problems over obtaining visas and even accessing the visa processing centres (Sigona, 2022) – and, even with these problems, there is a huge difference in this approach compared to the likelihood of being sent to Rwanda: 'The Home Office has said that people who arrived in the UK after crossing the Channel will be among the first group notified that it plans to send them to Rwanda.' (Cooney, 2022)

Political responses to new arrivals

We know too that sanctuary can be a political 'hot potato', especially with pressure from right-wing media and politicians and, in Chapter 2 particularly, we have looked at the impact that politics have had on the UK's stance towards new arrivals from the 1940s to the present day.

These political stances are, of course, reflected in local politics as well as at national level and can have a major impact on how local authorities and other agencies respond to the needs of new arrivals. We have noted in Chapters 4 and 6 some of the very positive responses by libraries: these mostly would not have been possible without strong support and leadership from local authorities (and other organisations) – for example, as both Barry Clark and Julie Mckirdy note, Sandwell Library Service were able to develop the work which led to their being awarded as the UK's first Library of Sanctuary because of the political support from Sandwell Metropolitan Borough Council.

Libraries and new arrivals

As the book shows, libraries have been responding positively to new arrivals for the last 70 years or so at least, and it is particularly heartening to see how many libraries are now wanting to engage with new arrivals, perhaps by supporting the principles of and becoming Libraries of Sanctuary (it was exciting to see just how many libraries of different types joined the CILIPS webinar, 'Libraries and Museums of Sanctuary', in March 2022).

So, what can go wrong?

As history shows us, libraries frequently get involved in major initiatives but often only for a short time – funding may dry up, or spending priorities change, or political directions may alter. We noted this, for example, in Chapter 4 in relation to the Welcome To Your Library initiative, where, whilst some of the work has continued in some places to this day, in other places it has not because, primarily, funding priorities changed (and the funding had not been mainstreamed).

Also in Chapter 4, we noted the impact of funding cuts in the 1970s, 1980s and 1990s on libraries' provision for new arrivals, and, of course, the increasing impact of austerity on libraries' budgets since 2010.

CONCLUSIONS 147

In passing, it is also worth noting here that library 'fashions' may change too – for example, the growth of a certain type of chequebook managerialism in the 1990s meant that some public libraries changed their focus.

What can we do to start to make things right?

- Longer-term planning: on a broader level, what we do know is that, to make any kind of difference, we need to be engaged with this work for 'the long haul'. I vividly remember hearing someone speak about the effort that would be required to overcome the issues caused by the loss of employment in parts of Wales in the 1990s, and that it would take at least 25 years to begin to make a difference. With the kind of political and organisational mindset we find frequently in libraries, local authorities and other organisations, there is no long-term view – this needs to change. We need to be able to convince our users, politicians and policymakers that supporting new arrivals – and thereby the wider community – is at the heart of what libraries do.
- Prioritising: as noted in Chapter 3, CILIP published in 2019 the strategy paper, *Libraries, Information and Knowledge Change Lives* (CILIP, 2019a), which set out new priorities for the profession. As this was adopted – and 'Changing Lives' has become a core of librarianship in the UK – there should no longer be any doubt about the need to prioritise working towards social justice, and, specifically, to support new arrivals.
- 'This is all political': in the past, I have had a lot of discussions with library staff who feel that any sort of social justice and community engagement work is somehow 'too political' for a library. As noted above, with the CILIP 'Changing Lives' strategy now at the heart of our work, responses to new arrivals should be high profile; and there is an urgent need for more research, more developing and sharing of good practice, and better reflective practice to understand fully what a difference we can make and how we can tackle seriously those issues outlined earlier in the book: racism, the hostile environment, the lack of awareness of who new arrivals are and what they may need.
- Funding: we have noted throughout the book how funding for library provision has fluctuated. Following on from the previous point, politicians and policymakers also need to put in place levels of funding to ensure that libraries can properly support new arrivals.
- Provision by libraries: this work also needs to be taken on by all kinds of library and information service. Whilst the responses from some sectors have been terrific, I have also been disappointed by the lack of engagement with this work by others: despite some general calls via

148   LIBRARIES AND SANCTUARY

CILIP mailings for information and assistance, together with some targeted mailing, the responses from some library sectors have been non-existent, and, despite their alleged involvement, only one University of Sanctuary library service actually replied. We know that health libraries must provide for new arrivals, but none came forward with evidence of this.

- Awareness: following on from the last point, it is critical that all people who work in libraries develop and maintain an awareness of the social, community and political background to their work.
- Sharing of good practice: particularly as good practice starts to develop now in the light of the Libraries of Sanctuary movement, we need to find ways of sharing this in order that everyone can learn from each other – and this sharing should also take place cross-sectorally within libraries and across other disciplines too (we see in Appendix 7, for example, just how much we can learn from Leicester Museums & Galleries).
- Sharing of information: a number of key issues – such as sources of supply of library materials – still need continuing exploration, and it is important that results are shared widely.

Albeit with some ups and downs, libraries in the UK have demonstrated strongly over the last 70 years or so just how they can engage with and support new arrivals (and other socially excluded groups and individuals). I hope that this book illustrates this – and also points the way towards further developments that all library services can implement to ensure that new arrivals really do receive the welcome to the UK that they merit.

Appendices

Appendix 1: Main countries of origin of people seeking asylum

According to the Home Office (Home Office, 2022), in 2021–22, the main countries of origin of people seeking asylum were:

- Iran
- Iraq
- Eritrea
- Albania
- Syria
- Afghanistan
- Sudan
- Vietnam
- Pakistan
- India.

In addition, the UK also hosts resettled refugees: 'Unlike asylum seekers, who can apply for asylum only in the UK, resettled refugees are identified abroad by the UN, and then transferred to the UK.' (Walsh, 2021, 3). 'From 1 January 2010 to 30 June 2020, 29,506 people were resettled in the UK under its four resettlement schemes . . . ' (p. 11). Around 70% of these people were Syrian citizens. The remainder were from: Somalia; Iraq; Democratic Republic of Congo; Sudan; Ethiopia; Bhutan; Eritrea; Afghanistan; and the Occupied Palestine Territories (p. 14). From early 2022 onwards, the UK has also been hosting people who have fled Ukraine.

150   LIBRARIES AND SANCTUARY

Appendix 2: Immigration status

'Immigration status' is the kind of permission people have to be in the UK.[147, 148]

These include:

- A person seeking asylum.
- Refugee Status: 'Given to a person who has been recognised as a Refugee under the definition in the UN Convention on Refugees 1951. Normally five years Leave to Remain. People with Refugee Status are eligible to apply for Indefinite Leave to Remain (ILR) towards the end of their initial 5-year grant of leave.' (Universities Scotland and Scottish Refugee Council, 2021, 10)
- Humanitarian Protection: 'If a person does not meet the criteria of the 1951 Refugee Convention but the Home Office believe a person is at risk of serious harm or human rights violations should they return to their home country, they may be granted Humanitarian Protection. As with Refugee Status, Humanitarian Protection is awarded for 5 years. People with Humanitarian Protection are eligible to apply for ILR at the end of their initial 5-year grant of leave.' (p. 11)
- Separated children and young people seeking sanctuary (Unaccompanied Asylum-Seeking Children) leave: 'Specifically given to children who cannot be returned to their country of origin because there are no safe reception arrangements in place in the country of origin. Leave until the young person is aged 17½ years old when arrangements will be made to return them to their country of origin on or near their 18th birthday. This is not a protection status and young people can challenge the Home Office for a protection status (Refugee Status or Humanitarian Protection) and while this is being considered they will not be returned to their home country.' (p. 14)
- Discretionary Leave: 'If the applicant's asylum claim has been processed and they have not been recognised as a Refugee nor been granted Humanitarian Protection, they may be granted Discretionary Leave, "Leave Outside the Immigration Rules" or Limited Leave.' (p. 11)
- Limited leave to remain.[149]
- Indefinite leave to remain.
- Visa.
- European Union citizen.

There are further complexities for young people, according to information on the London Assembly web page:

APPENDICES   151

- Many children and young people who arrived in the UK at a very young age and have lived here ever since may be undocumented. This means they might not have any legal immigration status.
- If you were born in the UK, this does not mean that you are automatically a British citizen. A birth certificate showing that you were born in the UK may not be enough. This can be for a number of reasons.

You may not automatically be a British citizen if:

  - At the time of your birth, your parents (either or both) did not have British citizenship
  - At the time of your birth, your parents (either or both) did not have indefinite leave to remain or permanent residence in the UK
  - At the time of your birth (after 01 July 2021) your parents did not receive EU Settlement Scheme Settled Status (this applies to children of EEA or Swiss citizens).

- People normally get nationality at birth. In the UK, most people get their nationality from their parents. But sometimes people find that they are not legally a national of any country. This might be because the country their parents are from does not let them inherit their parents' nationality for some reason. For example:

  - some countries do not accept children as nationals if they were born outside of that country and do not register with their embassy within a set amount of time
  - some countries do not let women pass on their nationality to their children
  - sometimes countries change their borders or new countries are created, and people are left unable to prove what country they belong to

People who are legally not a citizen of any country can apply to stay in the UK as a 'stateless' person.'

(Greater London Authority, 2021a)

The charity 'We Belong' estimates that there are some 332,000 children and young people growing up in the UK with precarious immigration status (We Belong, n.d.).

152 LIBRARIES AND SANCTUARY

Appendix 3: A note on funding
Introduction
At least since the 1960s – and probably longer – there has been a debate about how library developments should be funded: should additional money be sought (and where should it come from?), should existing budgets be redefined or, without these, can new work not be taken on?

This section looks briefly at some of the sources of funding and surrounding issues.

Home Office funding
As noted earlier, in the 1960s the 'problem' of provision of materials in community languages had been referred to the then Department of Education and Science – this was as part of an argument that public library provision could not be developed without additional central government funding.

In 1966, Section 11 of the Local Government Act made funds available to meet the needs of people '. . . belonging to ethnic minorities whose language or customs differ from those of the rest of the community.' (Great Britain, 1966). This included 75% of the salary costs of staff required to make special provision in the public library for these groups – but this was intended to be a temporary measure. However, as noted by Nicola Matthews and Vincent Roper (Matthews and Roper, 1994), there was no guidance as to the types of posts that could be funded, and local authorities were expected to find the remaining 25% of salary from their mainstream budget; it was also widely thought at the time – and echoed by Matthews and Roper – that such provision was viewed as 'added on' to the mainstream service and therefore seen only as an 'extra'. As Jaswinder Gundara and Ronald Warwick commented, whilst giving the impression that public libraries were embracing multicultural provision, in fact: '. . . one or two individuals have responsibility for running such a service (to ethnic minority groups), thus liberating the others to provide a traditional, middle class-oriented, Eurocentric service.' (Gundara and Warwick, 1981, 69)

There was also increasing evidence that these post-holders (often given limiting job titles such as 'Ethnic Minority Librarian') were sidelined, for example not getting the same opportunities as other staff for promotion (see for example Matthews and Roper, 1994) and by being regarded as 'separate' rather than part of the mainstream library service (see for example Khan, 1987); they were also often responsible for an enormous range of tasks – as Philippa Ireland said:

Unlike the mainstream library service, which employed staff with responsibility for specific aspects of the service (purchasing, cataloguing, marketing, outreach and so on), the community librarian's job entailed a variety of functions: training, responsibility for buying all specialist materials on the library's behalf, budgetary control, cataloguing, working with the defined user group, arranging, holding and participating in talks and events for the community, user education, and the publication of directories, bibliographies, newsletters and similar materials.

(Ireland, 2010, 108)

In addition, Ziggi Alexander thought that '. . . their brief is too wide and their powers non-existent.' (Alexander, 1982, 30); and she also expressed a widely held concern: 'One of the dangers of this trend is that other members of staff are encouraged to abdicate their responsibilities to the whole community.'

During the 1980s, there were several re-evaluations of Section 11 funding amid criticisms of how much it was actually achieving. New criteria for Section 11 funding were announced in 1990, and, from 1992: 'The new Section 11 grant can only be used to fund projects defined as a coherent overall plan aimed at addressing, through one or more linked approaches, an identified (special) need, and which break down barriers experienced by ethnic minority communities.' (Matthews and Roper, 1994, 6)

However, this change actually increased the precarious nature of the posts:

Ethnic minority specialists effectively will have depreciating career opportunities and a lack of the support and encouragement needed for any member of staff. Under the previous Section 11 criteria, these staff could have felt that they were 'added on' to the system rather than specialists providing a service to fill a gap the existing system was failing to meet. By the very nature of the new criteria, it would appear that ethnic minority post holders will suffer still further.

(p. 7)

Shiraz Durrani also highlighted this in his *Open to All?* 'Working Paper', quoting a Black library and information worker:

There were five Black librarians on Section 11 funding in our borough. This funding was abolished, and there was no means for us to assimilate. Management after Union pressure decided to create two mainstream posts to replace the five – one of the same grade, one on a lower grade . . . three experienced Black librarians lost their jobs.

(Durrani, 2000, 281)

154   LIBRARIES AND SANCTUARY

In 1999, the Section 11 grant was replaced by the Ethnic Minority Achievement Grant (EMAG):

> This new grant was distributed to local authorities on a formula basis relating to the number of learners using EAL [English as an Additional Language] and the number of pupils from 'underachieving' minority ethnic groups, combined with a Free School Meals indicator. The grant was intended to 'Narrow achievement gaps for those minority ethnic groups who are underachieving and to meet particular needs of pupils for whom English is an additional language'. Most of the money was devolved to schools and monitored by the local authority, whilst a percentage was held back to pay for advisory teachers and consultants centrally.
>
> (Bell Foundation, 2021)

In 2011, the EMAG was mainstreamed into the Direct Schools Grant and was no longer ring-fenced.

The issues around separate funding and Section 11 were also highlighted by Patrick Roach and Marlene Morrison in an article promoting their research, in which they said:

> The demise of racial equality and of multicultural service developments in libraries has been linked with the decline of so called 'special' funding opportunities (such as funding under the Section 11 programme). What does this tell us about how public librarians see their relationship to ethnic minority communities, and what activities are worthy of receiving mainstream funding? When funds are short, are multicultural and race equality programmes/initiatives in libraries the first to disappear?
>
> (Roach and Morrison, 1998b, 360)

Urban Programme

In the mid-1970s there was a renewed focus on the needs of inner-city areas, and the government funded:

> ... a series of experimental programmes to combat what was then called 'urban deprivation'. Compared with the scale of the USA's Poverty Program of the same period the money may have been rather small, nevertheless £80m was poured into the experiment. The Urban Programme, Educational Priority Areas, CDPs [Community Development Projects], Inner Area Studies, Quality of Life projects and many more like them were seeded all over the country ...
>
> (Community Development Projects, 1977, 3)

As noted here, this included the Urban Programme:

> The government proposed to initiate an urban programme of expenditure mainly on education, housing, health and welfare in areas of special social need. Those were localised districts which bear the marks of multiple deprivation, which may show itself, for example, by way of notable deficiencies in the physical environment, particularly housing; overcrowding of houses; family sizes above the average; persistent unemployment; a high proportion of children in trouble or in need of care; or a combination of these. A substantial degree of immigrant settlement would also be an important factor, though not the only factor, in determining the existence of special social need.
>
> ('Urban Programme Circular no 1', quoted in: Community Development Projects, 1977, 10)

Urban Programme funding was used to develop some provision for new arrivals: for example, it was noted in 1983 that Glasgow District Libraries received an extension to their Urban Aid Grant for library materials for Urdu, Punjabi, Hindi, Chinese and Bengali communities, as there had been difficulties over the supply of books and transliteration for cataloguing (Kelly, 1983); Kirklees was one of the first authorities to receive an Urban Aid grant to build up a large collection of Asian materials (*Assistant Librarian*, 1985).

In the mid-1970s the Urban Programme's scope was increased to form Inner City Partnerships: '. . . the establishment of Partnerships between central and local government in Liverpool; Birmingham; London Docklands; Hackney & Islington; Manchester & Salford; Lambeth; and Newcastle & Gateshead' (Nabarro, 1980, 25).

Continued searches for more funding

Research by Madeleine Cooke in 1979 highlighted both the continuing need for sources of external funding and the importance of making better use of existing resources:

> Although individual authorities must continue to seek alternative sources of financial support from bodies such as the Gulbenkian United Kingdom Trust to fund specific innovatory projects, it is essential that the public library service as a whole should find other ways to improve provision for people of minority ethnic origin, and this can only be achieved through the more effective use of existing resources of both materials and specialist staff skills, and a coordinated programme of future service developments.
>
> (Cooke, 1979, 35)

156 LIBRARIES AND SANCTUARY

Project funding: Paul Hamlyn Foundation funding

As we noted earlier, funding from PHF had a significant impact on the development of provision by public libraries (via the Welcome to Your Library projects). However, short-term project funding is not without its problems. As Helen Carpenter noted:

> The Reading and Libraries Challenge Fund was designed to enable innovation, but at times original project targets and objectives were overly ambitious and too dependent on the passion, commitment and initiative of individuals. Without proper support or connection made to strategic planning, there was a tendency for work to stop when project funding ceased.
>
> (Carpenter, 2010, 16)

Although she was referring to work in museums and galleries, Bernadette Lynch was also critical of the reliance on project funding:

> During the study it became clear that, in terms of public engagement practice, the system of short-term project funding that supports museums and galleries actively discourages reflection, serving to perpetuate an illusion that the work is more effective than it is. The imperative to attract further funding contributes to a fear of reflection and a perceived 'insecurity' of organisations and their senior management in opening up discussion of the work.
>
> (Lynch, 2012, 10)

Incidentally, it is worth noting that these criticisms of project funding are not new; for example, they were noted by DCMS in their Policy Action Team report in c. 1999:

> We have, however, identified various important barriers to the wider development of the contribution arts and sport can make to neighbourhood renewal:
>
> - community development projects are often focused on the requirements of particular funding organisations or programmes (inputs and outputs), rather than on the needs of those on the receiving end (outcomes)
> - community development projects are often funded on a short-term, project basis, whereas a longer period, supported on a more 'mainstream' basis, will often be needed for sustainable benefits to accrue . . .
>
> (Policy Action Team 10, c. 1999, 34):

The funding position now

The libraries that are developing their provision for new arrivals, especially those becoming Libraries of Sanctuary, are funding this from their mainstream core funding. They are also working with partners to benefit from their 'in-kind' funding. Occasional 'pots' of additional funding are becoming available: a couple of very recent examples for public libraries follow.

The **Libraries Opportunities for Everyone (LOFE)** innovation fund was launched in December 2016 in order to support projects that developed innovative library service activity to benefit disadvantaged people and places in England; this included funding that supported families, health and wellbeing, digital activities.

East Sussex Library Service focused on '. . . communities (both of people and place) in areas of high deprivation' and targeted 'A well-established community of refugees and migrants in the Hastings area with limited English skills, engaged through a local drop-in centre.' Their provision via LOFE included: 'Dual language rhyme time and story times with refugees and migrants.' (Quotations from: Bidey, Mustata and Rembiszewski, 2018, 27)

The **Libraries Improvement Fund** (awarded 2021–22) is 'To enable library services across England to invest in a range of projects to upgrade buildings and technology so they are better placed to respond to the changing ways people are using them.' (Arts Council England, n.d.). Although no specific information about the successful applications seems to be available at the time of writing, this could well be used to support provision for new arrivals.

158 LIBRARIES AND SANCTUARY

Appendix 4: A brief look at the supply of library materials

As noted in Chapter 4: 'Libraries' responses in the UK – historical background', a constant running theme has been the supply of books and other materials.

One model for provision was that developed by the Polish Library which was established in the 1940s, lending collections of books in Polish to libraries across the UK (see for example Sen and Listwon, 2009), and which continues today (Biblioteka Polska POSK w Londynie, 2021).

During the 1960s and 1970s, as Claire M. Lambert noted (Lambert, 1969), a number of library authorities were building up individual collections; during the 1970s, Birmingham Library Service took this a step forward and established its collection as a 'Library of Asian Languages', lending titles in bulk to other local authorities (Dolan, 1992); by 1976 it had a stock of some 18,000 books (Library Advisory Council and Community Relations Commission, 1976).

The Cooperative of Indic Language Library Authorities (CILLA) was founded in 1980 by LASER.[150] The aims were: to improve the quality of cataloguing of Indic language material throughout the LASER region and to lay down guidelines for standardisation; to increase the possibility of interlending the material, in particular by creating a worthwhile union catalogue; to provide facilities for book selection meetings for all LASER authorities wishing to take the CILLA service; to increase the bibliographical control of Indic language material; and to increase co-operation between Indic language specialists in the LASER authorities (see for example Lipniacka, 1994b; Plaister, 1985). By the early 1990s CILLA had grown to include groupings in the South-West, Midlands, northern England and Scotland (Lipniacka, 1994a, 181).

In parallel, schemes were being developed elsewhere in the UK, including SEALS[151] in the West Midlands Regional Library System, which covered '. . . languages of the European Union, i.e. French, German, Spanish and Italian, and is more a co-operative regional purchasing scheme than a circulating library.' (Lipniacka, 1994b, 167)

Again according to Ewa Lipniacka, in the early 1990s, CILLA, The Polish Central Circulating Library, SEALS, the Bradford Subscription Library (Indic language material), the Westminster Chinese Circulating Library and several others got together under the auspices of the Library and Information Co-operation Council to form LINGUALINC, an umbrella group for the co-operatives providing access to materials in community languages (see Lipniacka, 1994b, 167–168).

However, there were still issues over supply. As an article in *Assistant Librarian* noted in 1985:

The India Office Library was the first to meet the demand from public libraries [for] Asian languages. Its eventual reluctance to satisfy the growing needs of the public libraries brought the Birmingham Library of Asian Languages into existence. The service of the latter, warmly welcomed then, would have proved much more effective if adequate resources had been provided.

(Kirklees Libraries, 1985, 18)

The result was that Kirklees embarked on book buying direct from the Indian subcontinent, funded in part by grants (for further information, please see Appendix 3).

At the beginning of the 21st century, there was quite a wide range of primarily UK-based suppliers – including some larger companies that catered for libraries' needs – but, by 2022, the number had dwindled again. The following is by no means comprehensive, but may help in terms of finding current suppliers (updated 2022):

African Books Collective

www.africanbookscollective.com

Includes books from smaller African publishers and includes titles in languages such as Swahili and Yoruba.

Al Saqi Bookshop

www.alsaqibookshop.com

Stocks a wide range of subjects in English related to the Arab World, as well as books on all subjects in Arabic.

Arthur Probsthain (and **SOAS Bookshop**)

www.teaandtattle.com/bookshop

'Oriental and African bookseller'.

Bay Foreign Language Books Ltd

www.baylanguagebooks.co.uk

'We specialise in language learning material – especially dictionaries – for over 200 languages.'

Books Asia

www.booksasia.co.uk

Stock in nine Indic languages, including Bengali, Gujarati, Hindi, Punjabi, Tamil and Urdu. Also in 12 Non-Indic languages, including Arabic, Chinese, Farsi, Hungarian, Polish, Romanian and Turkish.

Casalini

www.casalini.it

European languages.

160 LIBRARIES AND SANCTUARY

DK Agencies
www.dkagencies.com
Books from India, Bangladesh, Bhutan, Nepal, Pakistan and Sri Lanka.
Grant and Cutler @ Foyles
www.grantandcutler.com
Specialises in the major Western European languages and Russian (and all living languages from Afrikaans to Zulu). Substantial stocks in Arabic and the Eastern European languages, particularly Polish.
Hanxin
http://hanxin.co.uk/
Library supplier of Chinese books from Hong Kong, mainland China, as well as Taiwan.
Harrassowitz
www.harrassowitz.de
European languages.
LOTE Online for Kids
https://lote4kids.com
Database of digital books in world languages.
International Children's Digital Library
http://en.childrenslibrary.org
Access to children's books to read online. Stocks a range of African languages, including Amharic, Arabic, Croatian, English, European languages, Farsi, French, German, Greek, Gujarati, Hindi, Japanese, Portuguese, Russian, Serbian, Slovak, South Asian languages, Spanish, Swahili, Tagalog, Tamil, Turkish and Urdu.
IraniBook.com
www.iranibook.com
Online bookshop (which also sells magazines, CDs, DVDs, toys, cards and posters) as well as rare and old books in Farsi.
little-linguist.co.uk
www.little-linguist.co.uk
Supplier of children's foreign-language learning books and resources, including in: Albanian, Arabic, Bengali, Chinese, Croatian, English, Farsi, French, German, Italian, Japanese, Korean, Kurdish, Lithuanian, Polish, Portuguese, Russian, Somali, Spanish, Tamil, Turkish, Urdu and Welsh.
MantraLingua
www.mantralingua.com
Multilingual education resources, including in: Albanian, Arabic, Bengali, Chinese, Croatian, Czech, English, Farsi, French, German, Greek, Gujarati, Hindi, Italian, Japanese, Korean, Kurdish, Lithuanian, Polish, Portuguese, Punjabi, Romanian, Russian, Somali, Spanish,

Swahili, Tagalog, Tamil, Thai, Turkish, Urdu, Vietnamese, Welsh and Yoruba.

Scansom Publishers

www.scansom.com

Based in Sweden, Scansom Publishers is the leading publisher and distributor in Somali-language materials. Also distribute books in Amharic, Tigrinya, Swahili and a range of Asian languages. (NB the website doesn't seem to have been updated since 2018.)

Shalimar Books

https://indianbooksuk.com

Distributor of Indian books in the UK.

Star Books

https://starbooksuk.com

Languages include:

Indic – Bengali, Gujarati, Hindi, Panjabi, Tamil, Urdu, Assamese, Marathi, Nepali, Malayalam.

European – French, Italian, Greek, Portuguese, Spanish, German.

Eastern European – Bosnian, Croatian, Serbian, Russian, Polish, Latvian, Lithuanian, Czech, Slovakian, Romanian.

African – Somali, Afrikaans.

Appendix 5: Outline for a course, 'Working with New Arrivals'

Half-day course, approx. 3 hours

Course aims

- to provide a greater understanding of new arrivals and their needs
- to share good practice
- to examine what services we need to develop
- to consider how we might all be involved in providing library and information services for new arrivals.

Course outline

Welcome & Introductions
  Introduction to key themes/aims of the day
Overview – who are new arrivals to the UK?
What do we know about newly arrived communities in this area? And the wider region?
What has been the response of libraries (and the cultural sector) in the past? And what is the current response – UK-wide? What's the response locally?
What are the barriers to the take-up of library services by new arrivals?
How can we improve our library provision? What could we do immediately? Longer term?
Plenary session/Evaluation

APPENDICES 163

Appendix 6: Some sources of information about new arrivals locally and regionally

Here are some suggestions to help you start to discover information about new arrivals in your area.

There may be specific local/regional guides, for example *Integration Works: the role of organisations in refugee integration in Yorkshire and the Humber* (Brown, Walkey and Martin, 2020).

On a regional – and, in Scotland, Wales and Northern Ireland, on a country-wide – level there are Strategic Migration Partnerships: 'Strategic Migration Partnerships (SMPs) are local authority-led partnerships which provide structures and forums of engagement for effectively dealing with migration at a local, regional and national level. SMPs work to meet the needs of National and Local Governments, and local communities.' (West Midlands Strategic Migration Partnership, 2021)

These include:

- East Midlands Strategic Migration Partnership, www.emcouncils.gov.uk/Migration-Hub
- East of England Strategic Migration Partnership, https://smp.eelga.gov.uk
- London Strategic Migration Partnership, www.london.gov.uk/what-we-do/communities/migrants-and-refugees/london-strategic-migration-partnership-lsmp
- North East Migration Partnership, www.nemp.org.uk
- North West Regional Strategic Migration Partnership, https://northwestrsmp.org.uk
- South East Strategic Partnership for Migration (SESPM), www.secouncils.gov.uk/about-us/migration-partnership
- South West Strategic Migration Partnership, https://swcouncils.gov.uk/policy-strategy/policy-swsmp
- West Midlands Strategic Migration Partnership, www.wmsmp.org.uk/about-us
- Yorkshire and Humberside: Migration Yorkshire, www.migrationyorkshire.org.uk
- Wales Strategic Migration Partnership, www.wlga.wales/wales-strategic-migration-partnership
- Migration Scotland, www.migrationscotland.org.uk
- Northern Ireland Strategic Migration Partnership, www.nilga.org/nilga-networks/strategic-migration-partnership

Appendix 7: Effective communications

With immense thanks to Leicester Museums & Galleries for permission to reprint this from their Welcome leaflet.

What's most important is not what you say but how you say it . . . .

93% of communication is non-verbal, through body language and tone. This can be even more relevant when working with refugees and asylum seekers.

Here is some advice which will help make your communication with refugees and asylum seekers easier and more effective:

- Don't promise what you cannot deliver and do all you can to deliver what you promise.
- Do speak slowly and clearly without using jargon or technical language. Do keep any written information very short, clear and to the point. Include pictures or graphics wherever possible.
- Don't assume everyone will understand English. Do encourage them to speak English as this will give them confidence and enable them to participate.
- Do be patient and don't expect everyone to follow at the same pace.
- A friendly smile and a 'hello' can go a long way.
- Do maintain confidentiality and don't judge.
- Don't give out your personal phone number. Be clear about your own personal boundaries, including your time and maybe even your emotional boundaries.
- Do remember that there might be cultural differences in the acceptability of eye contact, handshaking, and maybe other social contact.
- Do ask people if they can afford a bus journey. Don't ask questions about their journeys to the UK or why they are claiming asylum as this may trigger trauma or distress.
- Don't be disappointed – many refugees and asylum seekers are not always able to follow through with commitments as easily as we can because their lives are so uncertain.
- Don't underestimate the negative impact of the 'hostile environment' promoted by some elements of UK society.
- Do try to empower and facilitate rather than rescue and take over.
- Do try to collaborate. Don't underestimate the skills and talents of who you are working with. Many refugees and asylum seekers are well educated as they had to leave skilled positions when they came to this country.

APPENDICES 165

- Do empower and give opportunities. Don't foster a 'them and us' culture.
- Do offer everyone the opportunity to participate, even the quiet ones, but respect their decision if they choose not to.
- Do check that people have understood any instructions and don't assume that they have just because they nod or say yes. This is particularly important when taking photos and seeking permission to post on social media. People will often agree but haven't always understood what they are agreeing to or where the photos might be posted.
- Don't miss the opportunity to learn about different cultures.
- Do expect to have fun and to have lots of interesting conversations!

Appendix 8: Community cohesion

During the spring and summer of 2001 there were a number of disturbances in towns and cities in England (including Bradford, Burnley, Oldham and Stoke-on-Trent). The government's response was to establish a Ministerial Group on Public Order and Community Cohesion and also a Review Team to seek the views of local residents and community leaders. The Review Team produced a report (Home Office, 2001) which led to the widening use of the term 'community cohesion'. 'While continuing to emphasise the need to tackle inequalities, community cohesion programmes were radically different in that they attempted to build understanding between different groups and to build mutual trust and respect by breaking down stereotypes and misconceptions about the "other".' (iCoCo Foundation, 2022)

This definition was set out initially by the Local Government Association in its guidance for local authorities:

Community cohesion incorporates and goes beyond the concept of race equality and social inclusion.

The broad working definition is that a cohesive community is one where:

- there is a common vision and a sense of belonging for all communities;
- the diversity of people's different backgrounds and circumstances are appreciated and positively valued;
- those from different backgrounds have similar life opportunities; and
- strong and positive relationships are being developed between people from different backgrounds in the workplace, in schools and within neighbourhoods.

(Local Government Association, 2002, 6)

There were critics of the idea of community cohesion, primarily arguing that the way it was interpreted focused too strongly on race and did not, for example, take on board and explore fully other issues that can lead to conflict, such as class, inequality and poverty (see for example Ratcliffe, 2012; Burnett, 2004).[152]

However, organisations – especially local authorities – are continuing to use the term, linking it to inclusion (for example: Wrexham County Borough Council, 2022); to the Equality Act 2010 and the Public Sector Equality Duty (Tower Hamlets Council, n.d.); and also to their welcome for new arrivals – for example, at the time of writing, Birmingham has a community cohesion strategy in place, which highlights this work:

Birmingham is a welcoming city, and we are proud of our diversity of cultures, people, and communities. It is home to 1.15 million people, which includes people from more than 200 countries who have made Birmingham their home, and is one of the most diverse cities in the UK. This diversity brings with it a rich mix of creativity, entrepreneurship, skills and talent that all contribute to the city's social and economic vitality. Our city has a proud history of civic engagement and social action through which many different communities have been empowered to create thriving places to live and work. As a City of Sanctuary, Birmingham is committed to creating a culture of hospitality and support for people seeking refuge and asylum. We can and should build on all of these strengths to make sure that Birmingham is a great place of opportunity for everyone.

(Birmingham City Council, 2018, 8)

Research by the Scottish Community Development Centre, which looked at the '. . . resettlement experiences of refugees, communities and those who support them in providing sanctuary in Scotland' (Scottish Community Development Centre, 2018, 7) also considered community cohesion to be critical, and recommended under 'Building better communities' (p. 6):

- Improving frequency and quality of intercultural encounters
- Working to combat racism and hate crime
- Promoting mutual solidarity through tackling common issues
- Supporting receiving communities to engage with wider refugee and asylum policy.

Finally, the evaluation of a partnership between four museum services, 'Engaging Refugees and Asylum Seekers', showed just how the opportunity for new arrivals to meet contributed to their own sense of wellbeing and to community cohesion:

- [the initiative] is providing opportunities for individuals to meet and socialise within their own community groupings, and with people of other diverse backgrounds
- provides opportunities for refugees and asylum seekers to share their own cultural heritage and learn more about British culture and history
- makes a contribution to improving participants' general sense of wellbeing, reducing their sense of isolation, and boosting their self-esteem
- supports children and young people to do something positive and enjoyable
- is providing significant benefits to partner community and voluntary organisations
- provides secure environments in which people can learn, play and relax.

(Rodenhurst, 2007, 2)

Endnotes

1 They will certainly be receiving a welcome, as the Ministry of Housing, Communities and Local Government press release made clear:
   - 'Hong Kong BN(O) status holders and their families who settle in the United Kingdom will receive £43 million dedicated support package
   - 12 welcome hubs will help families and individuals access housing, education, and employment to build a life in the UK
   - Funding for councils to provide additional help for new arrivals where needed, including support with housing costs and learning English
   - Schools to receive dedicated Hong Kong educational resources to teach pupils about historic Hong Kong–British connection' (Ministry of Housing, Communities & Local Government, 2021).

2 'City of Sanctuary UK supports a UK-wide network to build a culture of welcome for people seeking sanctuary. We promote understanding, recognition and celebration of the ways in which people seeking sanctuary enrich society. Our goal is to create a network of places that are proud to offer safety to people seeking sanctuary, with local communities being inclusive and welcoming.' (Vincent, 2021b, 1)

3 Alison Phipps is the UNESCO Chair in Refugee Integration through Languages and the Arts at the University of Glasgow, where she is also Professor of Languages and Intercultural Studies, and Co-Convener of Glasgow Refugee, Asylum and Migration Network.

4 We could also consider whether a human rights approach to our work would be a valuable approach; as Henry McGhie argues (for museums):
   - 'Whether they realize it or not, museums, and indeed every individual who works in and with them, have duties to fulfil regarding human rights. In fact, every individual in society has duties to uphold the rights of others, just as they should expect to be able to attain their own rights.

170 LIBRARIES AND SANCTUARY

- If people are to exercise their rights and responsibilities, they need to know about them, care about them, understand how they relate to their lives and work, and to have effective, transparent institutions that fulfil their responsibilities and obligations.' (McGhie, 2020, 10)

5   Immigration and asylum barrister (and writer) Colin Yeo has helpfully broken down this definition:

'1 Possession of a fear that is well founded rather than fanciful

2 Of treatment that is so bad it amounts to being persecuted

3 For one of five reasons, referred to as 'Convention reasons': race, religion, nationality, membership of a particular social group or political opinion

4 Being outside one's country

5 Being unable or unwilling to obtain protection in that country' (Yeo, 2021).

6   'During Operation Herrick (2003–2014) the UK employed approximately 7,000 local Afghans to assist British forces in overcoming language and cultural barriers and to help them forge relationships with local communities in areas they were deployed in. Of those 7,000 locally employed civilians, 2,850 worked as interpreters and translators for British forces on the frontline, largely in Helmand province. Some of these people are entitled to relocation in the UK, or elsewhere in Afghanistan, and financial support.' (Mills and Gower, 2021, 4)

7   In January 2022, the House of Commons Library issued a revised briefing note to assist ' . . . Members of Parliament [who] are dealing with a lot of enquiries from constituents asking how relatives or friends in Afghanistan might be able to come to the UK.' (Gower, 2022, 4)

8   'The main objectives of the OAU were to rid the continent of the remaining vestiges of colonisation and apartheid; to promote unity and solidarity amongst African States; to coordinate and intensify cooperation for development; to safeguard the sovereignty and territorial integrity of Member States and to promote international cooperation.' (African Union, 2021)

9   *Convention Governing the Specific Aspects of Refugee Problems in Africa* (Organisation of African Unity, 1969).

10 *Cartagena Declaration on Refugees, 22 November 1984* (Colloquium on the International Protection of Refugees in Central America, 1984).

11 The Kino Border Initiative works across the US/Mexico border.

12 'Asylos is a global network of volunteers working to research country-of-origin information.' (Asylos, n.d.)

13 'There are estimated to be between 100,000 to 300,000 Gypsy and Traveller people and approximately 200,000 Roma people living in the UK. GRT people are linked by their Romani ethnicity or nomadic lifestyle, but 'GRT' is a broad term that incorporates a diverse range of groups and not all people who come under this term have Romani heritage or live nomadic lives. There are several distinct groups of Travelling and nomadic peoples in the UK including Romany

ENDNOTES 171

Gypsies, Irish Travellers, English Travellers, Scottish Travellers, Welsh Travellers, Showmen, Bargees and New Travellers.' (Cary, 2021)

14 'CoramBAAF is an independent membership organisation for professionals, foster carers and adopters, and anyone else working with or looking after children in or from care, or adults who have been affected by adoption. It is a successor organisation to the British Association for Adoption and Fostering (BAAF).' (CoramBAAF, 2021)

15 A recent report has also highlighted the trafficking and enslavement of indigenous peoples whose situation is frequently overlooked by anti-trafficking initiatives (Freedom United, 2021).

16 In a 2021 Council of Europe media release, it was noted that the UK had been urged to do more to identify and support victims of trafficking (Council of Europe, 2021).

17 The Mayor's Commission on African and Asian Heritage was established in 2003 by Ken Livingstone when he was Mayor of London: 'I established the Commission on African and Asian Heritage as part of my commitment to celebrate and champion London's hidden history. The Commission's remit was to develop the strategic framework and action plan for engaging London's mainstream and community heritage sectors in uncovering, promoting, documenting and preserving the many strands and stories that make up the real picture that is London's heritage.' (The Mayor's Commission on African and Asian Heritage, 2005, Mayor's foreword, 3)

18 The Home Office has produced a timeline table of legislative changes and their effects since 1983 (Home Office, 2021d).

19 A 2021 survey found that ' . . . 67% of UK respondents wrongly believed that the government allowed all or some Jewish immigration, when in fact the British government shut the door to Jewish immigration at the outbreak of the war.' (Mohdin and Hall, 2021)

20 It is also important to note the struggles that Jewish women faced: drawing on work by Wendy Webster (published as *Imagining home* (Webster, 1998)), Angela Davis (then in the Department of History, University of Warwick) has written about the struggles that Jewish women had to find their place in 1950s Britain, and reflecting on the discrimination and hostility they faced, both as Jewish women and foreigners (Davis, 2016).

21 As one example, there is a wealth of information about the influence of Caribbean new arrivals on the London Borough of Brent in their learning resource (Brent Museum and Archives, c. 2018).

22 Although it is worth noting that the government welcome was not entirely enthusiastic:
'The Empire Windrush, which made a single journey to the Caribbean, was one of many British troopships that brought [people] to the UK after World War 2.

172   LIBRARIES AND SANCTUARY

There were 110, mainly ex-servicemen, on the SS *Ormonde* that arrived in May 1947, and over 200 on the SS *Almanzora* in December 1947. It was the *Empire Windrush* that raise alarm Whitehall bells because there were more than 1,020 passengers on board, and the Labour Government took action to dissuade others who were planning to move to the motherland. They sent government personnel to Jamaica and they were obliged to inform potential settlers that there were no jobs for them in Britain and life would not be pleasant. The personnel did so with the knowledge that there was a massive labour shortage in the UK and that the British Government did not prefer coloured [sic] workers, but those of European heritage. White Australian or Canadian would not have been rejected as they would have been received as 'settlers'.' (Torrington, 2020)

23   'The Notting Hill riots took place in late August and early September 1958, and coincided with similar unrest in Nottingham. In the late 1950s, North Kensington (including Notting Hill) was an impoverished area of London, with high crime rates and a shortage of housing. Tensions between members of the white working class and the new African Caribbean residents broke into open violence in 1958 and 1959 with attacks by white youths ("Teddy Boys") on Caribbean people and properties, followed by counter-attacks by members of the Caribbean population.' (University of Warwick Modern Records Centre, 2020)

24   This was an allusion to Virgil's *Aeneid* which he quoted: 'as I look ahead, I am filled with foreboding; like the Roman, I seem to see "the River Tiber foaming with much blood".' (Taken from: Wikipedia, 2022b)

25   It is instructive to look at how this Bill was introduced into Parliament by the then Home Secretary, R. A. Butler, using many of the trigger phrases that are still in use: 'The justification for the control which is included in this Bill, which I shall describe in more detail in a few moments, is that a sizeable part of the entire population of the earth is at present legally entitled to come and stay in this already densely populated country. It amounts altogether to one-quarter of the population of the globe and at present there are no factors visible which might lead us to expect a reversal or even a modification of the immigration trend which I am about to describe.' (Hansard, 1961)

26   According to a blogpost by the People's History Museum: 'The Immigration Act 1971 was a main focus of CAIL's [Campaign Against the Immigration Laws] campaigning. It came into effect on 1 January 1973. The Act was designed to simplify the UK's immigration laws, building on the Commonwealth Acts of 1962 and 1968. It restricted the entry of Commonwealth citizens to the UK, introduced by the 1945 Labour government, who had previously been encouraged to fill post-war labour shortages.
This concession to Commonwealth citizens with British family connections was

racist. Cabinet minutes from the time show that in agreeing to the Immigration Act 1971 ministers knew that their decision to exempt those with a UK-born parent or grandparent would attract criticism for being in favour of the 'white Commonwealth', however this racism could be defended on the grounds that Britain had a special relationship with Australia, Canada and New Zealand.' (Kufeldt, 2021)

27 'Political and Economic Planning (act. 1931–1978), a group composed of leading figures from business, government, and academia, conducted inquiries into issues affecting British government and society in the twentieth century.' (Whiting, 2008)

28 There was also a report published giving the technical details of the survey of racial minorities (Airey, 1976).

29 The Home Affairs Committee continued: 'We believe that the concept of institutional racism set out by the Macpherson report remains important today and that institutions must be able to challenge themselves and be held publicly to account for addressing racism within structures or policies as well as within individual attitudes. We recommend that the Equality and Human Rights Commission undertakes work to determine a framework against which individual institutions including police forces can be rigorously assessed.' (Great Britain. Home Affairs Committee, 2021)

30 Net migration is the difference between the number of people leaving the UK to live abroad and the number entering to live here. It is worth noting that this is very much an estimated figure: as a recent House of Commons Library Briefing Paper noted, the Office for National Statistics has, in the last few years, made two major revisions to its estimates, for example because, the 2011 Census ' . . . showed that the population of England and Wales was 464,000 higher than expected . . . The ONS concluded that the "largest single cause is most likely to be underestimation of long-term immigration from central and eastern Europe in the middle part of the decade".' (Sturge, 2021, 9)

31 This argument is developed in a brief article for *Social Europe*, in which Sheri Berman (Professor of Political Science at Barnard College) suggests that diminishing the importance of immigration as a political topic could help undercut support for parties on the political right – and, to do this, we need to deal ' . . . forthrightly and effectively with these concerns . . . ' (Berman, 2021).

32 'Between September 2015 and November 2016, a team of researchers led by the Centre for Trust, Peace and Social Relations (CTPSR) at Coventry University, working in collaboration with the University of Birmingham's Institute for Research into Superdiversity and the Centre on Migration, Policy and Society at the University of Oxford, conducted research into the 'migration crisis' at the borders of Southern Europe.' (Crawley et al., 2018, 13)

174 LIBRARIES AND SANCTUARY

33 There is a lot more detailed information on migration routes in this book, as well as outlines of what drove people to flee their homelands (Crawley et al., 2018).

34 Islamic State.

35 Boko Haram is one of the largest Islamist militant groups in Africa (see, for example: Council on Foreign Relations, 2022).

36 Full Fact, the independent fact-checking organisation, confirmed in 2022 that there was evidence that the Labour Party had used the term in relation to enforcing immigration rules (Turnnidge, 2022).

37 There is further exploration of the origins of the name in an article in *The Guardian*: could it be a codename randomly applied? Or an esoteric Biblical reference? Or a nod to something more sinister? 'Northern European languages often share many old Norse and proto-Germanic roots; the word *vaken* in Swedish (from the old Norse) equates to awake or awaken in English and *erwache* or *erwachen* in modern German . . . Dietrich Eckart, who has been labelled 'the spiritual father of national socialism', wrote a famous poem in 1922 called *Deutschland Erwache* (Germany Awake).' (Hattenstone, 2018).

38 'In April 2011, the Coalition government launched a crowdsourcing initiative, the 'Red Tape Challenge', which invited the public to identify regulations to be improved or removed . . .
The Red Tape Challenge was conceived of to give voice to the perceived high levels of popular frustration with 'red tape'. However, after the process concluded, various analyses found that most of the comments submitted were in favour of protecting or enhancing regulation, rather than calls for eliminating red tape.' (Rose, 2020, 1)

39 The Joint Council for the Welfare of Immigrants ' . . . was founded on 23 September 1967 at a crowded meeting of 240 representatives of immigrant communities and anti-racism groups at the Dominion Cinema in Southall. The meeting was called in response to the introduction of new and harsh restrictions on movement, the rising tide of racist attacks against the UK's migrant communities, and the failure of the authorities to protect them . . . In the half century since then, we have been on the front lines of every big battle for the rights and welfare of people who move.' (Joint Council for the Welfare of Immigrants, n.d.)

40 In 2018, James Ker-Lindsay was Professor of Politics and Policy at St Mary's University, Twickenham, and Senior Research Fellow at LSEE-Research on South East Europe, European Institute, London School of Economics and Political Science.

41 'On 22 May 2017, an Islamist extremist suicide bomber detonated a shrapnel-laden home-made bomb as people were leaving the Manchester Arena following a concert by American singer Ariana Grande.' (Wikipedia, 2021f)

42 'Push-backs are a set of state measures by which refugees and migrants are forced back over a border – generally immediately after they crossed it – without consideration of their individual circumstances and without any possibility to apply for asylum or to put forward arguments against the measures taken. Push-backs violate – among other laws – the prohibition of collective expulsions stipulated in the European Convention on Human Rights.' (European Center for Constitutional and Human Rights, n.d.)

43 'Granica Group is a grassroots initiative uniting 14 non-governmental organizations working for human rights and supporting refugees and migrants in Poland.' (Grupa Granica, 2021)

44 Felix Bender is a postdoctoral fellow at KU Leuven, focusing on migration and asylum.

45 'UNITED for Intercultural Action is the European network against nationalism, racism, fascism, and in support of migrants and refugees.' (UNITED, n.d)

46 The same blogpost also included an interesting insight: 'People without a migration background have become a numerical minority in numerous western European cities, such as London, Amsterdam, Rotterdam and Vienna. Looking at the generation of children aged 15 and younger, these numbers are increasing, indicating that this is a lasting phenomenon.' (Kraus and Daenekindt, 2021)

47 This research formed part of the SEREDA Project, carried out by the Institute for Research into Superdiversity (IRiS) at the University of Birmingham, which looked at ' . . . the incidence and nature of SGBV experienced by women, men and child refugees who have fled conflict in the Levant Region.' (University of Birmingham. Institute for Research into Superdiversity, 2021)

48 People seeking sanctuary had also been housed in Penally Training Camp, but, after considerable criticism and opposition – and a highly critical inspection by Her Majesty's Inspectorate of Prisons, which ' . . . highlighted the deteriorating mental health of residents as well as a lack of COVID protection and fire safety.' – the Camp was handed back to the Ministry of Defence in March 2021 (Observer Reporter, 2021).

49 This drew the ire of then Home Secretary, Priti Patel: 'The damage and destruction at Napier barracks is not only appalling but deeply offensive to the taxpayers of this country . . . This site has previously accommodated our brave soldiers and army personnel – it is an insult to say that it is not good enough for these individuals.' (Patel, 2021).

50 The inspection was carried out by inspectors from the Independent Chief Inspector of Borders and Immigration and Her Majesty's Inspectorate of Prisons.

51 There are also calls for people seeking sanctuary in the UK either to be turned back (to France) or transported to a base further afield for 'processing' –

suggestions at the moment include Cyprus and Ascension (Policy Exchange, 2022).

52 The Sangatte Refugee Camp was built by the Red Cross and closed formally in 2002.

53 The 'Calais Jungle' was a refugee camp that had grown up following the closure of Sangatte – it was cleared in 2016.

54 Chris Philp MP, then Immigration Minister.

55 The report examines the effects on young people who have refugee status, are seeking asylum, have limited leave to remain or indefinite leave to remain, or are undocumented.

56 This is the programme for EU citizens to register their entitlement to stay in the UK.

57 UK newspapers *The Sun, Mail Online, The Independent, The Guardian, Express, Mirror, The Telegraph*; and the BBC and ITV.

58 The 2021 United Nations Climate Change Conference, more commonly referred to as COP26, was the 26th United Nations Climate Change conference.

59 Ian Cummins is Senior Lecturer in the School of Health and Society at Salford University, and author of *Welfare and Punishment* (Cummins, 2021b).

60 She is also quoted as saying: 'Those defending the broken system – the traffickers, the do-gooders, the lefty lawyers, the Labour Party – they are defending the indefensible' (BBC News, 2020).

61 Nando Sigona was Professor of International Migration and Forced Displacement and Director of the Institute for Research into Superdiversity, University of Birmingham.

62 Michaela Benson was Professor in Public Sociology, Lancaster University.

63 'The Identitarian movement or Identitarianism is a pan-European nationalist . . . far-right . . . political ideology asserting the right of Europeans and peoples of European descent to culture and territories claimed to belong exclusively to them.' (Wikipedia, 2021d)

64 'The Euro-Mediterranean Human Rights Monitor is a youth-led independent, nonprofit organization that advocates for the human rights of all persons across Europe and the MENA region, particularly those who live under occupation, in the throes of war or political unrest and/ or have been displaced due to persecution or armed conflict.' (Euro-Mediterranean Human Rights Monitor, 2020)

65 This is explored further in an article by researchers at Nottingham Trent University, 'The impact of poor healthcare provision in UK immigration removal centres' (Kellezi, Wakefield, and Bowe, 2021).

66 Tom Vickers is also the author of a book which looks more widely at migration in terms of border controls and class, *Borders, Migration and Class in an Age of Crisis: producing workers and immigrants* (Vickers, 2020a).

ENDNOTES 177

67 'This report presents the findings of an audit of service user data collected by caseworkers delivering DOTW's Hospital Access Project between July 2018 and July 2020. The study population is 27 individuals who have been assessed by an NHS service as not 'ordinarily resident' in the UK and have been refused access to services. It includes those who have had services withheld pending payment upfront.' (Doctors of the World, 2020, 3)

68 'Southall Black Sisters, a not-for-profit, secular and inclusive organisation, was established in 1979 to meet the needs of Black (Asian and African-Caribbean) women. Our aims are to highlight and challenge all forms gender-related violence against women, empower them to gain more control over their lives; live without fear of violence and assert their human rights to justice, equality and freedom.
For more than three decades we have been at the forefront of challenging domestic and gender-related violence locally and nationally, and have campaigned for the provision of proper and accountable support services to enable women and their children to escape violent relationships and live in dignity.' (Southall Black Sisters, 2020a).

69 At the same time, we need to be aware that there are some underlying currents of racism in Scotland, and the idea of welcoming new arrivals is closely bound up with the country's economic needs. (see for example Nicolson, 2021).

70 'Gulwali Passarlay was sent away from Afghanistan as a young boy, fleeing the conflict that had claimed his father's life. After an extraordinarily tortuous journey across eight countries, Gulwali arrived in the UK a year later and has devoted his new life to education.' (Passarlay and Ghouri, 2015, 365)

71 In 2015, I interviewed a number of librarians at the CILIP Conference to see what they thought about the CILIP Libraries Change Lives Award. Comments were an interesting mix of wanting to know more, and echoes of the earlier responses: 'Work in a scientific special library isn't about changing lives'; 'What's wrong with working in a library to make money? Legal libraries don't relate to social justice.'
Initially called the Community Initiative Award, the CILIP Libraries Change Lives Award ran from 1992 to 2018, and ' . . . recognised excellence and innovation in the UK library and information sector, celebrating initiatives that have equality, diversity and social justice at their heart.' (CILIP, n.d.-d)

72 '"Othering" is the way members of one social group distance themselves from, or assert themselves over, another by construing the latter as being fundamentally different (the 'Other').' (Thornbury, 2012)

73 'The Erasmus Programme ('EuRopean Community Action Scheme for the Mobility of University Students') is a European Union (EU) student exchange programme established in 1987.' (Wikipedia, 2021g)

74 German bread is so ingrained in our culture that UNESCO has declared it as a

178 LIBRARIES AND SANCTUARY

part of the Nationwide Inventory of Intangible Cultural Heritage (UNESCO German Commission, n.d.). English 'bread' would just qualify as 'Toast' in Germany (a.k.a. has to be toasted to taste nice and usually only children like it).

75 'The Society of College, National and University Libraries (SCONUL) represents all university libraries in the UK and Ireland, irrespective of mission group, as well as national libraries and many libraries with collections of national significance.' (SCONUL, 2021a)

76 L. S. Jast's pamphlet was described as: 'A paper read before the thirty-eighth annual meeting of the Library Association, at Caxton Hall, London, S.W., on Tuesday, August 31st, 1915, and now published separately by resolution of that meeting' (Trove, n.d.).

77 Ewa Lipniacka was the then Chief Cataloguer for LASER (the London and South East Region library interlending bureau) and Co-ordinator of CILLA (the Co-operative of Indic Language Library Authorities – see Appendix 4), as well as being the Deputy Chair of the Polish Library Management Committee at the Polish Social and Cultural Centre.

78 She likens their self-provision to that of Jewish communities from Eastern Europe, who had started arriving from c. 1900 onwards.

79 Also referred to as 'immigrant' communities: in 1972, Peter Norman wrote about 'Library services for immigrants', introducing some of the work developing in Lambeth (Norman, 1972); and, in the following year, there was a workshop on public libraries and the 'needs of immigrants' held at the Polytechnic of North London (Liaison, 1973).

80 In 2009, I was invited to write a reassessment of Claire Lambert's article, including outlining the development of provision from 1969 to 2009, and that reassessment article covers the 1970s and 1980s in some detail (Vincent, 2009).

81 'At Luton . . . three exhibitions have been arranged in the course of the past year or so, entitled respectively, 'Focus on the Caribbean', 'Focus on India', and 'Focus on Pakistan'. These exhibitions were planned well in advance, and lasted for one week. Their staging involved considerable co-operation with the local immigrant families as well as with the Victoria and Albert Museum, The Commonwealth Institute and the High Commissions of the countries concerned.' (Lambert, 1969, 49)

82 Writing in the early 1970s, Janet Hill was highly critical of this term: 'In terms of *active* librarianship, this well-worn phrase is nothing more than an archaic misnomer, and should be dropped from our professional vocabulary. It implies that all such activities are additions, frills, and extras to the basic service, instead of being an integral part of it.' (Hill, 1973, 29, emphasis hers). Janet Hill was then Children's Librarian of the London Borough of Lambeth. As well as editing *Books for Children: the homelands of immigrants* (Hill, 1971), she published *Children are People* (Hill, 1973), an outstanding critique of many libraries'

ENDNOTES 179

approaches to provision for young people, and was the 1972 winner of the Eleanor Farjeon Award – 'The Eleanor Farjeon Award is made for distinguished service to the world of British children's books and is given to someone whose commitment and contribution is deemed to be outstanding' (Wikipedia, 2021h).

83 'Special programmes for the Indian and Pakistani children have also been held at libraries in the London Borough of Newham. The Children's Librarian in the borough is fortunate in having an Indian colleague and with her help she is making a point of encouraging the children to use the library, finding them suitable books and recognizing them as special groups with their own particular book needs and problems. During the school holidays two programmes have been arranged and these consisted not only of folk tales and songs in their own languages but also of sitar recitals. The librarians have noted a growing curiosity among these children in their countries of origin, the culture and language of their parents, and feel strongly that this must be encouraged and answered in order that the children can feel a pride in belonging to two cultures, and do not become citizens of this country without an understanding of their inheritance.'(Lambert, 1969, 50)

84 Geoff Mills was formerly Head of Community Library Services, Birmingham.

85 The complete journal run has also been digitised by the University of Wisconsin-Madison Libraries (University of Wisconsin-Madison Libraries, n.d.).

86 At the time, Hazel Waters was senior librarian at the Institute of Race Relations.

87 Co-founder Rosemary Stones described the award in a 1988 article: 'It's important to remember that in 1975 books with active, enterprising girls, books in First Languages or books which presented the authentic Black British or ordinary state school experience were both few and far between and hard to find if you were not a children's book specialist . . . Alongside our campaigning work on children's books, we wanted to do something positive, something that would draw attention to new or neglected work from children's writers and illustrators who were reaching the parts not usually reached. An Award – the singling out for praise and attention of progressive books – seemed to us to be a flamboyant and entertaining way both to promote new kinds of writing for children and focus critical attention on 'other' concerns.' (Stones, 1988). I was a member of the award panel.

88 Social psychologist David Milner undertook research which led to the publication of the influential *Children and Race* (Milner, 1975), revisited in 1983 (Milner, 1983).

89 Bob Dixon was a teacher, poet, peace activist and writer who had also taught at Risinghill School, and was the author of two significant books on children's fiction (Dixon, 1977a; 1977b).

90 CISSY (the Campaign to Impede Sex Stereotyping in the Young) published a range of pamphlets and newsletters (e.g. CISSY, 1979).

180 LIBRARIES AND SANCTUARY

91 The Library Advisory Council (a.k.a. the Advisory Council on Libraries) was established by Section 2 of the Public Libraries and Museums Act 1964, and abolished in 2015–16 (Great Britain. Statutory Instrument, 2015).

92 'The Community Relations Commission was set up under the Race Relations Act 1968 to replace the National Committee for Commonwealth Immigrants . . . The Commission was abolished by the Race Relations Act 1976, which amalgamated it with the Race Relations Board to form the Commission for Racial Equality.' (The National Archives, n.d.-b)

93 'The fund supports bibliographic and other research in its fields of interest, in particular: the interactions between libraries, booksellers and publishers; the implications of information technology for the publishing chain; publications and their use. Awards are made only to organisations or people in the UK.' (Times Higher Education, 2000)

94 Madeleine Cooke, formerly County Services Librarian, Leicestershire Libraries and Information Service and champion of library and information provision for the whole community.

95 'The emergence of Black Supplementary Schools was a form of self-help when faced with a national education system perceived to be prejudiced and inadequate for the needs of black children. In several areas of London and in cities such as Birmingham and Huddersfield, black teachers came together to organise supplementary schools.
The supplementary schools were run by volunteer teachers, community activists and parents. The schools were held part time in addition to the state education pupils were receiving, usually taking place in the evenings or on a Saturday. Subjects included Pan African History and Culture, English, Mathematics and Geography. Summer schools and excursions were also included where possible. They also aimed to build the self-esteem of children so that they could stand up against prejudice.' (George Padmore Institute, c. 2011)

96 She noted one interesting development: North Yorkshire County Library had arranged for 17 titles (popular children's books) to be translated into Vietnamese and published (Simsova, 1982, 59).

97 This Green Paper was *Financing our Public Library Service: four subjects for debate* (Office of Arts and Libraries, 1988).

98 Anthony Olden was then Senior Lecturer at the Centre for Information Management, Thames Valley University.

99 Also interestingly, the report notes that this kind of work attracts the danger of media accusations of 'loony left-ness' (Roach and Morrison, 1998a, 18) – and cites Kate Myers's term 'equiphobia': ' . . . an irrational hatred and fear of anything to do with equal opportunities' (Klein, 1997).

100 The report also listed the then known existing refugee support groups in the UK.

101 This project was '... based at Leeds Metropolitan University and conducted in partnership with the London Borough of Merton (Libraries), Sheffield Libraries, Archives and Information and John Vincent, an independent consultant. The research was conducted between October 1998 and April 2000, with financial support from, successively, the British Library Research and Innovation Centre, the Library and Information Commission, and Re:source.' (Muddiman et al., 2000a, 2)

102 Incidentally, one of the spin-offs from this research project was the establishment of The Network, founded in 1999. The Network's full title is 'The Network – tackling social exclusion in libraries, museums, archives and galleries' (and was originally founded as the 'Social Exclusion Action Planning Network').

103 Adult Continuing Education and Training.

104 'The DCMS/Wolfson Public Libraries Challenge Fund was a partnership between DCMS and The Wolfson Foundation to enhance the facilities and services provided by public libraries in England. The Fund ran annually between 1997 and 2002 and has provided over £13 million funding for 139 public library based projects.' (Department for Culture, Media and Sport, 2003, 52)

105 'The Reading and Libraries Challenge Fund was designed to effect long-term change to the way libraries and other institutions work with young people and others with limited access to books and reading. It closed in 2006 having supported 60 organisations across England, Wales and Scotland.
There were three streams of the Fund:
- Right to Read – access to books and reading for children and young people in public care
- Free with Words – access to books and reading for prisoners and young offenders
- Libraries Connect – focused on communities, such as refugees and asylum seekers, which are not benefiting from the services public libraries offer' (Paul Hamlyn Foundation, 2020)

106 The Award was given to Merton for their outstanding Refugee Resources Collection and Service:
- 'Chosen from 33 entries nationwide, Merton Libraries' pioneering project seeks to help asylum seekers and refugees become self-sufficient and make a new life.
- Library staff regularly visit a local drop-in centre where they issue books and other materials in a range of identified ethnic languages.
- Groups are walked to the nearest library to show how easy it is to gain access to a wealth of information and the library service has organised a range of arts and cultural events focusing on the lives of refugees.' (London Borough of Merton, 2001)

107 'One authority that has recognized [the importance of training] is Nottingham City Libraries, who introduced specific training sessions for working with Refugees and Asylum Seekers in 2004. The sessions were run in partnership with the Education and Asylum Support Team as well as Connexions and Refugee Action. They included raising awareness of the issues affecting Refugees and Asylum Seekers and building staff confidence to work with these communities.' (Eaton, 2007, 18)

108 I have explored this issue further (in relation to funding for LGBTQ+ pieces of work, but the same principles apply) in a book chapter published in 2019 (Vincent, 2019).

109 Barry Clark was Chief Librarian of Sandwell Library and Information Service.

110 'Bearwood Action for Refugees is a not-for-profit charitable organisation working with local individuals, groups and schools to help refugees. We deliver a range of community fundraising events, and promote awareness, befriending, support and solidarity for refugees and asylum seekers living in Birmingham and the Black Country and those seeking safe passage across Europe.' (Birmingham City of Sanctuary, 2022)

111 As noted above, the Sangatte Refugee Camp was built by the Red Cross and closed formally in 2002. The 'Calais Jungle' was a refugee camp that had grown up following the closure of Sangatte – it was cleared in 2016.

112 'We serve the whole community, particularly asylum seekers, refugees and newcomers, with kindness and respect, to affirm the rights and dignities of vulnerable people across Sandwell, West Birmingham and the Black Country. Brushstrokes now welcomes people from over 100 countries.
The work with refugees continues to expand, helping them to rebuild their lives and settle into new homes, education and work in Sandwell. The core activities are driven by the needs of the people who use the services, both in the community and those identified on outreach visits.' (Brushstrokes Community Project, n.d.)

113 There are a number of articles outlining some of the background to this work (Vincent, 2020a; Vincent, 2020b; Vincent and Clark, 2020).

114 The discussion on barriers is taken from the *Libraries of Sanctuary Resource Pack* (Vincent, 2021b), informed by Olubukola Adekanmbi's research (Adekanmbi, 2019) – which, in turn, had been informed by the earlier research in Toronto by M. Shadrack Mwarigha (Mwarigha, 2002). It also draws on the framework created by DCMS as part of their work in tackling social exclusion in public libraries (Department for Culture, Media and Sport, 1999).

115 According to research by Newcastle University, this has been exacerbated by the effects of COVID-19: 'Digital inequality meant that many asylum seekers and refugees were struggling to access the online spaces that have become especially important for connectivity and wellbeing during the pandemic.' (Finlay, Hopkins and Benwell, 2021, 13).

116 Some new arrivals are particularly affected: 'Non-UK nationals are required to obtain leave to enter or remain in order to live in the UK, unless they have the right of abode or are exempt from immigration control. When leave to enter or remain is granted, conditions may be imposed on the person relating to employment and access to public funds. Different conditions apply depending on the type of leave that the person has been granted. When limited leave to enter is granted to a person to visit, study, work, or join family in the UK, they will have the "no recourse to public funds" (NRPF) condition imposed. A person who does not have any leave to enter or remain when they are required to have this will also have no recourse to public funds.' (NRPF Network, n.d.)

117 There is growing recognition of the key role that arts, culture and heritage organisations play in supporting new arrivals, developing partnerships to take this further and helping to create opportunities for engaging with new arrivals successfully (see for example a study of Yorkshire and the Humber: Brown, Walkey, and Martin, 2020).

118 'To achieve Library of Sanctuary status, the service had to look at three key areas: Learn, Embed and Share. Part of the learning process involved awareness training for library staff and volunteers to dispel popular myths and misinformation around sanctuary seeking. The sessions were delivered by the project manager at CLEAR [City Life Education and Action for Refugees] and around 50 staff and volunteers attended.' (Local Government Association, 2021)

119 This may seem a bit obvious, but it is worth emphasising – reading is a terrific way of developing empathy, as outlined, for example, in the annual EmpathyLab guide and booklist (see for example EmpathyLab, 2021). 'EmpathyLab is the first organisation to build children's empathy, literacy and social activism through a systematic use of high-quality literature. Our strategy builds on new scientific evidence showing the power of reading to build real-life empathy skills.' (EmpathyLab, 2021)

120 'Empathy is our ability to imagine and share someone else's feelings and perspectives ... Empathy is made up of 3 elements:
- FEELING: where we resonate with other people's feelings
- THINKING: where we use reason and imagination to work out how someone else feels
- ACTING: where we are inspired to help others, having experienced what they are feeling' (EmpathyLab, n.d.)

121 There is a clear outline of what it means to be anti-racist in guidance from the Chartered Management Institute:
- 'To be anti-racist is to proactively uphold the idea of racial equality.
- Anti-racism is a system that promotes the creation of policies, practices, and procedures for racial equality.

- Being anti-racist requires active resistance to and dismantling of the system of racism.' (Chartered Management Institute, 2020, 9)

122 There is an interesting exploration – and deeper analysis of what it means to be 'racist' or 'anti-racist' – in writings by the US author, professor, anti-racist activist and historian, Ibram X. Kendi (see for example Kendi, 2019):
'We are surrounded by racial inequity, as visible as the law, as hidden as our private thoughts. The question for each of us is: What side of history will we stand on? A racist is someone who is supporting a racist policy by their actions or inaction or expressing a racist idea. An antiracist is someone who is supporting an antiracist policy by their actions or expressing an antiracist idea. 'Racist' and 'antiracist' are like peelable name tags that are placed and replaced based on what someone is doing or not doing, supporting or expressing in each moment. These are not permanent tattoos. No one becomes a racist or antiracist. We can only strive to be one or the other. We can unknowingly strive to be a racist. We can knowingly strive to be an antiracist. Like fighting an addiction, being an antiracist requires persistent self-awareness, constant self-criticism, and regular self-examination.' (Kendi, 2020)

123 Kate Pickett is professor of epidemiology, deputy director of the Centre for Future Health, and associate director of the Leverhulme Centre for Anthropocene Biodiversity, all at the University of York. She is co-author, with Richard Wilkinson, of *The Spirit Level* (Wilkinson and Pickett, 2009) and *The Inner Level* (Wilkinson and Pickett, 2018).

124 A good starting-point is the City of Sanctuary website home page, https://cityofsanctuary.org.

125 An excellent example of one such city-wide directory of organisations is BARMS (Birmingham Asylum Refugee & Migrant Support), 'An online directory of organisations, services and groups committed to welcoming, supporting and resettling asylum seekers, refugees and migrants in Birmingham.' (BARMS, 2021)

126 The role of the Local Authority Asylum Support Liaison Officer (LAASLO) is 'To facilitate the smooth transition of new refugees from government-supported accommodation into mainstream society during their 28-day "move on" period and help facilitate the return of failed asylum seekers' (Department for Communities and Local Government and Home Office, n.d., 1)

127 'The Stop Hate in Norfolk Protocol aims to create a common standard for tackling hate incidents across Norfolk. It sets out how different organisations in Norfolk – whether public, private, voluntary or community – will work together, to make it easier for residents to report hate incidents and crime.' (Norfolk Constabulary, 2021)

128 This web page also provides a link to a search of the Library Service Catalogue.

ENDNOTES 185

129 It is worth noting that, as far back as the 1970s, similar initiatives were being developed. In Birmingham, for example, newly arrived people did not necessarily have proof of address evidence to enable them to join the library, and parents were concerned that their children would damage books on loan. The library service 'bent the rules' by no longer insisting on proof of address, instead accepting that an advice centre worker, a teacher or other professional could 'vouch' for a person without accepting personal responsibility for lost or damaged books. Library staff were happy to reassure parents that fines would not be imposed if reasonable care was taken. The aim was to encourage library use. (Taken from interview with Geoff Mills, 2022)

130 As noted previously, Brushstrokes is a local charity that aims to affirm and defend the rights and dignities of people of Smethwick. They concentrate on supporting people seeking sanctuary and new arrivals in adapting to a new life here. They support people from Sandwell, West Midlands and beyond. (see Brushstrokes Community Project, n.d.)

131 In an article in 2004, Andrew Hudson commented that libraries were purchasing books in community languages but were paying less attention to buying material to support EAL – and that ' . . . the stock provided has often been the same as that used in adult literacy schemes'. (Hudson, 2004, 8) He also made a powerful point about libraries' role: 'Libraries should not be an extension of the immigration service, so the legal resident status of any borrower is not our concern, but providing a service is.' (p. 9)

132 'Inspire: Culture, Learning and Libraries is a charitable community benefit society delivering cultural and learning services across Nottinghamshire.' (Inspire, 2021b)

133 'Maktabah will be staffed by librarians from the local Oxford Syrian community and welcomes everyone to browse books in Arabic, English and Kurdish. Maktabah means literally 'a place of learning', and we hope that the pop-up library becomes a place where people learn from each other.' (Bodleian Libraries, 2021b)

134 'Simple Acts are everyday actions we can all do to stand with refugees and make new connections in our communities.' (Refugee Week, 2022).

135 Taken from the talk by Jamie Darwen (Equality, Diversity and Inclusivity Projects Lead, University of the West of England) at the SWRLS 2021 AGM (Darwen, 2021).

136 'The RTÉ television series *What in the World?* has filmed in over 50 countries across the globe. To mark that milestone, as well as almost two decades on the air, RTÉ and Irish Aid have commissioned a brand-new travelling exhibition entitled *50 Countries, 50 Stories.*
The new dedicated exhibition brings a wide range of stories together for the first time. Throughout 2020, Irish audiences will have the chance to see this free exhibition as it tours libraries across the country.' (RTÉ, 2020)

186 LIBRARIES AND SANCTUARY

137 One of the key findings from the evaluation of Welcome To Your Library was '. . . the need for libraries to work within a wider policy context, not at the periphery of local government services, and place their work at the heart of the strategic agenda of what government is aiming to achieve in terms of social inclusion and community cohesion . . . ' (ADP Consultancy, 2007, 1)

138 'The Minority Ethnic Achievement Service staff work throughout Wirral and aim to: raise achievement; remove language barriers; provide access to the curriculum; raise self-esteem; encourage social integration' (Wirral Council, 2021).

139 'Fun Palaces supports local people to co-create their own cultural and community events, across the UK and worldwide, sharing and celebrating the genius in everyone.' (Fun Palaces, n.d.)

140 There is more information about the College and their Resource Centres online (Bridgwater & Taunton College, 2021).

141 'The Life in the United Kingdom test is a computer-based test constituting one of the requirements for anyone seeking Indefinite Leave to Remain in the UK or naturalisation as a British citizen. It is meant to prove that the applicant has a sufficient knowledge of British life and sufficient proficiency in the English language. The test is a requirement under the Nationality, Immigration and Asylum Act 2002. It consists of 24 questions covering topics such as British values, history, traditions and everyday life.' (Wikipedia, 2021e)

142 'The mission of the Standby Task Force, is to provide volunteer online digital responses to humanitarian crises, local emergencies, and issues of local or global concern . . . Standby Task Force provides humanitarian organisations with real-time Crisis Mapping and situational awareness support. We're a volunteer-based network of trained digital humanitarians who represent the first wave in Online Community Emergency Response Teams.' (UN Volunteers, n.d.)

143 'We are dedicated to documenting the people's history of the 1947 India-Pakistan Partition, a globally disruptive event that created one of the largest mass refugee crises of the last century.' (1947 Partition Archive, 2021)

144 'Operation Syrian Refugees was Canada's response to the humanitarian crisis in Syria. Over the span of 100 days, beginning in November 2015, we worked with Canadians from coast to coast to coast, private sponsors, non-governmental organizations and provincial, territorial, municipal governments and international partners to welcome more than 25,000 Syrian refugees by the end of February 2016.' (Government of Canada, 2020)

145 'A settlement worker can help you find out how to:
- get free help finding a job
- learn English and attend free classes
- get a driver's licence

ENDNOTES 187

- join newcomer programs
- and much more.' (Toronto Public Library, 2021)

146 'Welcome to our friends from Syria' (Toronto Public Library, 2015).

147 The UK charity Right to Remain has produced a toolkit for understanding the UK immigration and asylum system, which is kept up to date online (Right to Remain, n.d.).

148 LawStuff (run by Coram Children's Legal Centre) also has a web page of information about children and young people's immigration status (LawStuff, n.d.).

149 The organisation We Belong, has investigated the impact of limited leave to remain [LLR] on young people, arguing that it: ' . . . moves young people out of step with their peers: disrupting and limiting their ambitions, educational attainment, and opportunities. As a result, as this report highlights, LLR makes it all but impossible for young migrants to feel fully part of the country where they have grown up and call home, undoing years of integration in the process.' (Bawdon, 2021, 3)
A *Guardian* article in November 2021 on this report suggested that 'Thousands of students who have lived in the UK since childhood are being subjected to a regime described as even harsher than the Home Office's 'hostile environment' tactics when they apply for study loans . . . ' (Taylor, 2021)

150 The London and South East Region library interlending bureau.

151 The SElection, Acquisition and Loan System.

152 There is a rather dated – but still useful – summary of work by libraries around community cohesion, written by me in 2005 (Vincent, 2005).

References

1947 Partition Archive (2021) 1947 Archive. www.1947partitionarchive.org.

Abdelhady, Dalia, Martin Joormann and Nina Gren (2021) 'Welcoming' European welfare states are forcing refugees through mazes of harmful rules. *The Conversation*, 1 February 2021. https://theconversation.com/welcoming-european-welfare-states-are-forcing-refugees-through-mazes-of-harmful-rules-152704.

Abraham-Hamanoiel, Alejandro (2021) *Breaking the Frame: representation of migrants, refugees and asylum seekers in British news broadcasting*. London: The Refugee Journalism Project. https://drive.google.com/file/d/1WQMMqTjpNMftcO7HTT3YFq7KUYl2-_Be/view.

Achiume, E. Tendayi (2018) *End of Mission Statement of the Special Rapporteur on Contemporary Forms of Racism, Racial Discrimination, Xenophobia and Related Intolerance at the Conclusion of Her Mission to the United Kingdom of Great Britain and Northern Ireland*. United Nations Office of the High Commissioner for Human Rights. www.ohchr.org/en/statements/2018/05/end-mission-statement-special-rapporteur-contemporary-forms-racism-racial?LangID=E&NewsID=23073.

Adekanmbi, O F (2019) Investigating and proffering solutions to the information seeking behaviour of immigrants in the United Kingdom. *Library Philosophy and Practice*, February 2019, 1–11. https://digitalcommons.unl.edu/libphilprac/2336.

Adeleke, Oluwayemisi (2021) Poverty and migration. *Academia Letters*, April 2021. www.academia.edu/47740585/Poverty_and_Migration.

ADP Consultancy (2007) *Welcome To Your Library: evaluation report*. London: London Libraries Development Agency. www.welcometoyourlibrary.org.uk/content_files/files/WTYLEvaluationReportrevisedversion.pdf.

190 LIBRARIES AND SANCTUARY

Advice Development Project (2004) *Welcome to Your Library: an evaluation report by the Advice Development Project*. London: Advice Development Project. www.seapn.org.uk/uploads/files/ADPEvaluationReportWTYLPilotFinalwithfore word.pdf.

African Union (2021) About the African Union https://au.int/en/overview.

Ahmed, Zahir (2007) *Reading and Libraries Challenge Fund: Libraries Connect – 'A Sense of Belonging – Refugee Access Point'*. Leeds: Leeds City Council. www.seapn.org.uk/uploads/files/LeedsPaulHamlynFinalreporSept07Eversion.pdf.

Airey, Colin R. (1976) *A Technical Report on a Survey of Racial Minorities*. London: Social and Community Planning Research Centre for Sample Surveys.

Alexander, Ziggi (1982) *Library Services and Afro-Caribbean Communities*. London: Association of Assistant Librarians.

Allegretti, Aubrey (2021) Two UK government LGBT advisers quit with rebuke of 'ignorant' ministers. *The Guardian*, 11 March 2012. www.theguardian.com/world/2021/mar/10/government-adviser-quits-over-hostile-environment-for-lgbt-people?CMP=Share_iOSApp_Other.

Allen, William, and Madeleine Sumption (2015) UK Migration Policy since the 2010 General Election. *Full Fact*. https://fullfact.org/immigration/uk-migration-policy-2010-general-election.

American Library Association (2019) Core Values of Librarianship. www.ala.org/advocacy/intfreedom/corevalues.

Amnesty International (2021a) *Amnesty International Report 2020/21: the state of the world's human rights*. www.amnesty.org/download/Documents/POL1032022021ENGLISH.PDF.

Amnesty International (2021b) LGBTI rights. www.amnesty.org/en/what-we-do/discrimination/lgbt-rights.

Anonymous Immigrant, and Rumana Hashem (2020) 'Too black to be Moroccan' and 'too Afrikan to be Black-British': a conversation about unsafe lives of black-Afrikan refugees in Britain. *Displaced Voices: a Journal of Archives, Migration and Cultural Heritage*, 1: 17-24. www.livingrefugeearchive.org/wp-content/uploads/2020/07/Too-black-to-be-Moroccan-Hashem-v2-July-2020.pdf.

Anti-Bullying Alliance, and Friends, Families and Travellers (2020) *Bullied, Not Believed and Blamed: the experiences of Gypsy, Roma and Traveller pupils: recommendations for schools and other settings* London: National Children's Bureau. https://anti-bullyingalliance.org.uk/sites/default/files/uploads/attachments/School%20Report%20and%20Findings%20for%20action%20against%20bullying%20of%20Gypsies%2C%20Roma%20and%20Travelling%20children%20in%20schools_V4_0.pdf.

Anti-Slavery International (2021) Slavery in the UK. www.antislavery.org/slavery-today/slavery-uk.

Arts Council England (n.d.) [2021?]. Cultural Investment Fund.

www.artscouncil.org.uk/our-open-funds/cultural-investment-fund.

Assistant Librarian (1985) Kirklees services in Asian languages. *Assistant Librarian*, **78** (2), February.

Astbury, Raymond (1989a) Preface. In *Putting People First: some perspectives of community librarianship*, edited by Raymond Astbury. Newcastle-under-Lyme: AAL Publishing.

Astbury, Raymond, ed. (1989b) *Putting People First: some perspectives of community librarianship*. Newcastle-under-Lyme: AAL Publishing.

Asylos (n.d.) What we do. https://www.asylos.eu/what-we-do.

Asylum Insight (2016) History of asylum. www.asyluminsight.com/history-of-asylum.

Baldwin, Philip (2021) Join the fight for LGBTQI+ asylum claimants. *Diva*. https://divamag.co.uk/2021/06/16/join-the-fight-for-lgbtqi-asylum-claimants.

Baring Foundation (2021) *Creatively Minded and Ethnically Diverse: increasing creative opportunities for people with mental health problems from ethnically diverse backgrounds*. https://cdn.baringfoundation.org.uk/wp-content/uploads/BF_Creatively-minded-ethnically-diverse_WEB_LR.pdf.

BARMS (2021) Welcome to Birmingham Asylum Refugee & Migrant Support [home page]. https://barms.org.uk.

Barnard, Catherine, and Fiona Costello (2021) EUSS, looked-after children and care leavers. *UK in a Changing Europe*, 12 February 2021. https://ukandeu.ac.uk/euss-looked-after-children-and-care-leavers/?mc_cid=321d6a9485&mc_eid=14eb8e2c73.

Bartholomew, Jem [interviewer] (n.d.) [c. 2021]. A 13-year journey through the UK's labyrinthine asylum system. *The Big Issue* (Refugee Special). https://main-bigissue-thebigissue.content.pugpig.com/2021/08/20/refugees-story-addiss-13-year-journey/content.html.

Bath & North East Somerset Libraries (bathnes_libraries) (2021) 'Refugee Week'. Instagram, 20 June, www.instagram.com/p/CQWDZ27Ik_1/?utm_source=ig_embed.

Bawdon, Fiona (2021) *The Deintegration Generation: a report by We Belong – Young Migrants Standing Up*. London: We Belong. https://webelong.org.uk/sites/default/files/uploads/We%20Belong%20The%20Deintegration%20Generation.pdf.

BBC News (2015) Immigration Bill clears first Commons hurdle. 13 October 2015, www.bbc.co.uk/news/uk-politics-34508958.

BBC News (2016) Migrant crisis: migration to Europe explained in seven chart'. 4 March 2016. www.bbc.co.uk/news/world-europe-34131911.

BBC News (2017) The child immigrants 'bussed' out to school to aid integration. 30 January 2017. www.bbc.co.uk/news/uk-england-leeds-38689839.

BBC News (2020) Priti Patel pledges to fix 'broken' asylum system in UK. 4 October 2020. www.bbc.co.uk/news/uk-politics-54404554.

BBC News (2022) How many Ukrainians have fled their homes and where have they gone? 13 May 2022. www.bbc.co.uk/news/world-60555472.

BBC News Northern Ireland (2021) Carrickfergus: police investigate posts about asylum seekers. 23 July 2021. www.bbc.co.uk/news/uk-northern-ireland-57948637.

Bell Foundation (2021) EAL provision. www.bell-foundation.org.uk/eal-programme/guidance/eal-provision.

Bender, Felix (2022) Apprehend, detain, deport—towards a securitised EU?. *Social Europe*, 21 February 2022. https://socialeurope.eu/apprehend-detain-deport-towards-a-securitised-eu.

Berman, Sheri (2021) Dealing with the right-wing populist challenge. *Social Europe*, 12 April 2021. www.socialeurope.eu/dealing-with-the-right-wing-populist-challenge.

Betts, Alexander (2013) *Survival Migration: failed governance and the crisis of displacement*. Ithaca/London: Cornell University Press. https://d3p9z3cj392tgc.cloudfront.net/wp-content/uploads/2019/03/07114253/9780801477775.pdf.

Biblioteka Polska POSK w Londynie (2021) Central Circulating Library. http://polishlibrarylondon.co.uk/centrala-bibliotek-ruchomych/?lang=en.

Bidey, Tim, Viviana Mustata and Perla Rembiszewski (2018) *Evaluation of the Libraries: Opportunities for Everyone innovation fund – final report*. London: Department for Digital, Culture, Media & Sport. https://assets.publishing.service.gov.uk/government/uploads/system/uploads/att achment_data/file/754746/Evaluation_of_the_LOFE_fund_final_report.pdf.

Birmingham City Council (2018) *Community Cohesion Strategy for Birmingham: forward together to build a fair and inclusive city for everyone*. www.birmingham.gov.uk/downloads/file/12487/community_cohesion_strategy_pdf_version.

Birmingham City of Sanctuary (2022) Bearwood Action for Refugees. https://birmingham.cityofsanctuary.org/support/bearwood-action-for-refugees.

Black, Alistair (1996) *A New History of the English Public Library: social and intellectual contexts 1850–1914*. Leicester: Leicester University Press.

Black, Alistair (2000a) *The Public Library in Britain 1914–2000*. London: The British Library.

Black, Alistair (2000b) Skeleton in the cupboard: social class and the public library in Britain through 150 years. *Library History*, **16** (1), 3–12. doi: https://doi.org/10.1179/lib.2000.16.1.3.

Black, Alistair, and Dave Muddiman (1997) *Understanding Community Librarianship: the public library in post-modern Britain*. Aldershot: Avebury.

Blinder, Scott, and Lindsay Richards (2020) UK public opinion toward immigration: overall attitudes and level of concern. The Migration Observatory.

https://migrationobservatory.ox.ac.uk/resources/briefings/uk-public-opinion-toward-immigration-overall-attitudes-and-level-of-concern.

Bodleian Libraries (2021a) Bodleian Libraries Afghan Scholars Programme. www.bodleian.ox.ac.uk/csb/fellowships/afghan-scholars-programme.

Bodleian Libraries (2021b) Visit - Syria and Silence: Maktabah. https://visit.bodleian.ox.ac.uk/event/space-for-reading#.

Boffey, Daniel, and Toby Helm (2016) Vote Leave embroiled in race row over Turkey security threat claims. *The Observer*, 22 May 2016. www.theguardian.com/politics/2016/may/21/vote-leave-prejudice-turkey-eu-security-threat.

Boswell, Caitlin (2022) *'We Also Want to be Safe': undocumented migrants facing COVID in a hostile environment.* London: The Joint Council for the Welfare of Immigrants. www.jcwi.org.uk/Handlers/Download.ashx?IDMF=37f4816f-fc08-41a3-8257-565621c85efd.

Boswell, Caitlin, and Chai Patel (2021) *When the Clapping Stops: EU care workers after Brexit.* London: The Joint Council for the Welfare of Immigrants. www.jcwi.org.uk/Handlers/Download.ashx?IDMF=15c60f7e-17ff-4fa0-8f5d-df00cf2c5967.

Bowdoin, Natalia Taylor, Chris Hagar, Joyce Monsees, Trishanjit Kaur, Trae Middlebrooks, Leatha Miles-Edmonson, Ashanti White, Touger Vang, Musa Wakhungu Olaka, Charles Agai Yier, Clara M. Chu and Barbara J. Ford (2017) Academic libraries serving refugees and asylum seekers. *College & Research Libraries News*, **78** (6). https://crln.acrl.org/index.php/crlnews/article/view/16676/18140.

Bowles, Vickery (2021) Welcoming newcomers. 'One World One Library Network' – Working Internationally for Libraries Conference 2021, 25 June 2021. https://vimeo.com/showcase/8656926/video/578071693.

Bradford College Library Online (2021a) Cultural Capital: Black History. https://library.bradfordcollege.ac.uk/unitedvalues/BlackHistory.

Bradford College Library Online (2021b) Cultural Capital: refugees and asylum seekers. https://library.bradfordcollege.ac.uk/unitedvalues/refugees.

Brahmbhat, Shobha (1990) *Public Library Provision to the Asian communities in Nottinghamshire with Special Reference to Those from the Indian Sub-continent: a Master's Dissertation, submitted in partial fulfilment of the requirements for the award of the Master of Arts degree of the Loughborough University of Technology.* Loughborough University of Technology. https://repository.lboro.ac.uk/articles/Public_library_provision_to_the_Asian_co mmunities_in_Nottinghamshire_with_special_reference_to_those_from_the_Indi an_sub-continent/9414338.

Brent Museum and Archives (c. 2018) *Brent's Windrush Generation Learning Resource.* www.brent.gov.uk/media/16416864/windrush_generation_learning_resource_acce ssible.pdf.

194 LIBRARIES AND SANCTUARY

Bridgwater & Taunton College (2021) Learning Resource Centres. www.btc.ac.uk/the-college/campuses/bridgwater-campus/learning-resource-centres.

Brighton & Hove City Council (2020) Brighton & Hove Libraries awarded Library of Sanctuary status. 17 June 2020. https://www.brighton-hove.gov.uk/news/2020/brighton-hove-libraries-awarded-library-sanctuary-status.

Brighton & Hove City Council (2021) Refugee Week 2021 with Brighton & Hove libraries 14 to 20 June. www.brighton-hove.gov.uk/libraries-leisure-and-arts/libraries/refugee-week-2021.

British Library (2021) Projects: Community Engagement. www.bl.uk/projects/community-engagement.

Brown, Philip, Daniel Allen, Sindy Czureja, Liviu Dinu, Szymon Glowacki, Gabi Hesk, Sylvia Ingmire, Philip Martin, Orsolya Orsos, Maria Palmai and Terezia Rostas (2016) *Supporting Roma voices*. Salford: The University of Salford Sustainable Housing & Urban Studies Unit. https://usir.salford.ac.uk/id/eprint/44112/1/SRV-Final-Report-Dec-2016.pdf.

Brown, Philip, Claire Walkey and Philip Martin (2020) *Integration Works: the role of organisations in refugee integration in Yorkshire and the Humber*. Huddersfield: University of Huddersfield. https://huddersfield.app.box.com/s/qias4ks55sazc445jaili2zvf06krjst.

Browne, Evie (2017) *Evidence on Education as a Driver for Migration*. Brighton: Institute of Development Studies (K4D Helpdesk Report). https://assets.publishing.service.gov.uk/media/598086a0ed915d022b00003c/K4D_HDR_Migration_and_Education.pdf.

Brushstrokes Community Project. (n.d.) www.brushstrokessandwell.org.uk.

Buchanan, John (1972) *Black Britons: a select bibliography on race*. London: London Borough of Lambeth.

Bukhari, Sumbal, and Lauren LaTulip (2012) Conversation Café. *CILIP Update*, August, 38–40.

Bulman, May (2020) They're branded economic migrants – now young men trying to cross Channel tell us why they really want to reach UK. *Independent*, 6 October 2020. www.independent.co.uk/news/world/europe/channel-crossing-border-calais-economic-migrants-refugees-b555289.html.

Bulman, May (2021a) 500 Windrush victims waiting more than a year for compensation. *Independent*, 3 May 2021. www.independent.co.uk/news/uk/home-news/windrush-scandal-compensation-victims-b1840175.html.

Bulman, May (2021b) Britain closes the door on unaccompanied child refugees. *Independent*, 26 January 2021. www.independent.co.uk/news/uk/home-news/child-refugees-legal-route-home-office-b1792353.html.

Bulman, May (2021c) Home Office put refugees in barracks after fears better housing would 'undermine confidence' in system. *Independent*, 2 February 2021.

www.independent.co.uk/news/uk/home-news/asylum seekers-napier-barracks-home-office-b1793951.html.

Bulman, May (2021d) Hundreds of thousands of migrants 'much less likely' to get vaccine due to hostile environment fears, MPs warn. *Independent*, 6 March 2021. www.independent.co.uk/news/uk/home-news/migrants-undocumented-vaccine-hostile-environment-covid-b1812985.html?mc_cid=7bea1b772c&mc_eid=7d8713d 645.

Burke, Susan K. (2008) Use of public libraries by immigrants. *Reference & User Services Quarterly*, **48** (2), 164–74.

Burne, Julia (2021) Views of people seeking asylum on the COVID vaccines. *City of Sanctuary Blog*, 8 February 2021. https://blog.cityofsanctuary.org/2021/02/08/views-of-people-seeking-asylum-on-the-covid-vaccines.

Burnett, Jon (2004) 'Community, cohesion and the state'. *Race & Class*, **45** (3), March, 1–18.

Burnett, Jon (2016) *Racial Violence and the Brexit State*. London: Institute of Race Relations. https://irr.org.uk/app/uploads/2016/11/Racial-violence-and-the-Brexit-state-final.pdf.

Byron, Margaret (2020) Men deported to Jamaica are being set up for failure. *The Conversation*, 9 December 2020. https://theconversation.com/men-deported-to-jamaica-are-being-set-up-for-failure-151261.

Calò, Francesca, Simone Baglioni, Tom Montgomery and Olga Biosca (2021) 'Regulating Fortress Britain: migrants, refugees and asylum applicants in the British labour market.' In *Migrants, Refugees and Asylum Seekers' Integration in European Labour Markets: a comparative approach on legal barriers and enablers*, edited by Veronica Federico and Simone Baglioni. Basel: Springer (IMISCOE Research Series), 235–58. https://link.springer.com/content/pdf/10.1007%2F978-3-030-67284-3_12.pdf.

CAN (2021) It's a wrap for our Libraries of Sanctuary project. 9 December 2021. https://can.uk.com/2021/12/09/its-a-wrap-for-our-libraries-of-sanctuary-project.

Carpenter, Helen (2004) *Welcome To Your Library Project: developing public library services for asylum seekers and refugees in the London Boroughs of Brent, Camden, Enfield, Merton, Newham*. London: London Libraries Development Agency. www.seapn.org.uk/uploads/files/WTYL_PC_FINAL_REPORT.pdf.

Carpenter, Helen (2007) *The role of Public Libraries in Multicultural Relationships: report by Helen Carpenter for Winston Churchill Memorial Trust*. London: Winston Churchill Memorial Trust. www.seapn.org.uk/uploads/files/WCMTfinalreport210108.pdf.

Carpenter, Helen (2010) *Leading Questions: learning from the Reading and Libraries Challenge Fund*. www.phf.org.uk/publications/leading-questions.

Cart, Michael (1992) Here there be sanctuary: the public library as refuge and retreat. *Public Library Quarterly*, **12** (4), 5–23. doi: https://doi.org/10.1300/J118v12n04_02.

Cary, Matt (2021) GRT History Month 2021. www.london.gov.uk/city-hall-blog/grt-history-month-2021.

Cavalli, Nicolò (2019) *CSI 34: did hate crime double after Brexit?* Oxford: Centre for Social Investigation, Nuffield College. http://csi.nuff.ox.ac.uk/wp-content/uploads/2019/06/CSI34_hate-crime.pdf.

Chambers's Journal (1875) Free libraries. *Chambers's Journal of Popular Literature, Science and Arts*, 3 April 1875, 215–17. https://babel.hathitrust.org/cgi/pt?id=coo.31924069261729&view=1up&seq=227&q1=3%20April%201875.

Chartered Management Institute (2020) *Moving the Dial on Race: a practical guide on workplace inclusion.* www.managers.org.uk/wp-content/uploads/2020/10/moving-the-dial-on-race-practical-guidance-cmi-race-2020.pdf.

Christie, Gary, and Helen Baillot (2020) *The Impact of COVID-19 on Refugees and Refugee-assisting Organisations in Scotland.* Glasgow: Scottish Refugee Council. www.scottishrefugeecouncil.org.uk/wp-content/uploads/2020/09/Covid-impact-survey.pdf.

CILIP (2018) *Ethical Framework: clarifying notes.* https://cdn.ymaws.com/www.cilip.org.uk/resource/resmgr/cilip/policy/new_ethical_framework/ethical_framework_clarifying.pdf.

CILIP (2019a) *Libraries, Information and Knowledge Change Lives.* (CILIP Position Paper). https://drive.google.com/file/d/1TOq6oBuGRE7dpSxjPVEiMi528E7LuIMe/view.

CILIP (2019b) Libraries, information and knowledge change lives. www.cilip.org.uk/page/changinglives.

CILIP (n.d.-a) [2021] Working internationally for libraries. www.cilip.org.uk/page/workinginternationally.

CILIP (n.d.-b) [2021] *Working Internationally for Libraries: project report.* London: CILIP. https://drive.google.com/file/d/1HjUkYvx0BCKoPr0LRKX9PYEqPFpW4rFW/view.

CILIP (n.d.-c) [c. 2018] CILIP's ethical framework. www.cilip.org.uk/page/ethics.

CILIP (n.d.-d) [post 2019] Libraries Change Lives Award. www.cilip.org.uk/page/LibrariesChangeLiv.

CISSY (1979) *Non sexist picture books.* London: Campaign to Impede Sex Stereotyping in the Young.

City of Sanctuary Local Authority Network (2021) City of Sanctuary Local Authority Network statement of solidarity for the people of Afghanistan. 18 August 2021. https://la.cityofsanctuary.org/2021/08/18/city-of-sanctuary-local-authority-network-statement-of-solidarity-for-the-people-of-afghanistan.

City of Sanctuary UK (2021) It's time for global action for climate refugees – you can help. *City of Sanctuary*, 17 September 2021. https://cityofsanctuary.org/2021/09/17/its-time-for-global-action-for-climate-refugees-you-can-help/.

City of Sanctuary UK (2022) Sanctuary Awards. https://cityofsanctuary.org/awards.

City of Toronto (2021) 'Equity, diversity & inclusion. www.toronto.ca/city-government/accessibility-human-rights/equity-diversity-inclusion.

City of Westminster (2021) Westminster Chinese Library. www.westminster.gov.uk/leisure-libraries-and-community/library-opening-times-and-contact-details/westminster-chinese-library.

Clark, Barry (n.d.) [c. 2019]. *Thimblemill – Library of Sanctuary (Case Study)*. Leeds: City of Sanctuary. https://libraries.cityofsanctuary.org/wp-content/uploads/sites/157/2020/04/Thimblemill-Library-of-Sanctuary-Case-Study.pdf.

Clarke, Chris (2021) *Level Best: diversity, cohesion and the drive to level up*. London: HOPE not Hate Charitable Trust (Hopeful Towns). https://c38b684e-8f15-4ff8-b290-3b8ce6267869.filesusr.com/ugd/078118_8a8f1baf858b48178f1c35f2f12bc38b.pdf.

Cloudesley, Simon, and Justine Humphrey (2018) Feeding minds and souls. *Information Professional*, 28 October, 40–3. www.cilip.org.uk/page/EchoRefugeelibrarygreeceathens.

Clough, Eric, and Jacqueline Quarmby (1978) *A Public Library Service for Ethnic Minorities in Great Britain*. London: Library Association.

Coleman, Patricia (1981) *Whose Problem? The public library and the disadvantaged*. Newcastle under Lyme: Association of Assistant Librarians.

Colloquium on the International Protection of Refugees in Central America, Mexico and Panama (1984) *Cartagena Declaration on Refugees, 22 November 1984*. www.refworld.org/cgi-bin/texis/vtx/rwmain?page=search&docid=3ae6b36ec&skip=0&query=cartagena%20declaration.

Community Development Projects (1977) *Gilding the Ghetto: the state and the poverty experiments*. London: Community Development Projects Inter-Project Editorial Team.

Cooke, Madeleine (1979) *Public Library Provision for Ethnic Minorities in the United Kingdom: the report of an investigation carried out on behalf of the British National Bibliography Research Fund, between January–May 1979*. Leicester: Leicestershire Libraries and Information Service.

Cooke, Madeleine (1988) Multicultural library services. In *British Library and Information Work 1981–85*, edited by David W. Bromley and Angela Allott. London: Library Association, 203–18.

Cooke, Madeleine, John Feather and Ian Malley (1991) *Co-operative Arrangements for the Management of Stock in Languages other than English: the report of a review commissioned by the Library and Information Co-operation Council*. Leicester: Leicestershire Library and Information Plan.

Cooke, Madeleine, John Feather, and Ian Malley (1993) The management of stock in minority languages in British public libraries. *Journal of Librarianship and Information Science*, **25**, 79–84.

Cooke-Escapil, Louise (2021) Libraries of Sanctuary: supporting migrant communities. *Libfocus*, 12 April 2021. www.libfocus.com/2021/04/libraries-of-sanctuary-supporting.html.

Cooney, Christy (2022) First refugees to be told this week of their relocation to Rwanda. *The Guardian*, 9 May 2022. www.theguardian.com/uk-news/2022/may/09/first-refugees-to-be-toldd-this-week-of-their-relocation-to-rwanda.

Coram Children's Legal Centre (2017) New status for children brought to the UK under the 'Dubs Amendment'. www.childrenslegalcentre.com/section-67-leave.

CoramBAAF (2021) About us. https://corambaaf.org.uk/about.

Cotrona, Sofia (2021) 'What would Scottish culture be without immigrant artists?'. *Art UK*, 30 August 2021. https://artuk.org/discover/stories/what-would-scottish-culture-be-without-immigrant-artists.

Council of Europe (2021) Human trafficking: UK urged to better identify and assist victims, convict traffickers. Strasbourg: Council of Europe. https://search.coe.int/directorate_of_communications/Pages/result_details.aspx?ObjectId=0900001680a4358a.

Council on Foreign Relations (2022) Boko Haram in Nigeria. *Global Conflict Tracker*, 28 March 2022. www.cfr.org/global-conflict-tracker/conflict/boko-haram-nigeria.

Cowell, Peter (1893) How to popularise a free library. *The New Review*, **9** (53), 440–8.

Craig, Gary (2011) *The Roma: a study of national policies*. Brussels: European Commission DG Employment, Social Affairs and Equal Opportunities. www.york.ac.uk/inst/spru/research/pdf/EURoma.pdf.

Craig, Gary (2020) The hidden scourge of modern slavery. *Transforming Society*, 16 March 2020. www.transformingsociety.co.uk/2020/03/16/the-hidden-scourge-of-modern-slavery.

Crawley, Heaven (2021) How COVID-19 became a cover to reduce refugee rights. *The Conversation*, 10 March 2021. https://theconversation.com/how-covid-19-became-a-cover-to-reduce-refugee-rights-156247.

Crawley, Heaven, Franck Düvell, Katharine Jones, Simon McMahon and Nando Sigona (2018) *Unravelling Europe's 'Migration Crisis': journeys over land and sea*. Bristol: Policy Press ('Shorts').

Croker, Susan K. (1975) Library services to Indian and Pakistani immigrants in Great Britain. In *Library Services to the Disadvantaged*, edited by William Martin. London: Bingley, 119–29.

Cromarty, Hannah (2020) *Rough Sleeping Immigration Rule: who does it affect and how?* London: House of Commons Library ('Insight'). https://commonslibrary.parliament.uk/rough-sleeping-immigration-rule-who-does-it-affect-and-how/?mc_cid=d2abc2898f&mc_eid=7d8713d645.

Cummins, Ian (2021a) More Thatcherite than Thatcher: understanding UK welfare and penal policy today. *Transforming Society*, 29 January 2021. www.transformingsociety.co.uk/2021/01/29/more-thatcherite-than-thatcher-understanding-uk-welfare-and-penal-policy-today.

Cummins, Ian (2021b) *Welfare and Punishment: from Thatcherism to austerity*. Bristol: Bristol University Press.

Darwen, Jamie (2021) University of Sanctuary. In SWRLS AGM, online, 26 November 2021. https://uwe.cloud.panopto.eu/Panopto/Pages/Viewer.aspx?id=e5396790-d8f2-4919-ad58-ae1800e292c3.

Davies, Matilda (2021) Asylum seeker who sold a kidney to flee homophobic Pakistan wins crucial legal battle in bid to remain in UK. *PinkNews*, 29 January 2021. www.pinknews.co.uk/2021/01/29/gay-asylum-seeker-uk-scotland-ar-glasgow-pakistan-home-office-lgbt.

Davis, Angela (2016) Belonging and 'unbelonging': Jewish refugee and survivor women in 1950s Britain. *Women's History Review*, **26** (1), 130–46. https://www.tandfonline.com/doi/full/10.1080/09612025.2015.1123028.

Dawson, Bethany (2021) Coronavirus has fuelled new forms of antisemitism, charity says. *Independent*, 11 February 2021. www.independent.co.uk/news/uk/home-news/antisemitism-covid-coronavirus-cst-b1800352.html.

Day, Alison (1971) *The Library in the Multi-racial Secondary School: a Caribbean book list*. London: Community Relations Commission.

de Noronha, Luke (2020) *Deporting Black Britons: portraits of deportation to Jamaica* Manchester: Manchester University Press.

Dennison, James, and Noah Carl (2016) The ultimate causes of Brexit: history, culture, and geography. *British Politics and Policy at LSE*, 18 July 2016. https://blogs.lse.ac.uk/politicsandpolicy/explaining-brexit.

Department for Communities and Local Government, and Home Office (n.d.) *Local Authority Asylum Support Liaison Officer Job Description*. London: DCLG/Home Office. www.local.gov.uk/sites/default/files/documents/171123%20LAASLO%20job%20 description_FINAL.pdf.

Department for Culture, Media and Sport (DCMS) (1999) *Libraries for All: social inclusion in public libraries – policy guidance for local authorities in England*. London: DCMS. https://webarchive.nationalarchives.gov.uk/ukgwa/20080306063652mp_/ http://www.culture.gov.uk/NR/rdonlyres/42818901-0EA3-4AE5-B1C2-1689ABC069BD/0/Social_Inclusion_PLibraries.pdf

Department for Culture, Media and Sport (DCMS) (2003) *Framework for the Future: libraries, learning and information in the next decade*. London: DCMS. https://libraries.communityknowledgehub.org.uk/sites/default/files/framework_f or_the_future3.pdf.

Detzler, Matt (2020) I am not a virus – anti-Chinese racism and coronavirus. *TUC Wales*, 1 September 2020. www.tuc.org.uk/blogs/i-am-not-virus-anti-chinese-racism-and-coronavirus.

Dixon, Bob (1977a) *Catching Them Young 1: sex, race and class in children's fiction.* London: Pluto Press.

Dixon, Bob (1977b) *Catching Them Young 2: political ideas in children's fiction.* London: Pluto Press.

Doctors of the World (2020) *Delays & Destitution: an audit of Doctors of the World's Hospital Access Project (July 2018-20).* London: Doctors of the World. www.doctorsoftheworld.org.uk/wp-content/uploads/2018/11/Delays-and-destitution-An-audit-of-Doctors-of-the-Worlds-Hospital-Access-Project-July-2018 -20.pdf.

Dodd, Vikram (2022) Bianca Williams decries 'culture of racism' as Met police officers face misconduct charges. *The Guardian*, 27 April 2022. www.theguardian.com/uk-news/2022/apr/27/five-met-officers-to-face-misconduct-charges-over-bianca-williams-stop-and-search.

Dolan, John (1992) Birmingham – as a whole. In *The Whole Library Movement: changing practice in multi-cultural librarianship*, edited by Ziggi Alexander and Trevor Knight. Newcastle-under-Lyme: Association of Assistant Librarians, 16–25.

Doras (2016) Portlaoise Social Inclusion Week: 11th-21st March 2016. 7 March 2016. https://doras.org/portlaoise-social-inclusion-week.

Duffy, Bobby, and Tom Frere-Smith (2014) *Perceptions and Reality: public attitudes to immigration.* London: Ipsos MORI. www.ipsos.com/sites/default/files/publication/1970-01/sri-perceptions-and-reality-immigration-report-2013.pdf.

Duggan, Jack (2021) Library service steps up to help summer camp ran by Northampton youth club for asylum-seeking children. *Northampton Chronicle & Echo*, 26 July 2021. www.northamptonchron.co.uk/lifestyle/family-and-parenting/library-service-steps-up-to-help-summer-camp-ran-by-northampton-y outh-club-for-asylum-seeking-children-3324314.

Durrani, Shiraz (1999) Black communities and information workers in search of social justice. *New Library World*, **100** (1151), 265–78.

Durrani, Shiraz (2000) Struggle against racial exclusion in public libraries: a fight for the rights of the people (Working Paper 13). In *Open to All? The public library and social exclusion*, edited by Dave Muddiman, Shiraz Durrani, Martin Dutch, Rebecca Linley, John Pateman and John Vincent. London: Resource, 254–349. www.seapn.org.uk/uploads/files/vol3wp13.pdf.

Durrani, Shiraz (2001) *Social and Racial Exclusion Handbook for Libraries, Archives, Museums and Galleries.* 2nd edn. Nadderwater, Exeter: The Social Exclusion Action Planning Network.

http://vitabooks.co.uk/wp-content/uploads/sites/6/2020/09/Social-racial-exclusion-handbook-2ed-Aug-2001.pdf.

Dyck, Jordan (2019) *The Findings of the LGBT African Asylum Seeker Research Project*. London: Metropolitan Community Church of North London. http://mccnorthlondon.org.uk/wp-content/uploads/2019/09/LGBT-African-Asylum-Seeker-Research-Project-Report.pdf.

East of England Local Government Association Strategic Migration Partnership (2020) Our work. https://smp.eelga.gov.uk.

East Renfrewshire Council (2021) Free sanitary products. www.eastrenfrewshire.gov.uk/free-sanitary-products.

Eaton, Jessie (2007) *'Welcome To Your Library': a study of public library services for refugees and asylum seekers in Sheffield and Liverpool*. Sheffield: University of Sheffield. https://dagda.shef.ac.uk/dispub/dissertations/2006-07/External/Eaton_Jessie_MALib.pdf.

ECHO (2022) *English books in ECHO Mobile Library*. Athens, Greece: ECHO Mobile Library.

ECHO (n.d.-a) About. https://echolibrary.org/about.

ECHO (n.d.-b) The library. https://echolibrary.org/library.

Edmond-Pettitt, Anya, Maël Galisson and Frances Timberlake (2021) Where does 'Fortress Britain' begin and end? *Institute of Race Relations*, 30 Jun 2021. https://irr.org.uk/article/where-does-fortress-britain-begin-and-end.

Ekman, Mattias (2019) Anti-immigration and racist discourse in social media. *European Journal of Communication*, **34** (6), 606–18. https://journals.sagepub.com/doi/pdf/10.1177/0267323119886151.

Elkin, Judith (1971) *Books for the Multi-racial Classroom: a select list of children's books, showing the backgrounds of India, Pakistan and the West Indies*. Birmingham: Library Association Youth Libraries Group (YLG Pamphlet no.10).

Ellul, Rosanna, Rose McCarthy and Melanie Haith-Cooper (2020) Destitution in pregnancy: forced migrant women's lived experiences. *British Journal of Midwifery*, **28** (11), November, 778–87.

EmpathyLab (n.d.) Research & Strategy: what is empathy? www.empathylab.uk/research.

EmpathyLab (2021) About us. www.empathylab.uk/about.

End Violence Against Women (2022) IOPC finds cultural issues of misogyny and racism in the Met Police. 1 February 2022. www.endviolenceagainstwomen.org.uk/iopc-cultural-issues-misogyny-racism-met-police.

Equality and Human Rights Commission (2020) *Public Sector Equality Duty Assessment of Hostile Environment Policies*. London: Equality and Human Rights Commission. www.equalityhumanrights.com/sites/default/files/public-sector-equality-duty-assessment-of-hostile-environment-policies.pdf.

202 LIBRARIES AND SANCTUARY

Esthimer, Marissa (2016) Protecting the forcibly displaced: Latin America's evolving refugee and asylum framework. *Migration Information Source*, 14 January 2016. www.migrationpolicy.org/article/protecting-forcibly-displaced-latin-america-evolving-refugee-and-asylum-framework.

Euro-Mediterranean Human Rights Monitor (2020) Who we are. www.euromedmonitor.org/en/About

European Center for Constitutional and Human Rights (n.d.) Push-back. www.ecchr.eu/en/glossary/push-back.

European Union Agency for Fundamental Rights (2016) *Second European Union Minorities and Discrimination Survey: Roma – selected findings*. https://fra.europa.eu/sites/default/files/fra_uploads/fra-2016-eu-minorities-survey-roma-selected-findings_en.pdf.

Fekete, Liz (2001) The emergence of xeno-racism. *Institute of Race Relations*, 28 September 2001. https://irr.org.uk/article/the-emergence-of-xeno-racism.

Fekete, Liz (2020) Divesting from immigration policing – the abolitionist challenge. *Institute of Race Relations*, 5 November 2020. https://irr.org.uk/article/divesting-from-immigration-policing-the-abolitionist-challenge/?utm_source=newsletter&utm_medium=email&utm_campaign=we_need_to_talk_about_state_racism&utm_term=2020-11-05.

Filipova-Rivers, Maggie (2021) How can councils foster welcome and inclusion in their community? City of Sanctuary Conference 2021, online, 23 September 2021. https://cityofsanctuary.org/wp-content/uploads/2021/09/LAs-presentation-Workshop.pdf.

Finlay, Robin, Peter Hopkins and Matthew Benwell (2021) *'It's Like Rubbing Salt on the Wound': the impacts of Covid-19 on asylum seekers and refugees*. Newcastle upon Tyne: Newcastle University. https://eprints.ncl.ac.uk/file_store/production/278292/9CA31F73-22E2-4362-B45B-1EC82308EA7E.pdf.

Fox, Jon (2012) The experience of East European migrants in the UK suggests that there is racism towards newcomers regardless of racial difference. *LSE Comment*, 22 September 2012. https://blogs.lse.ac.uk/europpblog/2012/09/22/rascism-migrants.

Freedom United (2021) 'We've been sold a lie': Caribbean workers abused on British strawberry farms. 13 October 2021. www.freedomunited.org/news/caribbean-workers-abused.

Frodin, Angela (2001) Gloucestershire builds website for refugees and asylum seekers. *Public Libraries & Social Exclusion Action Planning Network Newsletter*, (27) July. 7–8. www.seapn.org.uk/newsletters-archive.

Fryer, Peter (1984) *Staying Power: the history of black people in Britain*. London: Pluto Press.

Fun Palaces (n.d.) About Fun Palaces. https://funpalaces.co.uk/about-fun-palaces.

Fursland, Eileen, and Henrietta Bond (2020) *Caring for Unaccompanied Asylum-seeking Children and Young People from Vietnam*. London: CoramBAAF.

REFERENCES   203

Fursland, Eileen, and Kevin Lowe (2020) *Caring for Unaccompanied Asylum-seeking Children and Young People*. London: CoramBAAF.

Gentleman, Amelia (2018) Perspectives on the Windrush generation scandal: an account by Amelia Gentleman (British Library: Windrush Stories). 4 October 2018. www.bl.uk/windrush/articles/perspectives-on-the-windrush-generation-scandal-an-account-by-amelia-gentleman.

Gentleman, Amelia (2020) *The Windrush Betrayal: exposing the hostile environment*. London: Guardian Faber Publishing.

Gentleman, Amelia (2021a) Home Office unlawfully stopped family joining Windrush woman, court rules. *The Guardian*, 6 May. www.theguardian.com/uk-news/2021/may/06/home-office-unlawfully-discriminating-against-windrush-families-court-rules.

Gentleman, Amelia (2021b) Why things don't bode well for Afghans seeking asylum in the UK. *The Guardian*, 17 August 2021. www.theguardian.com/uk-news/2021/aug/17/why-things-dont-bode-well-for-afghans-seeking-asylum-in-the-uk.

Gentleman, Amelia, and Diane Taylor (2021) Outcry over plan to deport Jamaican nationals who came to UK as children. *The Guardian*, 5 August 2021. www.theguardian.com/uk-news/2021/aug/05/outcry-over-plan-to-deport-jamaican-nationals-who-came-to-uk-as-children?mc_cid=81d602f206&mc_eid=7d8713d645.

George Padmore Institute (c. 2011) Black education movement. www.georgepadmoreinstitute.org/collections/the-black-education-movement-1965-1988.

Girvan, Alyssa (2018) *The History of British Immigration Policy (1905–2016): timeline resource, June 2018*. Norwich: University of East Anglia/Refugee History. https://static1.squarespace.com/static/5748678dcf80a1ffcaf26975/t/5b27e23d8a922df0ca10ddeb1/1529340490557/Immigration+Timeline.pdf.

Glasgow Women's Library (2011) She sells 'She Settles in the Shields'. . .. https://womenslibrary.org.uk/2011/11/11/she-sells-she-settles-in-the-shields.

Goldsmiths University of London Library (2019) 'Celebrating Black History Month'. *Library blog*. https://sites.gold.ac.uk/library-blog/celebrating-black-history-month.

Goodfellow, Maya (2020) *Hostile Environment: how immigrants became scapegoats*. London: Verso.

Government of Canada (2020) #WelcomeRefugees: Canada resettled Syrian refugees. www.canada.ca/en/immigration-refugees-citizenship/services/refugees/welcome-syrian-refugees.html.

Gower, Melanie (2022) *UK Immigration Routes for Afghan Nationals*. House of Commons Library. https://researchbriefings.files.parliament.uk/documents/CBP-9307/CBP-9307.pdf.

Great Britain (1948) *British Nationality Act 1948, Chapter 56*. London: HM Stationery Office. www.legislation.gov.uk/ukpga/Geo6/11-12/56/enacted.

Great Britain (1966) Local Government Act 1966.
www.legislation.gov.uk/ukpga/1966/42/section/11.

Great Britain. Home Affairs Committee (2021) *The Macpherson Report: twenty-two years on*. edited by House of Commons Seelect Committee. London: UK Parliament.
https://publications.parliament.uk/pa/cm5802/cmselect/cmhaff/139/13903.htm.

Great Britain. Statutory Instrument (2015) *The Public Bodies (Abolition of the Library Advisory Council for England) Order*. London: The Stationery Office.
www.legislation.gov.uk/uksi/2015/850/pdfs/uksi_20150850_en.pdf.

Greater London Authority (2021) Checking your immigration status. 15 December 2021. www.london.gov.uk/what-we-do/communities/migrants-and-refugees/guidance-young-londoners-citizenship-residence/checking-your-immig ration-status.

Greater Manchester Immigration Aid Unit (2019) *Assessing the Age of Children Seeking Asylum: disputes between local authorities*. Manchester: Greater Manchester Immigration Aid Unit. https://gmiau.org/speaking-out/children/age-assessments.

Greater Manchester Immigration Aid Unit (2020) *A Guide to the Age Assessment Process: a guide by young people who have been age assessed*. Manchester: Greater Manchester Immigration Aid Unit. https://gmiau.org/speaking-out/children/age-assessments.

Grierson, Jamie (2020) Kent inspectors find wet and cold migrants held in cramped containers. *The Guardian*, 23 October 2020.
www.theguardian.com/uk-news/2020/oct/23/kent-inspectors-find-wet-and-cold-migrants-held-in-cramped-containers.

Griffiths, Melanie, and Colin Yeo (2021) The UK's hostile environment: deputising immigration control. *Critical Social Policy*, **41** (4), 521–44.
https://journals.sagepub.com/doi/pdf/10.1177/0261018320980653.

Grupa Granica (2021) Grupa Granica – home. https://m.facebook.com/grupagranica.

Guardian Staff (2018) 'It's inhumane': the Windrush victims who have lost jobs, homes and loved ones. *The Guardian*, 20 April 2018.
www.theguardian.com/uk-news/2018/apr/20/its-inhumane-the-windrush-victims-who-have-lost-jobs-homes-and-loved-ones.

Guderjan, Marius, Hugh Mackay and Gesa Stedman, eds (2020) *Contested Britain: Brexit, austerity and agency*. Bristol: Bristol University Press,.

Gundara, Jaswinder (1981) *Indian Women in Britain: a study of information needs*. London: Polytechnic of North London, School of Librarianship (Occasional Publication no. 2).

Gundara, Jaswinder, and Ronald Warwick (1981) Myth or reality?. *Assistant Librarian*, **74** (5), 67–73.

Hadjazi, Youcef (2021) Illustrating queer migrant journeys. *People's History Museum*, 1 February 2021. https://phm.org.uk/blogposts/illustrating-queer-migrant-journeys.

REFERENCES 205

Haith-Cooper, Melanie (2020) Hungry, homeless and pregnant: the migrant women facing destitution in the UK. *The Conversation*, 12 November 2020. https://theconversation.com/hungry-homeless-and-pregnant-the-migrant-women-facing-destitution-in-the-uk-146518.

Hamada, Rachel, Emiliano Mellino, Vicky Gayle, Sarah Haque, Ruth Bushi, Robyn Vinter and Siriol Griffiths (2021) Most GP surgeries refuse to register undocumented migrants despite NHS policy. *Bureau of Investigative Journalism*, 15 July 2021. www.thebureauinvestigates.com/stories/2021-07-15/most-gp-surgeries-refuse-to-register-undocumented-migrants.

Hamlin, Rebecca (2021) *Crossing: how we label and react to people on the move*. Stanford, California: Stanford University Press.

Hansard (1961) *HC Deb 16 November 1961 vol 649 c803*. https://api.parliament.uk/historic-hansard/commons/1961/nov/16/commonwealth-immigrants-bill.

Hargrave, Russell, and Jonathan Thomas (2021) *Stuck in the Middle with You: capturing contribution and closing the integration gap at the heart of the UK immigration system's approach to safe and legal routes for refugees*. London: The Social Market Foundation. www.smf.co.uk/wp-content/uploads/2021/03/Stuck-in-the-middle-with-you-Mar-2021.pdf.

Hastings Community of Sanctuary (2021) A heartwarming welcome on Hastings beach. *Hastings Community of Sanctuary Blog*, 15 November 2021. https://hastings.cityofsanctuary.org/2021/11/15/a-heartwarming-welcome-on-hastings-beach.

Hattenstone, Simon (2018) Why was the scheme behind May's 'Go Home' vans called Operation Vaken? *The Guardian*, 26 April 2018. 'Opinion'. www.theguardian.com/commentisfree/2018/apr/26/theresa-may-go-home-vans-operation-vaken-ukip.

Haynes, Mike (2019) The sorry story of Fortress Britain and its war on refugees. *rs21*, 4 January 2019. www.rs21.org.uk/2019/01/04/the-sorry-story-of-fortress-britain-and-its-war-on-refugees.

Heap, Emily-Jane (2021) One visit to a Kent asylum seeker centre aged 12 turned a refugee's life around. *KentLive*, 15 May 2021. www.kentlive.news/news/kent-news/one-visit-kent-asylum-seeker-5419239?utm_source=twitter.com&utm_medi um=social&utm_campaign=sharebar.

Hewett, Andy (2021) *Living in Limbo: a decade of delays in the UK asylum system*. London: Refugee Council. https://media.refugeecouncil.org.uk/wp-content/uploads/2021/07/01191305/Living-in-Limbo-A-decade-of-delays-in-the-U K-Asylum-system-July-2021.pdf.

Hewitt, Adam (2021) Hope for Justice: working to end modern slavery. *People's History Museum*, 18 October 2021. https://phm.org.uk/blogposts/hope-for-justice-working-to-end-modern-slavery.

Hill, Janet, ed. (1971) *Books for Children: the homelands of immigrants*. London: Institute of Race Relations.

Hill, Janet (1973) *Children are People*. London: Hamish Hamilton.

Hirsch, Afua (2018) *Brit(ish): on race, identity and belonging*. London: Vintage

Home Office (2001) *Community Cohesion: a report of the Independent Review Team chaired by Ted Cantle*. http://image.guardian.co.uk/sys-files/Guardian/documents/2001/12/11/communitycohesionreport.pdf.

Home Office (2013) *Immigration Bill – Factsheet: overview of the Bill*. https://assets.publishing.service.gov.uk/government/uploads/system/uploads/attachment_data/file/249251/Overview_Immigration_Bill_Factsheet.pdf.

Home Office (2021a) National statistics: why do people come to the UK? To work. 25 November 2021. www.gov.uk/government/statistics/immigration-statistics-year-ending-september-2021/why-do-people-come-to-the-uk-to-work.

Home Office (2021b) National statistics: why do people come to the UK? To study. 25 November 2021. www.gov.uk/government/statistics/immigration-statistics-year-ending-september-2021/why-do-people-come-to-the-uk-to-study.

Home Office (2021c) National statistics: why do people come to the UK? For family reasons'. 25 November 2021. www.gov.uk/government/statistics/immigration-statistics-year-ending-september-2021/why-do-people-come-to-the-uk-for-family-reasons.

Home Office (2021d) *Policy and Legislative Changes Affecting Migration to the UK: timeline*. www.gov.uk/government/publications/policy-and-legislative-changes-affecting-migration-to-the-uk-timeline?utm_source=93847da8-299c-4933-ad65-d2ad86422170&utm_medium=email&utm_campaign=govuk-notifications&utm_content=daily.

Home Office (2022) How many people do we grant asylum or protection to?. 24 February 2022. www.gov.uk/government/statistics/immigration-statistics-year-ending-december-2021/how-many-people-do-we-grant-asylum-or-protection-to.

HOPE not Hate and Migration Exchange (2021) *Migration and the Far Right: briefing 1*. https://cityofsanctuary.org/wp-content/uploads/2021/01/HnHET_Migration-and-the-Far-Right_2021-01-v1-1.pdf.

House of Commons. Public Accounts Committee (2020) *Oral Evidence: Asylum Accommodation and Support Transformation Programme*. edited by Public Accounts Committee. London: UK Parliament. (HC 683). https://committees.parliament.uk/oralevidence/958/default.

House of Commons. Women and Equalities Committee (2019) *Tackling Inequalities Faced by Gypsy, Roma and Traveller Communities: Seventh Report of Session 2017–19. Report, together with formal minutes relating to the report*. (HC360). https://publications.parliament.uk/pa/cm201719/cmselect/cmwomeq/360/360.pdf.

Howley, Brendan (2018) Libraries as values-driven participatory culture hubs. *Information Today*, **35** (5), 15–16.

Hudson, Andrew (2004) Library services for people for whom English is an additional language. *Impact, the Journal of the Career Development Group*, **7** (1), April, 7–10.

Human Rights Watch (2020) Covid-19 fueling anti-Asian racism and xenophobia worldwide. 12 May 2020. www.hrw.org/news/2020/05/12/covid-19-fueling-anti-asian-racism-and-xenophobia-worldwide.

Hutchings, Paul B., and Katie E. Sullivan (2019) Prejudice and the Brexit vote: a tangled web. *Palgrave Communications*, **5** (5). doi: https://doi.org/10.1057/s41599-018-0214-5.

IBCB (n.d.) [post 2018] A Bibliography of the Interracial Books for Children Bulletin. https://ibcbulletin.info.

iCoCo Foundation (2022) About community cohesion. https://tedcantle.co.uk/about-community-cohesion.

Inc Arts (2020) *A Statement for the UK.* www.whatnextculture.co.uk/wp-content/uploads/2020/10/BAMEOver-A-Statement-for-the-UK-2.pdf.

Independent Chief Inspector of Borders and Immigration (2021) An inspection of the use of contingency asylum accommodation – key findings from site visits to Penally Camp and Napier Barracks. 8 March 2021. www.gov.uk/government/news/an-inspection-of-the-use-of-contingency-asylum-accommodation-key-findings-from-site-visits-to-penally-camp-and-napier-barracks.

Inspire (2021a) Refugee stories. www.inspireculture.org.uk/reading-information/reading-recommendations/equality-diversity/refugee-stories.

Inspire (2021b) About us. www.inspireculture.org.uk/about-us.

International Federation of Library Associations and Institutions (2020) Library map of the world: Toronto Public Library and Government collaborate to welcome and support Syrian refugees. https://librarymap.ifla.org/stories/Canada/Toronto-Public-Library-And-Government-Collaborate-To-Welcome-And-Support-Syrian-Refugees/153.

International Labour Organisation (2021) *ILO Global Estimates On International Migrant Workers – Results and Methodology.* www.ilo.org/wcmsp5/groups/public/—-dgreports/—-dcomm/—-publ/documents/publication/wcms_808935.pdf.

International Organisation for Migration (2016) *Mixed Migration: flows in the Mediterranean and beyond – compilation of available data and information, 2015.* www.iom.int/sites/g/files/tmzbdl486/files/situation_reports/file/Mixed-Flows-Mediterranean-and-Beyond-Compilation-Overview-2015.pdf.

Ionesco, Dina (2019) Let's talk about climate migrants, not climate refugees. *Sustainable Development Goals*, 6 June 2019. www.un.org/sustainabledevelopment/blog/2019/06/lets-talk-about-climate-migrants-not-climate-refugees.

208 LIBRARIES AND SANCTUARY

IPCC (2022a) *Climate Change 2022: impacts, adaptation, and vulnerability – contribution of Working Group II to the Sixth Assessment Report of the Intergovernmental Panel on Climate Change.* www.ipcc.ch/report/ar6/wg2.

IPCC (2022b) Press release. www.ipcc.ch/report/ar6/wg2/resources/press/press-release/.

Ipsos MORI (2021) Proportion of Britons who want to see immigration reduced falls to lowest level since 2015. *Ipsos MORI*, 22 January 2021. www.ipsos.com/ipsos-mori/en-uk/proportion-britons-who-want-see-immigration-reduced-falls-lowest-l evel-2015.

Ireland, Philippa (2010) *Material Factors Affecting the Publication of Black British Fiction.* DPhil, Open University. https://core.ac.uk/download/pdf/154422823.pdf.

Ivybridge Foodbank (n.d.) [2021?] Give help: donate food. https://ivybridge.foodbank.org.uk/give-help/donate-food.

Jacques, Vera (1979) Storytelling in a multi-racial society. In *Practical Guides: storytelling,* edited by Margaret Marshall. Birmingham: Youth Libraries Group of the Library Association, 18–25.

Jamroz, Ewa (2018) *National Roma Network 2015–2017: developments, learning and action.* Leeds: Migration Yorkshire. www.migrationyorkshire.org.uk/userfiles/file/publications/MY-finalNRNreport-Oct2018.pdf.

Jast, L. Stanley (1915) *What Public Libraries Can Do During and After the War.* London: Library Association. https://trove.nla.gov.au/work/26807448.

Jeffries, Stuart (2014) Britain's most racist election: the story of Smethwick, 50 years on. *The Guardian*, 15 October 2014. www.theguardian.com/world/2014/oct/15/britains-most-racist-election-smethwick-50-years-on.

Jenkins, Simon (2022) Ukrainian refugees, meet Britain's 'hostile environment'. We should be ashamed. *The Guardian*, 7 March 2022. www.theguardian.com/commentisfree/2022/mar/07/ukrainian-refugees-britain-hostile-environment-europe.

Joint Council for the Welfare of Immigrants (n.d.) Our story. www.jcwi.org.uk/our-story.

Joint Council for the Welfare of Immigrants (n.d.) [2020] Windrush scandal explained. www.jcwi.org.uk/windrush-scandal-explained.

Jones, Denise (2007) *Welcome to Your Library: connecting public libraries and refugee communities – final report.* Liverpool: Liverpool Libraries and Information Services. www.seapn.org.uk/uploads/files/LiverpoolWTYLFinalReport0708.pdf.

Jones, Hannah, Yasmin Gunaratnam, Gargi Bhattacharyya, William Davies, Sukhwant Dhaliwal, Kirsten Forkert, Emma Jackson and Roiyah Saltus (2017) *Go Home? The politics of immigration controversies.* Manchester: Manchester University Press.

https://research.gold.ac.uk/id/eprint/20124/1/Jones,%20Gunaratnam,%20Bhatach
aryya,%20Davies,%20Dhaliwal,%20Forkert,%20Jackson%20and%20Saltus%20_%
20Go%20home_.pdf.

Kale, Sirin (2021) Out of thin air: the mystery of the man who fell from the sky. *The Guardian*, 15 April 2021, 'The long read'.
www.theguardian.com/world/2021/apr/15/man-who-fell-from-the-sky-airplane-stowaway-kenya-london.

Kaur-Ballagan, Kully, Glenn Gottfried and Holly Day (2020) *Attitudes Towards Immigration: survey conducted on behalf of IMIX*. London: Ipsos MORI.
www.ipsos.com/sites/default/files/ct/news/documents/2021-01/attitudes-towards-immigration-imix-2021.pdf.

Kellezi, Blerina, Juliet Wakefield, and Mhairi Bowe (2021) The impact of poor healthcare provision in UK immigration removal centres. *The Conversation*, 14 June 2021. https://theconversation.com/the-impact-of-poor-healthcare-provision-in-uk-immigration-removal-centres-161525.

Kelly, Ann M. (1983) 'Asian library services: Glasgow's approach'. *SLA News* (175), May 1983.

Kendi, Ibram X. (2019) *How to be an Antiracist*. London: Bodley Head.

Kendi, Ibram X. (2020) Ibram X. Kendi defines what it means to be an antiracist.
www.penguin.co.uk/articles/2020/june/ibram-x-kendi-definition-of-antiracist.html

Ker-Lindsay, James (2018) Did the unfounded claim that Turkey was about to join the EU swing the Brexit referendum?. *LSE*, 15 February 2018.
https://blogs.lse.ac.uk/politicsandpolicy/unfounded-claim-turkey-swing-brexit-referendum/#Author.

Khan, Naseem (1987) 'The arts Britain ignores' – how libraries can help. In *Libraries and the Arts in Action or Inaction? Proceedings of the Sheffield Conference, November 1985*, edited by Patricia Coleman. Sheffield: Sheffield City Libraries, 40–50.

Kiernan, Lynda (2020) Launch: Multicultural Portlaoise to receive Library of Sanctuary award. *Leinster Express*, 10 March 2020.
www.leinsterexpress.ie/news/portlaoise-/523988/multicultural-portlaoise-has-first-library-of-sanctuary.html.

Kino Border Initiative (2018) Education: a major reason for migration. *Kino Border Initiative Passages Newsletter*, 18 September 2018.
www.kinoborderinitiative.org/education-a-major-reason-for-migration.

Kirklees Libraries (1985) Kirklees services in Asian languages. *Assistant Librarian*, **78** (2) February, 18–19.

Kirklees Welcomes (2021) Refugee Week 2021. *#kirkleeswelcomes*, 2021.
https://welcometokirklees.blog/refugee-week-2021-14th-20th-june-we-cannot-walk-alone.

Kittiwake Trust (2021) The Kittiwake Trust Multilingual Library. https://multilinguallibrary.org.uk.

Klein, Reva (1997) Welcome to the new world of equiphobia. *TES*, 31 January 1997. www.tes.com/news/welcome-new-world-equiphobia.

Knight, Andrew, Deborah Mbofana, Priscilla Simpson and Eileen Smyth (2008) *Welcome to Your Library: exploring the role of libraries as promoters of health literacy and community cohesion*. Uxbridge, Middlesex: Healthy Hillingdon. www.seapn.org.uk/uploads/files/Andrew-Knights-paper.pdf.

Kraus, Lisa-Marie, and Stijn Daenekindt (2021) Why social mobility is key to explaining attitudes toward multiculturalism. *Social Europe*, 26 October 2021. https://socialeurope.eu/why-social-mobility-is-key-to-explaining-attitudes-toward-multiculturalism.

Kufeldt, Zofia (2021) A rediscovered campaign with resonance today. *People's History Museum*, 1 December 2021. https://phm.org.uk/blogposts/a-rediscovered-campaign-with-resonance-today.

Kuya, Dorothy (1973) *Sowing the Dragon's Teeth: racial bias in the books we teach*. Liverpool: Merseyside Community Relations Council.

Kvist, Else (2021) One year on and citizens are still paying the price of Brexit. *The Federal Trust for Education & Research*, 4 February 2021. https://fedtrust.co.uk/one-year-on-and-citizens-are-still-paying-the-price-of-brexit.

Lambert, Claire M. (1969) Library provision for the Indian and Pakistani communities in Britain. *Journal of Librarianship and Information Science*, 1, 41–61.

Laois County Library Service (2022) Portlaoise Library of Sanctuary. www.youtube.com/channel/UCyVQ4U9PjKpWugvSZnDlcDA.

Lavigueur, Nick (2021) New £800k library to open in Huddersfield complete with safe welcome space for migrants. *YorkshireLive*, 11 August 2021. www.examinerlive.co.uk/news/west-yorkshire-news/new-800k-library-open-huddersfield-21275038.

LawStuff (n.d.) Not from UK: your status. https://lawstuff.org.uk/not-from-the-uk/not-from-uk-your-status.

Leatham, Scott (2020) 'Natural climate solutions': we aren't seeing the wood for the trees. *Clean Slate*, 118, Winter 2020: 26–8. https://issuu.com/billyaikencat/docs/clean_slate_118/28.

Leeper, Helena (2017) *'New Arrivals': what services are public libraries in the UK offering to refugees & asylum seekers, and how can we improve services for the rising numbers of this vulnerable group? A study submitted in partial fulfilment of the requirements for the degree of MA Librarianship*. Sheffield. https://dagda.shef.ac.uk/dispub/dissertations/2016-17/External/Leeper_H.pdf.

Leeuwenberg, Jeffrey (1979) *The Cypriots in Haringey : a study of their literacy and reading habits*. London: Polytechnic of North London, School of Librarianship.

Leicester Libraries (2007) *Welcome to Your Library – final report*. Leicester: Leicester City Council. www.seapn.org.uk/uploads/files/WTYLFinalReportLeicester310308.pdf.

Leigh, J.G (1906) Free libraries and their possibilities. *The Economic Review, 1891–1914*, **16** (1), 32-42.

Lessard-Phillips, Laurence , Lin Fu, Antje Lindenmeyer, Jenny Phillimore and Rita Dayoub (2021) *Barriers to Wellbeing: migration and vulnerability during the pandemic*. London: Doctors of the World UK. www.doctorsoftheworld.org.uk/wp-content/uploads/2021/09/Barriers-to-wellbeing-09.21.pdf.

Liaison (1973) Announcement of workshop on the public library and needs of immigrants. *Liaison*, June, 44.

Library Advisory Council, and Community Relations Commission (1976) *Public Library Service for a Multi-cultural Society: a report produced by a joint working party of the Library Advisory Council and the Community Relations Commission*. London: Community Relations Commission.

Library Association (1977) *Public Libraries in a Multi-cultural Britain*.

Lingayah, Sanjiv (2021) *It Takes a System: the systemic nature of racism and pathways to systems change*. London: Beyond Race/Race on the Agenda. www.rota.org.uk/sites/default/files/researchpublications/It%20takes%20a%20system%20FINAL%20-%20January%202021.pdf.

Linley, Rebecca, and Bob Usherwood (1998) *New Measures for the New Library: a social audit of public libraries*. Sheffield: British Library (British Library Research & Innovation Centre Report 89). www.sheffield.ac.uk/polopoly_fs/1.128118!/file/CPLIS—-New-Measures-for-the-New-Library.pdf.

Lipniacka, Ewa (1994a) CILLA: the Co-operative of Indic Language Library Authorities. Preservation of ethnic cultural heritage: access to sources in culturally diverse societies conference (5–7 December 1994), Warsaw, 177–83. http://pbc.uw.edu.pl/271/1/Dziedzictwo.pdf.

Lipniacka, Ewa (1994b) Library provision for linguistic minorities. Preservation of ethnic cultural heritage: access to sources in culturally diverse societies conference (5–7 December 1994), Warsaw,163–74. http://pbc.uw.edu.pl/271/1/Dziedzictwo.pdf.

Live Music Now (2020) A Scottish music project shows support to musicians living as refugees and asylum seekers. 10 March 2020. www.livemusicnow.org.uk/lmn-news/title/A-Scottish-music-project-shows-support-to-musicians-living-as-refuge es-and-asylum seekers/item/69791.

Local Government Association (2002) *Guidance on Community Cohesion*. www.tedcantle.co.uk/publications/006%20Guidance%20on%20Community%20C ohesion%20LGA%202002.pdf.

Local Government Association (2021) Libraries of Sanctuary: changing perceptions of refugees in Southampton. www.local.gov.uk/case-studies/libraries-sanctuary-changing-perceptions-refugees-southampton.

Lock, Larry (2020) The Refugee Convention: who are refugees and asylum seekers?. *Free Movement*, 5 June 2020. www.freemovement.org.uk/refugee-convention.

London Borough of Merton (2001) Merton wins national library award. https://news.merton.gov.uk/2001/06/22/pressrelease-96.

Lubbock, John (1891) Free libraries. *The New Review*, **4** (20), 60–6.

Lynch, Bernadette (2012) *Whose Cake is it Anyway? A collaborative investigation into engagement and participation in 12 museums and galleries in the UK*. London: Paul Hamlyn Foundation. www.phf.org.uk/wp-content/uploads/2014/10/Whose-cake-is-it-anyway.pdf.

McColvin, Lionel Roy (1942) *The Public Library System of Great Britain: a report on its present condition with proposals for post-war reorganization*. London: Library Association.

McGhie, Henry A. (2020) *Museums and Human Rights: human rights as a basis for public service*. Liverpool: Curating Tomorrow. https://curatingtomorrow236646048.files.wordpress.com/2020/12/museums-and-human-rights-2020.pdf.

McIntosh, Neil (1974) *The Extent of Racial Discrimination*. London: P.E.P. (Political and Economic Planning).

McKinlay, Lynne (2007) *Welcome To Your Library – final report*. Gateshead: Gateshead Council. www.seapn.org.uk/uploads/files/GquatesheadWTYLFinalreport2007.pdf.

MacPherson, William (1999) *The Stephen Lawrence Inquiry: report of an Inquiry by Sir William MacPherson of Cluny* (0101426224). London: Stationery Office Limited. https://assets.publishing.service.gov.uk/government/uploads/system/uploads/att achment_data/file/277111/4262.pdf.

Makoii, Akhtar Mohammad (2021) 'I wondered whether a bullet had my name on it: my terrifying 24-hour journey out of Afghanistan.' *The Guardian*, 11 December 2021. www.theguardian.com/world/2021/dec/11/i-wondered-whether-a-bullet-had-my-name-on-it-my-terrifying-24-hour-journey-out-of-afghanistan.

Malik, Nesrine (2020) For liberals, Brexit is a hard lesson in the politics of resentment. *The Guardian*, 14 December 2020, 'Opinion'. www.theguardian.com/commentisfree/2020/dec/14/liberals-brexit-politics-resentment.

Manchester Libraries (2021) Libraries of Sanctuary Status awarded to Manchester Libraries. *MANCLIBRARIES BLOG*, 15 June 2021. https://manclibraries.blog/2021/06/15/libraries-of-sanctuary-status-awarded-to-manchester-libraries.

Mansour, Essam (2018) Profiling information needs and behaviour of Syrian refugees displaced to Egypt: an exploratory study. *Information and Learning*

Sciences, **119** (3/4 (May)): 161–82.
www.researchgate.net/publication/325138313_Profiling_information_needs_and
_behaviour_of_Syrian_refugees_displaced_to_Egypt_An_exploratory_study.

Manzoor-Khan, Suhaiymah (2021) It's not just cricket. Racism against Yorkshire's south Asian Muslims has a long history. *The Guardian*, 21 November 2021, 'Opinion'. www.theguardian.com/commentisfree/2021/nov/21/cricket-racism-yorkshire-south-asian-muslims-azeem-rafiq.

Marshall, Margaret R. (1969) Libraries in Yorkshire industry. *Library History*, **1** (5): 164–9. doi: https://doi.org/10.1179/lib.1969.1.5.164.

Matthews, Nicola, and Vincent Roper (1994) Section 11 funding: its changes and implications for library provision for ethnic minority committees. *Library Management*, **15** (3), 5–13.

Mayor's Commission on African and Asian Heritage (2005) *Delivering Shared Heritage*. London: Greater London Authority.

Menendez, Elisa (2021) 'I'm not dying without a fight': Nigerian man who fled home because being gay is a crime. *Metro*, 15 June 2021. https://metro.co.uk/2021/06/15/pride-week-nigerian-man-who-sought-asylum-because-being-gay-is-a-crime-14769294.

Merritt, Angela (2007) *Newcastle City Council: Welcome to Your Library – final report*. Newcastle upon Tyne: Newcastle City Council. www.seapn.org.uk/uploads/files/WTYLFinalReportNewcastleDec07.pdf.

Migrant Voice (2020) *Heroes, Threats & Victims: UK media coverage of migration during the first COVID-19 lockdown*. London: Migrant Voice. www.migrantvoice.org/img/upload/Migrant_Voice_Media_Monitoring_Report_December_2020.pdf.

Mills, Claire, and Melanie Gower (2021) *Resettlement Scheme for Locally Employed Civilians in Afghanistan*. London: House of Commons Library. https://researchbriefings.files.parliament.uk/documents/CBP-9286/CBP-9286.pdf.

Milner, David (1975) *Children and Race*. Harmondsworth, Middlesex: Penguin Books.

Milner, David (1983) *Children and Race: ten years on*. London: Ward Lock Educational.

Ministry of Housing, Communities & Local Government (2021) National welcome for Hong Kong arrivals. London: Ministry of Housing, Communities & Local Government. www.gov.uk/government/news/national-welcome-for-hong-kong-arrivals.

Mitchell, Geoff (n.d.) [c. 2020]. Focus on asylum: a morning in the life of a LAASLO. www.birmingham.gov.uk/info/20057/about_birmingham/2011/city_of_sanctuary/10.

Mohdin, Aamna, and Rachel Hall (2021) Half of Britons do not know 6m Jews were murdered in Holocaust. *The Guardian*, 10 November 2021. https://www.theguardian.com/world/2021/nov/10/half-of-britons-do-not-know-6m-jews-were-murdered-in-holocaust.

Morrison, Sue (2011) *She Settles in the Shields: untold stories of migrant women in Pollokshields*. Glasgow: Glasgow Women's Library.

Mort, Lucy, Marley Morris and Evelina Grinuite (2021) *Jump Starting Integration: supporting communities to reconnect and thrive*. London: IPPR. www.ippr.org/files/2021-12/jump-starting-integration-december-21.pdf.

Mortimer, Josiah (2022) The Met Police 'is definitely racist' and at 'extreme end' of the problem says Black police chief. *My London*, 15 February 2022. www.mylondon.news/news/zone-1-news/met-police-is-definitely-racist-23107511.

Morton, Becky (2021) UK looking at bespoke Afghan refugee scheme – Dominic Raab. 17 August 2021. www.bbc.co.uk/news/uk-58238490.

Moss, Richard (2022) The hidden history of the UK's post war Polish refugees. *Museum Crush*, 16 March 2022. https://museumcrush.org/the-hidden-history-of-the-uks-post-war-polish-refugees.

Mračević, Danica (2020) Refugees are seen either as criminals or saints. *Our World Too*. https://ourworldtoo.org.uk/2021/01/24/refugees-are-seen-either-as-criminals-or-saints.

Muddiman, Dave, Shiraz Durrani, Martin Dutch, Rebecca Linley, John Pateman, and John Vincent (2000a) *Open to All? The public library and social exclusion. Vol. 1: Overview and Conclusions*. London: Resource (Library and Information Commission Research Report 84). www.seapn.org.uk/content_files/files/ota_volume_1_final_version_sept_211.doc.

Muddiman, Dave, Shiraz Durrani, Martin Dutch, Rebecca Linley, John Pateman and John Vincent (2000b) *Open to All? The public library and social exclusion. Vol. 2: Survey, Case Studies and Methods*. London: Resource (Library and Information Commission Research Report 85). www.seapn.org.uk/uploads/files/Open-to-All-The-Public-Library-and-Social-Exclusion.pdf.

Muddiman, Dave, Shiraz Durrani, Martin Dutch, Rebecca Linley, John Pateman, and John Vincent (2000c) *Open to All? The public library and social exclusion. Vol. 3: Working Papers*. London: Resource (Library and Information Commission Research Report 86).

Mulcahy, Ellie, Vanessa Joshua and Sam Baars (2021) *Higher Education on Hold: access to higher education for young people with insecure or unresolved immigration status*. London: King's College London. https://cfey.org/wp-content/uploads/2021/06/Higher-Education-on-Hold-Access-to-HE-for-young-people-with-insecure-immigration-status-By-The-Centre-for-Education-and-Youth.pdf.

Mulhall, Joe (2021) *Drums in the Distance: journeys into the global far right*. London: Icon Books.

Mwarigha, M. Shadrack (2002) *Towards a Framework for Local Responsibility: taking action to end the current limbo in immigrant settlement : Toronto*. Toronto: Maytree

Foundation. https://maytree.com/wp-content/uploads/
SummaryTowardsAFrameworkForLocalResponsibilityMwarighaMS2002.pdf.

Nabarro, Rupert (1980) Inner City Partnerships: an assessment of the first programmes. *The Town Planning Review*, **51** (1) January 1980, 25–38.

Nason, Nick (2017) Should refugees claim asylum upon arrival in their first 'safe' country?. *Free Movement*, 20 June 2017. www.freemovement.org.uk/refugees-claim-asylum-upon-arrival-first-safe-country.

National Crime Agency (n.d.) [2021?] Modern slavery and human trafficking. www.nationalcrimeagency.gov.uk/what-we-do/crime-threats/modern-slavery-and-human-trafficking.

Newcastle City Council (2021) Library of Sanctuary. www.newcastle.gov.uk/services/libraries-culture/accessibility-services/library-sanctuary.

Ng, Alex (1989) *The Library Needs of the Chinese Community in the United Kingdom.* London: British Library Research & Development Department (British Library Research Papers no. 56).

Ng, Kate (2021) How British east and southeast Asians are fighting racism during the pandemic. *Independent*, 13 January 2021. www.independent.co.uk/news/uk/home-news/coronavirus-racism-hate-crime-south-east-asians-b1770177.html.

Nicolson, Marcus (2021) Immigration: how Scotland sees itself and how migrants actually experience it. *The Conversation*, 9 December 2021. https://theconversation.com/immigration-how-scotland-sees-itself-and-how-migrants-actually-experience-it-173187.

Norfolk Constabulary (2021) Stop Hate in Norfolk (SHiN). www.norfolk.police.uk/stop-hate.

Norfolk County Council (2021) Tricky Period & Toiletries to Go. www.norfolk.gov.uk/libraries-local-history-and-archives/libraries/library-services/health-and-wellbeing/the-tricky-period.

Norman, Peter Leonard (1972) Library services for immigrants. *Library Association Record*, **74** (10), October, 195.

North Tyneside Libraries (n.d.) [2007] *Final Welcome To Your Libraries report – North Tyneside Libraries and Partners.* www.seapn.org.uk/uploads/files/WTYLFinalReportNTyneside2007.pdf.

NRPF Network (n.d.) Immigration status and entitlements – how immigration status affects eligibility for public funds and other services: overview. www.nrpfnetwork.org.uk/information-and-resources/rights-and-entitlements/immigration-status-and-entitlements/overview#.

Nwabuzo, Ojeaku, and Georgina Siklossy (2020) Why Europe has a racism problem. *Social Europe*, 8 October 2020. www.socialeurope.eu/why-europe-has-a-racism-problem.

O'Nions, Helen (2021) Why Priti Patel's plans to overhaul the asylum system make no legal sense. *The Conversation*, 25 March 2021. https://theconversation.com/why-priti-patels-plans-to-overhaul-the-asylum-system-make-no-legal-sense-157815.

Observer Reporter (2021) A farewell to former Penally Camp residents as asylum role ends today. *Tenby Observer*, 21 March 2021. www.tenby-today.co.uk/news/a-farewell-to-former-penally-camp-residents-as-asylum-role-ends-today-508858.

Office of Arts and Libraries (1988) *Financing our Public Library Service: four subjects for debate*. Vol. CM. 324. London: HMSO.

Olden, Anthony (1999) Somali refugees in London: oral culture in a Western information environment. *Libri*, **49**, 212–24. www.researchgate.net/publication/228606596_Somali_Refugees_in_London_Oral_Culture_in_a_Western_Information_Environment.

Olden, Anthony, Ching-Ping Tseng and Alli A. S. Mcharazo (1996) *Service for All? A review of the published literature on black and ethnic minority/multicultural provision by public libraries in the United Kingdom*. London: British Library Research and Development Department (British Library R&D report).

Oldfield, Marie, Jade Siu and Sadia Sheikh (2021) *An Unstable Environment: the economic case for getting asylum decisions right the first time*. London: Pro Bono Economics. www.probonoeconomics.com/Handlers/Download.ashx?IDMF=0f76a4b1-17cc-47ad-9e7b-ab099a5201e2.

Orchestra of St John's (2022). Displaced Voices: amplifying the voices of young refugees through music. www.osj.org.uk/osj-connections-old/displaced-voices.

Organisation of African Unity (1969) *Convention Governing the Specific Aspects of Refugee Problems in Africa*. Addis Ababa: OAU. https://au.int/sites/default/files/treaties/36400-treaty-oau_convention_1963.pdf.

Owen, Joe (2020) The Windrush scandal was a failure of law, policy, politics and bureaucracy. *Institute for Government*, 20 March 2020. www.instituteforgovernment.org.uk/blog/windrush-scandal-was-failure-law-policy-politics-and-bureaucracy.

Oxford Research Centre in the Humanities (2021) Syria and silence. www.torch.ox.ac.uk/syria-and-silence#.

Pacy, F. (1926) Public libraries in England. *Bulletin of the American Library Association*, **20** (10): 221–3.

Pai, Hsiao-Hung (2021) What is offensive is these governments' housing arrangements for asylum seekers. *openDemocracy*, 9 February 2021. www.opendemocracy.net/en/can-europe-make-it/what-is-offensive-is-these-governments-housing-arrangements-for-asylum seekers.

REFERENCES   217

Parker, Sadie (2021) Boris Johnson and the fall of the Roman Empire. *West Country Bylines*, 1 November 2021. https://westcountrybylines.co.uk/boris-johnson-and-the-fall-of-the-roman-empire.

Parkin, Simon (2022) 'I remember the feeling of insult': when Britain imprisoned its wartime refugees. *The Guardian*, 1 February 2022, 'The long read'. www.theguardian.com/world/2022/feb/01/when-britain-imprisoned-refugees-second-world-war-internment-camps.

Parveen, Nazia, and Wendy Huynh (2021) Confronting hate against east Asians – a photo essay. *The Guardian*, 19 May 2021. www.theguardian.com/artanddesign/2021/may/19/confronting-hate-against-east-asians-a-photo-essay.

Passarlay, Gulwali, and Nadene Ghouri (2015) *The Lightless Sky: an Afghan refugee boy's journey of escape to a new life in Britain*. London: Atlantic Books.

Patel, Priti (@pritipatel) (2021) A statement on the shocking scenes at Napier barracks. Twitter, 29 January 2021, https://twitter.com/pritipatel/status/1355207920091344897.

Pateman, Joe, and John Pateman (2021) *Public Libraries and Marxism*. Abingdon: Routledge.

Pateman, John (1999) Stephen Lawrence Executive Briefing. *Public Libraries & Social Exclusion Action Planning Network Newsletter*, (3) July 1999. www.seapn.org.uk/newsletters-archive.

Pateman, John (2003) *Developing a Needs Based Library Service*. Leicester: NIACE (Lifelines in Adult Learning, no.13).

Pateman, John, and Joe Pateman (2019) *Managing Cultural Change in Public Libraries: Marx, Maslow and management*. Abingdon: Routledge.

Pateman, John, and Ken Williment (2013) *Developing Community-led Public Libraries: evidence from the UK and Canada*. Farnham, Surrey: Ashgate.

Pati, Anita (2007) Booking a ticket to success. *The Guardian*, 2 May 2007. www.theguardian.com/society/2007/may/02/immigrationasylumandrefugees.asylum1.

Paul Hamlyn Foundation (2020) Reading and Libraries Challenge Fund. www.phf.org.uk/programmes/reading-libraries-challenge-fund.

Pettrachin, Andrea, and Leila Hadj Abdou (2022) Explaining the remarkable shift in European responses to refugees following Russia's invasion of Ukraine. *LSE EU Politics*, 9 March 2022. https://blogs.lse.ac.uk/europpblog/2022/03/09/explaining-the-remarkable-shift-in-european-responses-to-refugees-following-russias-invasion-of-ukraine.

Phipps, Alison (2020) UOS Conference: Keynote and Scholars Session. Universities of Sanctuary 2020. www.youtube.com/watch?v=NvhdOD9Qv6c.

Pickett, Kate (2021) Fissures that tear us apart and pressures that weigh us all down. *Social Europe*, 8 March 2021. www.socialeurope.eu/fissures-that-tear-us-apart-and-pressures-that-weigh-us-all-down.

Pinder, Sarah (2021) New statement of changes to the Immigration Rules: HC 913 (closing the door on Afghans). *Free Movement*, 15 December 2021. www.freemovement.org.uk/new-statement-of-changes-to-the-immigration-rules-hc-913-closing-the-door-on-afghans.

Plaister, Jean (1985) Co-operative of Indic Language, LASER Library Authorities (CILLA). *Community Librarian*, **3** (1), August.

Pohl, Julia Z. (2019) Gay in the age of Brnabić. 3 October 2019. www.asylos.eu/blog/gay-in-the-age-of-brnabic.

Poinasamy, Krisnah (2013) *The True Cost of Austerity and Inequality: UK case study*. Oxford: Oxfam. https://www-cdn.oxfam.org/s3fs-public/file_attachments/cs-true-cost-austerity-inequality-uk-120913-en_0.pdf.

Policy Action Team 10. (c. 1999). *The Contribution Arts and Sports Can Make*. London: DCMS (Policy Action Team reports). www.artshealthresources.org.uk/wp-content/uploads/2020/05/1999-PAT10-Report_Arts-sport-and-leisure.pdf.

Policy Exchange (2022) *Stopping the Small Boats: a 'Plan B' – a Policy Exchange proposal for addressing the crisis*. London: Policy Exchange. https://policyexchange.org.uk/wp-content/uploads/Stopping-the-Small-Boats-a-Plan-B.pdf.

Poole, Lynne, and Kevin Adamson (2008) *Report on the Situation of the Roma Community in Govanhill, Glasgow*. Glasgow: University of the West of Scotland. www.bemis.org.uk/resources/gt/scotland/report%20on%20the%20situation%20of%20the%20roma%20community%20in%20govanhill,%20Glasgow.pdf.

Prendergast, Mike (2007) *Welcome to Your Library Progress Report*. London: Southwark Council. www.seapn.org.uk/uploads/files/WTYLFinalReportSouthwarkDec07.pdf.

Prichard, R. J. (1991) Change and opposition in the 1980s: the UK Government's proposals for the public library service. *Library Review*, **40** (6). doi: 10.1108/EUM0000000001482. https://doi.org/10.1108/EUM0000000001482.

Pro Bono Economics (2021) Wrong Home Office decisions penalising refugees from war-torn countries. London: Pro Bono Economics. www.probonoeconomics.com/news/wrong-home-office-decisions-penalising-refugees-from-war-torn-countries?mc_cid=bdfd3ef915&mc_eid=7d8713d645.

Proctor, Richard, Hazel Lee and Rachel Reilly (1998) *Access to Public Libraries: the impact of opening hours reductions and closures 1986–1997*. Wetherby: British Library Research and Innovation Centre. www.sheffield.ac.uk/polopoly_fs/1.128096!/file/CPLIS—-Access-to-Public-Libraries.pdf.

Project Welcome (n.d.) About Project Welcome. https://publish.illinois.edu/projectwelcome/about/about-project-welcome.

Protecting Rights at Borders (2021) *Pushing Back Responsibility: rights violations as a 'Welcome Treatment' at Europe's borders*. Protecting Rights at Borders.

https://drc.ngo/media/mnglzsro/prab-report-january-may-2021-_final_10052021.pdf.

Pyper, Doug (2020) *The Public Sector Equality Duty and Equality Impact Assessments*. London: House of Commons Library (Briefing Paper no. 06591). http://researchbriefings.files.parliament.uk/documents/SN06591/SN06591.pdf.

Qian, Angela (2021) 'As borders closed, I became trapped in my Americanness': China, the US and me. *The Guardian*, 6 May 2021, 'The long read'. www.theguardian.com/news/2021/may/06/between-two-worlds-a-chinese-american-story.

Qureshi, Amreen, Marley Morris and Lucy Mort (2020) *Access Denied: the human impact of the hostile environment*. London: Institute for Public Policy Research. www.ippr.org/files/2020-09/access-denied-hostile-environment-sept20.pdf.

Qureshi, Fizza (2022) Statement. *Migrant' Rights Network Newsletter*, April 2022.

Raddon, Rosemary, and Christine Smith (1998) *Information Needs of Refugee Groups*. London: British Library Research and Innovation Centre (British Library Research and Innovation report).

Rainbow Migration (n.d.) Nisha's story.www.rainbowmigration.org.uk/case-studies/nishas-story.

Raitt, S K (1993) *Reading and Information Needs of Elderly Punjabis*. Loughborough University of Technology. https://repository.lboro.ac.uk/articles/Reading_and_information_needs_of_elderly_Punjabis/9415781/files/17035865.pdf.

Ratcliffe, Peter (2012) 'Community cohesion': reflections on a flawed paradigm. *Critical Social Policy*, 15 March 2012, 262–81.

Raven, Debby (1998) Real corkers: wine included. *Library Association Record*, **100** (9), 473.

Refugee Action (2016) Facts about refugees. www.refugee-action.org.uk/about/facts-about-refugees.

Refugee Action (n.d.) *What Sort of Help Might a Recently Arrived Refugee Need?* Manchester: Refugee Action. http://refugee-action.org.uk/wp-content/uploads/2016/10/How-to-welcome-new-refugees.pdf.

Refugee Council (2019) *Asylum Statistics Annual Trends, February 2019*. www.refugeecouncil.org.uk/wp-content/uploads/2019/04/Asylum_Statistics_Annual_Trends_Mar_2019.pdf.

Refugee Council (2020) The truth about asylum: asylum seekers and refugees – who's who?. www.refugeecouncil.org.uk/information/refugee-asylum-facts/the-truth-about-asylum.

Refugee Council (2021a) *An Analysis of Channel Crossings & Asylum Outcomes: November 2021*. https://media.refugeecouncil.org.uk/wp-content/uploads/2021/11/16095953/Channel-crossings-and-asylum-outcomes-November-2021.pdf.

Refugee Council (2021b) *'I Sat Watching Life Go by My Window for So Long': the experiences of people seeking asylum living in hotel accommodation.* https://media.refugeecouncil.org.uk/wp-content/uploads/2021/04/22152856/I-sat-watching-my-life-go-by-my-window-for-so-long-23rd-April-2021.pdf.

Refugee Council (2021c) *A Note on Barriers Experienced by Refugees and People Seeking Asylum When Accessing Health Services.* March 2021. https://media.refugeecouncil.org.uk/wp-content/uploads/2021/10/29174557/A-note-on-barriers-experienced-by-refugees-and-people-seeking-asylum-when-accessing-health-services_March_2021.pdf.

Refugee Week (2021) Together We Walked: a snapshot of Refugee Week 2021. https://refugeeweek.org.uk/together-walked-snapshot-refugee-week-2021.

Refugee Week (2022) Simple Acts. https://refugeeweek.org.uk/simple-acts/.

Renshaw, David (2021) 'The rug can be ripped at any point': how rapper Cashh reinvented himself after being deported. *The Guardian*, 13 August 2021. www.theguardian.com/music/2021/aug/13/caash-being-deported-return-of-the-immigrant.

Right to Remain (2021) *The New Asylum Inadmissibility Rules.* 3 February 2021. https://righttoremain.org.uk/the-new-asylum-inadmissibility-rules.

Right to Remain (n.d.) [2022?]. The Right to Remain toolkit: a guide to the UK immigration and asylum system. https://righttoremain.org.uk/toolkit.

Roach, Patrick, and Marlene Morrison (1998a) *Public Libraries, Ethnic Diversity and Citizenship.* Warwick: University of Warwick Centre for Research in Ethnic Relations and Centre for Educational Development, Appraisal and Research (British Library Research and Innovation Report 76).

Roach, Patrick, and Marlene Morrison (1998b) Pursuing the wind of change. *Library Association Record*, **100** (7) July, 358–60.

Roache, Madeline (2021) Death at the EU border: migrants pay the price of Belarus's 'hybrid warfare'. *ODR*, 15 November 2021. www.opendemocracy.net/en/odr/death-at-the-eu-border-migrants-pay-the-price-of-belaruss-hybrid-warfare.

Robin, Vicki (n.d.) [c. 2016]. History of Conversation Café. www.conversationcafe.org/history.

Robson, Ann (1976) The intellectual background of the public library movement in Britain. *Journal of Library History*, **11** (3), 187–205.

Rodenhurst, Kate (2007) *Engaging Refugees and Asylum Seekers: project review and social outcome evaluation, October 2005–March 2007.* National Museums Liverpool/Leicester City Arts and Museums Service/Salford Heritage Service/Tyne and Wear Museums. https://archive-media.museumsassociation.org/16122013-engaging-refugees-and-asylum seekers-report-2007.pdf.

REFERENCES 221

Rolfe, Heather, Sunder Katwala and Steve Ballinger (2021) *Immigration: a changing debate – analysis of new findings from the Ipsos MORI immigration attitudes tracker survey*. London: British Future. www.britishfuture.org/wp-content/uploads/2021/09/Immigration.A-changing-debate.pdf.

Rose, Emma (2020) *The 2011 Red Tape Challenge - outcomes and effectiveness*. Caversham: Reading, Unchecked UK. www.unchecked.uk/wp-content/uploads/2020/06/The-2011-Red-Tape-Challenge-outcomes-effectiveness.pdf.

RTÉ (2020) In the picture: What in the World? 50 countries, 50 stories. 17 January 2020. www.rte.ie/culture/2020/0116/1107909-in-the-picture-what-in-the-world-50-countries-50-stories.

Rumsby, Seb (2022) Economic migration: the root problem is not smugglers but global inequality. *The Conversation*, 4 February 2022. https://theconversation.com/economic-migration-the-root-problem-is-not-smugglers-but-global-inequality-174073.

Runnymede Trust (n.d.-a) The struggle for race equality – an oral history of the Runnymede Trust 1968–1988: Commonwealth Immigration Act 1968. www.runnymedetrust.org/histories/race-equality/38/commonwealth-immigration-act-1968.html.

Runnymede Trust (n.d.-b) The struggle for race equality – an oral history of the Runnymede Trust 1968–1988: Enoch Powell's 'Rivers of Blood' speech. www.runnymedetrust.org/histories/race-equality/49/enoch-powell-s-rivers-of-blood-speech.html.

Ryan, Ben, ed. (2018) *Fortress Britain? Ethical approaches to immigration policy for a post-Brexit Britain*. London: Jessica Kingsley Publishers.

Rybarczyk, Katarzyna (2021) Refugees fleeing Lebanon look to Europe – but Europe looks away. *Social Europe*, 21 October 2021. https://socialeurope.eu/refugees-fleeing-lebanon-look-to-europe-but-europe-looks-away.

Ryder, Julie, and John Vincent (2002) *Public Library Services for Refugees and Asylum Seekers: the results of the 'Words without Frontiers' survey*. Nadderwater, Exeter: The Network. www.seapn.org.uk/uploads/files/WWF-analysis-final-version.pdf.

Sabbagh, Rachel (1980) *Armenians in London: a case-study of the library needs of a small and scattered community*. London: Polytechnic of North London School of Librarianship.

Sajjad, Tazreena (2022) Ukrainian refugees are welcomed with open arms – not so with people fleeing other war-torn countries. *The Conversation*. https://theconversation.com/ukrainian-refugees-are-welcomed-with-open-arms-not-so-with-people-fleeing-other-war-torn-countries-178491.

Sanctuary Kirklees (2021) Congratulations Kirklees Library – now a Library of Sanctuary!. 12 August 2021. https://kirklees.cityofsanctuary.org/2021/08/12/302.

Schools of Sanctuary (2021) Gypsy, Roma and Traveller History Month. https://schools.cityofsanctuary.org/2021/05/26/resources-for-gypsy-roma-and-traveller-history-month-june.

Schools of Sanctuary (2022) About City of Sanctuary UK.
https://schools.cityofsanctuary.org/about-city-of-sanctuary-uk.

SCONUL (2021a) About SCONUL. www.sconul.ac.uk/page/about-sconul.

SCONUL (2021b) Statement of solidarity with librarians and archivists in Afghanistan. 6 September 2021. www.sconul.ac.uk/news/statement-of-solidarity-with-librarians-and-archivists-in-afghanistan.

SCONUL (2022) Statement of solidarity with library professionals in Ukraine – Mon, 28 Feb 2022. www.sconul.ac.uk/news/statement-of-solidarity-with-library-professionals-in-ukraine.

Scoop Media (2021) UK Government's anti-immigrant rhetoric is fueling racist attacks against asylum seekers. *Scoop Independent News*, 18 August 2021. www.scoop.co.nz/stories/WO2108/S00167/uk-governments-anti-immigrant-rhetoric-is-fueling-racist-attacks-against-asylum seekers.htm.

Scottish Community Development Centre (2018) *Widening the Welcome: exploring experiences of refugee resettlement approaches in Scotland.* https://static1.squarespace.com/static/5943c23a440243c1fa28585f/t/5bfc12cf8985839163cf1beb/1543246554344/Widening+the+Welcome+-+September+2018.pdf.

Scottish Refugee Council (2021) Refugee histories. 28 July 2021. www.scottishrefugeecouncil.org.uk/refugee-histories.

Sen, Barbara, and Anna Listwon (2009) Public library services and the Polish community in England: case study. *Library Review*, **58** (4), 290–300. https://eprints.whiterose.ac.uk/9299/1/Sen_9299.pdf.

Sergi, Domenico (2021) *Museums, Refugees and Communities.* London: Routledge.

Sheffield. Libraries Art Galleries and Museums Committee (1956) *The City Libraries of Sheffield: 1856–1956.*

Shukla, Nikesh, ed. (2017) *The Good Immigrant.* London: Unbound.

Sigona, Nando (2022) UK government's response to refugee crisis is too little, too confused, too slow. 10 March 2022. www.birmingham.ac.uk/news/2022/uk-governments-response-to-refugee-crisis-is-too-little-too-confused-too-slow.

Sigona, Nando, and Michaela Benson (2021) Debunking key myths about Britain's 'broken asylum system. *The Conversation*, 2 December 2021. https://theconversation.com/debunking-key-myths-about-britains-broken-asylum-system-172794.

Simsova, Sylva (1982) *Library Needs of the Vietnamese in Britain.* London: Polytechnic of North London, School of Librarianship and Information Studies (Research report 10).

Simsova, Sylva, and Wey Tze Chin (1982) *Library Needs of Chinese in London.* London: Polytechnic of North London, School of Librarianship and Information Studies (British Library Research and Development Reports no. 5718/Research report – Polytechnic of North London, School of Librarianship and Information Studies no. 9).

Smith, David John (1974) *Racial Disadvantage in Employment*. London: P.E.P. (Political and Economic Planning).

Smith, David John (1975) *Racial Minorities and Public Housing*. London: P.E.P. (Political and Economic Planning).

Smith, David John (1976) *The Facts of Racial Disadvantage: a national survey*. London: P.E.P. (Political and Economic Planning).

Smith, David John (1977) *Racial Disadvantage in Britain: the PEP report*. Harmondsworth, Middlesex: Penguin Books.

Smith, Reiss (2021) Queer asylum seekers left facing isolation, hunger and mockery – right here in the UK. *Pink News*, 1 May 2021. www.pinknews.co.uk/2021/05/01/lgbt-asylum seekers-uk-african-rainbow-family-donate-home-office-covid.

Sordyl, Marta, and Paulina Janus (2013) *Polish Insight Project*. London: London Borough of Lambeth. www.lambeth.gov.uk/sites/default/files/04022014%20Polish%20Insight%20Project.pdf.

South Tyneside Council (2007) *South Tyneside Welcome to Your Library – Final Report November 2007*. www.seapn.org.uk/uploads/files/STynesideWTYLFinalReportNov07.pdf.

Southall Black Sisters (2020a) About us: who are Southall Black Sisters? https://southallblacksisters.org.uk/about.

Southall Black Sisters (2020b) *The Domestic Abuse Bill & Migrant Women*. Southall, Middlesex: Southall Black Sisters (Briefing Paper 2). https://southallblacksisters.org.uk/wp-content/uploads/2020/03/DA-Bill-Briefing-Paper-2.pdf.

Southampton City Council (2020) Southampton City Libraries awarded 'Library of Sanctuary'. 5 October 2020. www.southampton.gov.uk/news/article.aspx?id=tcm:63-432472.

Stone, Jon (2017) InFact – Brexit lies: the demonstrably false claims of the EU referendum campaign. *Independent*, 17 December 2017. www.independent.co.uk/infact/brexit-second-referendum-false-claims-eu-referendum-campaign-lies-fake-news-a8113381.html.

Stones, Rosemary (1988) 13 other years: The Other Award 1975-1987. *Books for Keeps*, **53** November, 22. https://booksforkeeps.co.uk/article/awards-3.

Sturge, Georgina (2021) *Migration Statistics*. London: House of Commons Library (Briefing Paper, CBP06077). 27 April 2021. https://researchbriefings.files.parliament.uk/documents/SN06077/SN06077.pdf.

Sunderland Libraries (2007) *Sunderland Libraries: Welcome to Your Library – quarterly update, final project*. Sunderland: Sunderland City Council. www.seapn.org.uk/uploads/files/WTYLSunderlandFinalReportNov07.pdf.

Surrey County Council (2021) Supporting refugees in Surrey libraries.
www.surreycc.gov.uk/libraries/health-and-well-being-how-libraries-can-help/supporting-refugees-in-surrey-libraries.

Sykes, Paul (1979) *The Public Library in Perspective: an examination of its origins and modern role*. London: Clive Bingley.

Tanner, Claudia (2020) Refugees welcome! Meet the British families who open their homes to asylum seekers. *i*, 15 December 2020, 'Real Life'.
https://inews.co.uk/news/real-life/refugees-asylum seekers-host-home-room-accommodation-help-uk-hostile-environment-791700.

Taylor, Diane (2021) Students who have lived in UK since childhood denied loans – report. *The Guardian*, 23 November 2021.
www.theguardian.com/education/2021/nov/23/student-finance-england-young-migrants-lived-uk-childhood-denied-loans.

Taylor, Diane (2022) Windrush descendants lose high court fight to expand scheme. *The Guardian*, 14 January 2022.
www.theguardian.com/uk-news/2022/jan/14/windrush-descendants-lose-fight-to-expand-compensation-scheme?mc_cid=a4fe38d4c1&mc_eid=7d8713d645.

Taylor, Russell (2018) *Impact of 'Hostile Environment' Policy: debate on 14 June 2018*. London: House of Lords (Library Briefing).
https://lordslibrary.parliament.uk/research-briefings/lln-2018-0064.

The Mayor's Commission on African and Asian Heritage (2005) *Delivering Shared Heritage*. London: Greater London Authority.

The National Archives (n.d.-a) 'The Cabinet Papers: Commonwealth Immigration control and legislation'.
www.nationalarchives.gov.uk/cabinetpapers/themes/commonwealth-immigration-control-legislation.htm.

The National Archives (n.d.-b) Community Relations Commission: Minutes and Papers [catalogue description].
https://discovery.nationalarchives.gov.uk/details/r/C4103.

The Reading Agency (2021) Reading Ahead.
https://readingagency.org.uk/adults/quick-guides/reading-ahead.

Thornbury, Scott (2021) O is for Othering. *An A-Z of ELT*.
https://scottthornbury.wordpress.com/2012/04/08/o-is-for-othering.

Times Higher Education (2000) The British National Bibliography Research Fund.
www.timeshighereducation.com/news/the-british-national-bibliography-research-fund/179803.article.

Tondo, Lorenzo (2021) Revealed: 2,000 refugee deaths linked to illegal EU pushbacks. *The Guardian*, 5 May 2021. www.theguardian.com/global-development/2021/may/05/revealed-2000-refugee-deaths-linked-to-eu-pushbacks.

Tondo, Lorenzo, and Helena Smith (2021) EU states cooperating informally to deny refugees asylum rights – report. *The Guardian*, 12 May 2021.

www.theguardian.com/global-development/2021/may/12/eu-states-cooperating-informally-to-deny-refugees-asylum-rights-report.

Toronto Public Library (2015) Welcome to our friends from Syria. *New to Canada*, 8 December 2015. https://torontopubliclibrary.typepad.com/new_to_canada/2015/12/weclometoourfriendsfromsyria.html.

Toronto Public Library (2021) Settling in Toronto. www.torontopubliclibrary.ca/new-to-canada/toronto.jsp.

Torrington, Arthur (2020) Empire Windrush, British Governments and coloured immigration. *Windrush Foundation*, 7 July 2020. https://windrushfoundation.com/articles/empire-windrush-british-governments-and-coloured-immigration.

Tower Hamlets Council (n.d.) [after 2018]. Community cohesion. www.towerhamlets.gov.uk/lgnl/community_and_living/Community-cohesion/Community-cohesion.aspx.

Traies, Jane, ed. (2021) *Free To Be Me: refugee stories from the Lesbian Immigration Support Group*. Machynlleth: Tollington Press.

Trilling, Daniel (2021) The Napier barracks fire is an indictment of Britain's inhumane asylum system.' *The Guardian*, 2 February 2021. www.theguardian.com/commentisfree/2021/feb/02/napier-barracks-fire-britain-asylum-system-priti-patel.

Tsakiris, Manos (2021) Refugees in the media: how the most commonly used images make viewers dehumanise them. *The Conversation*, 19 November 2021. https://theconversation.com/refugees-in-the-media-how-the-most-commonly-used-images-make-viewers-dehumanise-them-171865.

Tsangarides, Natasha, and Liz Williams (2019) *Lessons not Learned: the failures of asylum decision-making in the UK*. London: Freedom from Torture. https://uklgig.org.uk/wp-content/uploads/2019/10/Lessons_Not_Learned_FINAL_Sept19.pdf.

Tuft, Nancy (1972) Black listed. *The Guardian*, 24 May 1972, 9.

Turnnidge, Sarah (2022) Did Labour invent the 'hostile environment'?. *Full Fact*, 17 March 2022. https://fullfact.org/immigration/michael-gove-hostile-environment-labour.

UK Parliament (2021) Race Relations Act 1965. www.parliament.uk/about/living-heritage/transformingsociety/private-lives/relationships/collections1/race-relations-act-1965/race-relations-act-1965.

UN Volunteers (n.d.) Standby Task Force. www.onlinevolunteering.org/en/node/392415.

UNESCO German Commission (n.d.) German bread culture. 'Nationwide Inventory of Intangible Cultural Heritage'. www.unesco.de/en/german-bread-culture.

UNITED (2021) The fatal policies of Fortress Europe.
http://unitedagainstrefugeedeaths.eu.

UNITED (n.d.) Fortress Europe: death by policy.
http://unitedagainstrefugeedeaths.eu/about-the-campaign/fortress-europe-death-by-policy.

United Nations High Commissioner for Refugees (1984) *Cartagena Declaration on Refugees: adopted by the Colloquium on the International Protection of Refugees in Central America, Mexico and Panama, Cartagena de Indias, Colombia, 22 November 1984.* https://web.archive.org/web/20170303220356/www.unhcr.org/45dc19084.html.

United Nations High Commissioner for Refugees (1992) Persons covered by the OAU Convention Governing the Specific Aspects of Refugee Problems in Africa and by the Cartagena Declaration on Refugees (Submitted by the African Group and the Latin American Group) EC/1992/SCP/CRP.6. 6 April 1992, www.unhcr.org/uk/excom/scip/3ae68cd214/persons-covered-oau-convention-governing-specific-aspects-refugee-problems.html.

United Nations High Commissioner for Refugees (2011) *The 1951 Convention Relating to the Status of Refugees and its 1967 Protocol.* www.unhcr.org/uk/about-us/background/4ec262df9/1951-convention-relating-status-refugees-its-1967-protocol.html.

United Nations High Commissioner for Refugees (2020) Resettlement. www.unhcr.org/resettlement.html.

United Nations High Commissioner for Refugees (n.d.-a) 'The 1951 Refugee Convention' www.unhcr.org/uk/1951-refugee-convention.html.

United Nations High Commissioner for Refugees (n.d.-b) *Convention and Protocol Relating to the Status of Refugees.* www.unhcr.org/protect/PROTECTION/3b66c2aa10.pdf.

Universities of Sanctuary (2021) Solidarity and compassion for the people of Afghanistan. 19 August 2021. https://universities.cityofsanctuary.org/2021/08/19/solidarity-and-compassion-for-the-people-of-afghanistan.

Universities Scotland and Scottish Refugee Council (2021) *Refugees Welcome: guidance for Universities on providing asylum seekers and refugees with access to Higher Education 2021.* www.universities-scotland.ac.uk/wp-content/uploads/2021/10/Refugees-Welcome-2021-final.pdf.

University of Birmingham (2021) Uncovering the failures of the asylum system faced by refugee victims of sexual and gender-based violence. www.birmingham.ac.uk/university/colleges/socsci/unfiltered-lives/iris/research.aspx.

University of Birmingham. Institute for Research into Superdiversity (2021) Sexual and gender based violence in the refugee crisis: from displacement to arrival (SEREDA). www.birmingham.ac.uk/research/superdiversity-institute/sereda/index.aspx.

University of East Anglia (2022) University of Sanctuary. www.ueasanctuary.org.

University of Glasgow (n.d.) MyGlasgow Students: Reach Out. www.gla.ac.uk/myglasgow/students/reachout.

University of Salford Library (2021) Refugee Week 2021: we cannot walk alone. https://salford.leganto.exlibrisgroup.com/leganto/readinglist/lists/9186323170001611?institute=44SAL_INST&auth=LOCAL.

University of Warwick Modern Records Centre (2020) The Notting Hill riots of 1958. https://warwick.ac.uk/services/library/mrc/studying/docs/racism/riots.

University of Wisconsin-Madison Libraries (n.d.) [pre-2019] The Literature Collection: browse the series – *Interracial books for children bulletin*. https://digicoll.library.wisc.edu/cgi-bin/Literature/Literature-idx?type=browse&scope=Literature.CIBCBulletin.

University of York Library (2020) *Migration and Refugees: an introductory reading list*. York: University of York. https://subjectguides.york.ac.uk/your-voice/migration.

Vasagar, Jeevan (2021) Britain should welcome Hongkongers, but not the 'good migrant' narrative. *The Guardian*, 3 February 2021. www.theguardian.com/commentisfree/2021/feb/03/britain-hong-kong-migration-imperial-stereotypes.

Vickers, Tom (2020a) *Borders, Migration and Class in an Age of Crisis: producing workers and immigrants*. Bristol: Bristol University Press.

Vickers, Tom (2020b) Borders, migration and class in times of COVID-19. *Transforming Society*, 27 October 2020. www.transformingsociety.co.uk/2020/10/27/borders-migration-and-class-in-times-of-covid-19.

Vincent, John (1986) *An Introduction to Community Librarianship*. Sheffield: Association of Assistant Librarians (AAL Pointers: 3).

Vincent, John (1999) Public libraries, children and young people and social exclusion (Working Paper 8). In *Open to All? The public library and social exclusion. Volume 3: Working Papers*, edited by Dave Muddiman, Shiraz Durrani, Martin Dutch, Rebecca Linley, John Pateman and John Vincent. London: Resource, 144–78. www.seapn.org.uk/uploads/files/vol3wp8.pdf.

Vincent, John (2001) Social Exclusion Action Planning Network Conference, 'Libraries, Museums, Galleries and Archives for All – Tackling Social Exclusion across the Sectors', 29 June 2001. *Public Libraries & Social Exclusion Action Planning Network Newsletter*, (27) July 2001, 2–3. www.seapn.org.uk/newsletters.

Vincent, John (2005) *Libraries and Community Cohesion: a paper for the South East Museum, Library and Archive Council*. Winchester: South East Museum, Library and Archive Council. www.seapn.org.uk/uploads/files/libraries_and_community_cohesion.pdf.

Vincent, John (2009) Public library provision for Black and minority ethnic communities - where are we in 2009? *Journal of Librarianship and Information Science*, **41** (5) 137–47.

Vincent, John (2015) How can we find out how many refugees and asylum seekers there are in our area?. www.seapn.org.uk/post/how-can-we-find-out-how-many-refugees-and-asylum seekers-there-are-in-our-area.

Vincent, John (2018) *Libraries Welcome Everyone: six stories of diversity and inclusion from libraries in England*. Manchester: Arts Council England. www.artscouncil.org.uk/sites/default/files/download-file/ACE_Libraries_welcome_everyone_report_July18.pdf.

Vincent, John (2019) Moving into the mainstream: is that somewhere we want to go in the United Kingdom? In *LGBTQ+ Librarianship in the 21st Century: emerging directions of advocacy and community engagement in diverse information environments*, edited by Bharat Mehra. Bingley, West Yorkshire: Emerald Publishing.

Vincent, John (2020a) Libraries of Sanctuary [talk to 'ILIG Informal', 12 February 2020]. www.youtube.com/watch?v=97DQE4H-Hjg.

Vincent, John (2020b) Libraries of Sanctuary. *Information Professional*, August/September, 44–6.

Vincent, John (2021a) Connecting libraries and refugee communities. *Information Professional*, October/November 2021, 38–41.

Vincent, John (2021b) *Libraries of Sanctuary Resource Pack*. 2nd edn. Leeds: City of Sanctuary. www.seapn.org.uk/uploads/files/COS-Library-resource-pack-Low-res-web-version-SINGLE-PAGE-11-10-21.pdf.

Vincent, John, and Barry Clark (2020) Libraries of Sanctuary. *Alexandria*, **30** (1) 5-15.

Vincent, John, and Muriel Hill (1999) Enfield Libraries' response to the 'Warwick Report'. *Public Libraries & Social Exclusion Action Planning Network Newsletter*, (8 (Old Series)) December 1999, 1–4. www.seapn.org.uk/newsletters-archive.

Vougioukalou, Sofia, Rosie Dow, Laura Bradshaw and Tracy Pallant (2019) Wellbeing and integration through community music: the role of improvisation in a music group of refugees, asylum seekers and local community members. *Contemporary Music Review*, **38** (5), 533–48. www.tandfonline.com/doi/full/10.1080/07494467.2019.1684075.

Walsh, Peter William (2020a) *Irregular Migration in the UK*. Oxford: The Migration Observatory (Briefing). https://migrationobservatory.ox.ac.uk/wp-content/uploads/2020/09/Briefing-Irregular-Migration-in-the-UK.pdf.

Walsh, Peter William (2020b) *Migrants Crossing the English Channel in Small Boats: what do we know?* Oxford: The Migration Observatory (Commentary). 16 October 2020. https://migrationobservatory.ox.ac.uk/resources/commentaries/migrants-crossing-the-english-channel-in-small-boats-what-do-we-know.

Walsh, Peter William (2021) *Asylum and Refugee Resettlement in the UK*. Oxford: The Migration Observatory (Briefing). 11 May 2021.

https://migrationobservatory.ox.ac.uk/wp-content/uploads/2021/05/Briefing-Asylum-and-refugee-resettlement-in-the-UK.pdf.

Waltham Forest Community Help Network (2021) Ways you can help. www.walthamforest.gov.uk/content/ways-you-can-help.

Waters, Hazel, and Jennifer Wilkinson (1974) A poverty of thinking. *Library Association Record*, **76** (1), 3–5.

We Belong (n.d.) What is the problem? www.webelong.org.uk/issue/what-problem.

Webster, Wendy (1998) *Imagining Home: gender, 'race' and national identity, 1945–1964*. London: University College London Press.

Welcome To Your Library Steering Group (2008) *Welcome To Your Library: final report – London Borough of Hillingdon*. Uxbridge, Middlesex: London Borough of Hillingdon. www.seapn.org.uk/uploads/files/WTYLFinalReportHillingdon.pdf.

Wellum, Jessica (1981) *Black Children in the Library: a brief survey of the library needs of pupils attending the West Indian supplementary education schemes in London*. London: School of Librarianship, Polytechnic of North London (Research report no. 8).

Whiting, R.C. (2008) Political and Economic Planning. In *Oxford Dictionary of National Biography*. Oxford: Oxford University Press.

Whyte, William (1967) Sacred space as sacred text: church and chapel architecture in Victorian Britain. *Theology*, **70** (568), 450–4. doi: https://doi.org/10.1177/0040571x6707056803.

Wikipedia (2021a) History of UK immigration control. https://en.wikipedia.org/wiki/History_of_UK_immigration_control#1968%E2%80%931978:_New_laws_and_European_Union_membership.

Wikipedia (2021b) Immigration to Canada. https://en.wikipedia.org/wiki/Immigration_to_Canada.

Wikipedia (2021c) Refugee. https://en.wikipedia.org/wiki/Refugee.

Wikipedia (2021d) Identitarian movement. https://en.wikipedia.org/wiki/Identitarian_movement.

Wikipedia (2021e) Life in the United Kingdom test. https://en.wikipedia.org/wiki/Life_in_the_United_Kingdom_test.

Wikipedia (2021f) Manchester Arena bombing. https://en.wikipedia.org/wiki/Manchester_Arena_bombing

Wikipedia (2021g) Erasmus Programme. https://en.wikipedia.org/wiki/Erasmus_Programme.

Wikipedia (2021h) Eleanor Farjeon Award. https://en.wikipedia.org/wiki/Eleanor_Farjeon_Award.

Wikipedia (2022a) 2022 Ukrainian refugee crisis. 31 March 2022. https://en.wikipedia.org/wiki/2022_Ukrainian_refugee_crisis.

Wikipedia (2022b) Rivers of Blood speech. https://en.wikipedia.org/wiki/Rivers_of_Blood_speech.

Wilkinson, Richard, and Kate Pickett (2009) *The Spirit Level: why more equal societies almost always do better*. London: Penguin Allen Lane.

Wilkinson, Richard, and Kate Pickett (2018) *The Inner Level: how more equal societies reduce stress, restore sanity and improve everyone's well-being*. London: Penguin Books.

Williams, Martin (2021) UK government rejected more than 32,000 Afghan asylum seekers. *Open Democracy*, 16 Aug 2021. www.opendemocracy.net/en/opendemocracyuk/uk-government-rejected-more-32000-afghan-asylum seekers/?mc_cid=52237cf5fc&mc_eid=e91604b40f.

Williams, Wendy (2020) *Windrush Lessons Learned Review: independent review by Wendy Williams*. London: HMSO (House of Commons papers, session 2019/21 ; HC 93). https://assets.publishing.service.gov.uk/government/uploads/system/uploads/att achment_data/file/874022/6.5577_HO_Windrush_Lessons_Learned_Review_WE B_v2.pdf.

Winder, Robert (2013) *Bloody Foreigners: the story of immigration to Britain*. London: Abacus.

Winterbottom, Eleanor (2021) Working Internationally for Libraries Virtual Conference. *Focus on International Library and Information Work* **52** (2), 14–18. https://cdn.ymaws.com/www.cilip.org.uk/resource/group/bd35bb32-65ad-475f-82be-dcfe36e1ec69/focus/focus52-2.pdf.

Wirral Council (2021) Minority Ethnic Achievement Service. www.wirral.gov.uk/schools-and-learning/minority-ethnic-achievement-service.

Woodhouse, John, and Yago Zayed (2020) *Public Libraries*. London: House of Commons Library (Briefing Paper 5875). https://researchbriefings.parliament.uk/ResearchBriefing/Summary/SN05875#full report.

Woodward, Sonya (2021) How Croeso Menai welcomed a Syrian family to North Wales. *Sponsor Refugees*, 7 April 2021. www.sponsorrefugees.org/how_croeso_menai_welcomed_a_syrian_family_to_n orth_wales.

Wrexham County Borough Council (2022) Equality, Human Rights and Community Cohesion. www.wrexham.gov.uk/service/equality-human-rights-and-community-cohesion.

Writers and Readers Publishing Cooperative (1975) *Racist and Sexist Images in Children's Books*. London: Writers and Readers Publishing Cooperative.

Yeo, Colin (2019) Are refugees obliged to claim asylum in the first safe country they reach?. *Free Movement*, 2 January 2019. www.freemovement.org.uk/are-refugees-obliged-to-claim-asylum-in-the-first-safe-country-they-reach.

Yeo, Colin (2021) What is the legal definition of a 'refugee'?. *Free Movement*, 15 June 2021. https://freemovement.org.uk/what-is-the-legal-meaning-of-refugee.

Younge, Gary (2019) Shocked by the rise of the right? Then you weren't paying attention. *The Guardian*, 24 May 2019, 'Opinion'. www.theguardian.com/commentisfree/2019/may/24/country-racist-elections-liberals-anti-racism-movement.

YoungMinds Welcome (n.d.) [2021?] *Feedback from Refugee and Asylum Seeking Parents*. London: YoungMinds. www.youngminds.org.uk/media/wx2l4fhj/youngminds-welcome-parents-feedback.pdf.

Yusuf, Mohamoud (2020) A new pact for asylum in Europe?. *Social Europe*, 11 November 2020. www.socialeurope.eu/a-new-pact-for-asylum-in-europe.

Zurich (2022) There could be 1.2 billion climate refugees by 2050. Here's what you need to know. *Zurich Magazine*, 25 January 2022. www.zurich.com/en/media/magazine/2022/there-could-be-1-2-billion-climate-refugees-by-2050-here-s-what-you-need-to-know.

Index

Abraham-Hamanoiel, Alejandro 51
academic libraries, 'Project Welcome' 139–41
accommodating people seeking sanctuary, status quo 46–7
Achiume, E. Tendayi 33
Adeleke, Oluwayemisi 12
ADP Consultancy 96
Afghan refugees/asylum seekers 7–8, 31, 67, 71–2
Afghan Scholars Programme 122
Ahmed, Zahir 97
Alexander, Ziggi 85–6, 153
Allegretti, Aubrey 35
American Library Association, ethics statements 65–6
Amnesty International 53–4
Anti-Slavery International 18
Astbury, Raymond 87
asylum 2–4
asylum decision-making, status quo 46
asylum seekers 5–6
  countries of origin 149
  definitions 6

Baillot, Helen 59
Barnet Libraries 124–5
barriers to library services 101–4
  environmental 102–3
  institutional 103–4
  perception and awareness 102
  personal and social 101–2
Bell Foundation 154
Bender, Felix 43
Bergen Libraries 125

Betts, Alexander 4
binary definitions, refugees 3–5
Birmingham City Council 166–7
Birmingham Library Service 158
Birmingham Public Libraries 81
Bodleian Libraries 122
Bowles, Vickery 143–4
Brennan, Donal 127–30
Brexit 40–2
  see also status quo
  rhetoric 52
British National Bibliography Research Fund 84
Brushstrokes Community Project 99–100
'Building Bridges' projects 124
'bussing' of schoolchildren 26

Carl, Noah 41
Carpenter, Helen 95–6, 98, 156
Cartagena Declaration 10–11
case studies
  Conversation Café 132–7
  Lambeth Libraries and the Polish community 130–2
  music and new arrivals 127–30
  Wirral Schools' Library Service Library of Sanctuary Scheme 126–7
Cavalli, Nicolò 42
children and young people, unaccompanied 17–18
Christie, Gary 59
CILIP, ethics statements 64
CILIP 'Changing Lives' strategy 147
CILIP Working Internationally Conference 123–4

CILLA (Cooperative of Indic Language Library Authorities) 158
City of Sanctuary 12, 21, 111
City of Sanctuary Local Authority Network 71–2
Clark, Barry 99
climate change, reason for seeking safety and sanctuary 11–12
Cloudesley, Simon 142–3
Clough, Eric 83
Coleman, Patricia 82, 84
Cologne, Hamburg & Bremen libraries 124
Commonwealth Immigrants Act 1962: 25
Commonwealth Immigrants Act 1968: 25–6
communications, effective 164–5
community cohesion 166–7
Community Relations Commission 80–1
contributions of new arrivals, celebrating 120–2
Conversation Café, case study 132–7
Cooke, Madeleine 84, 88, 155
Cooperative of Indic Language Library Authorities (CILLA) 158
Copenhagen & Allerød Libraries 124–5
CoramBAAF 17–18, 19
Cotrona, Sofia 60
countries of origin, asylum seekers 149
course: 'Working with New Arrivals' 162
COVID-19 impacts 50, 53–8
Craig, Gary 18–19
Crawley, Heaven 31, 32, 55
creating awareness for the wider community 122
current position, refugees 3
current suppliers, library materials supply 159–61

dangers for people trying to gain access to the UK 50
definitions
    see also terminology
    asylum seekers 6
    refugees 5–6
Dennison, James 41

Doctors of the World 54
Durrani, Shiraz 153
Dyck, Jordan 115

East Sussex Library Service, funding 157
ECHO Mobile Library 141–3
Edmond-Pettitt, Anya 44
EEC (European Economic Community) 26, 27
effective communications 164–5
EHRC (Equality and Human Rights Commission) 38
EIA (Equality Impact Assessment) 36
embedding positive action 111–23
    benefits of this work 122–3
    contributions of new arrivals 120–2
    creating awareness for the wider community 122
    information need 114–15
    library services for new arrivals 116–20
    library spaces use and promotion 120
    Refugee Week 120–1
    sympathetic advice and signposting 115
    targeted provision 122
    welcome need 111–14
    work experience and work 116
'Engaging Refugees and Asylum Seekers' 167
English Channel, people crossing the 48–9
environmental barriers to library services 102–3
environmental degradation, reason for seeking safety and sanctuary 11–12
Equality Act 2010: 35–6
Equality and Human Rights Commission (EHRC) 38
Equality Impact Assessment (EIA) 36
Esthimer, Marissa 10
ethics statements by library associations 63–6
Ethnic Minority Achievement Grant (EMAG) 154
Euro-Med Monitor 53
European Economic Community (EEC) 26, 27

INDEX 235

EU Settled Status Scheme (EUSS) 50

Fekete, Liz 47
Filipova-Rivers, Maggie 21
Freedom from Torture report 2019: 34–5
Freedom United 19
Frodin, Angela 93–4
fruit-pickers on UK farms 19
Fryer, Peter 25
funding 152–7
    East Sussex Library Service 157
    Ethnic Minority Achievement Grant
        (EMAG) 154
    funding difficulties 146–7
    Home Office funding 152–4
    Libraries Improvement Fund 157
    Libraries Opportunities for Everyone
        (LOFE) 157
    Paul Hamlyn Foundation (PHF)
        95–100, 156
    project funding 95–100, 156
    Urban Programme 154–5
Fursland, Eileen 17, 19

gender identity, reason for seeking
    safety and sanctuary 13–15
Gentleman, Amelia 7, 39–40
Ghouri, Nadene 61
Gloucestershire County Council,
    website for people seeking
    sanctuary 93–4
Goodfellow, Maya 30
Greater London Authority 151
Griffiths, Melanie 28, 34
Gypsy, Roma and Traveller people,
    reason for seeking safety and
    sanctuary 15–16

Hadjazi, Youcef 15
Hamada, Rachel 56
Hamlin, Rebecca 3–4
Hargrave, Russell 51
Hashem, Rumana 20
Hastings Community of Sanctuary 60
Heap, Emily-Jane 60
Hewitt, Adam 19
historical background, refugees 2
Home Office Factsheet 27–8

Home Office funding 152–4
'hostile environment' 32–5
House of Commons Women and
    Equalities Committee 16
House of Lords Library 32–3
Humphrey, Justine 142–3

'illegal immigration' 16–17
Immigration Act 1971: 26
Immigration Act 2016: 28
Immigration Bill 23–4
immigration enforcement, status quo 47
immigration status 150–1
immigration UK background 24–8
    1940s–1950s 24
    1960s–1970s 24–7
    1980s to date 27–8
    arrivers and leavers 29–30
    growing hostility 30–1
improvement initiatives 147–8
India Office Library 159
information needs of refugee groups
    91–2
information sources, new arrivals 164
Institute for Public Policy Research
    (IPPR) 38–9
institutional barriers to library services
    103–4
institutional racism 28–9
Intergovernmental Panel on Climate
    Change report was published
    (IPCC) 11
international agreements 9–11
    Cartagena Declaration 10–11
    Organisation of African Unity (OAU)
    10
    United Nations Refugee Convention
    9–10
Ionesco, Dina 11
IPPR (Institute for Public Policy
    Research) 38–9
Ipsos MORI 58
Ireland, Philippa 152–3
irregular migrants 16–17

JCWI (Joint Council for the Welfare of
    Immigrants) 37
Jenkins, Simon 8

Joint Council for the Welfare of Immigrants (JCWI) 37
Jones, Hannah 34

Kale, Sirin 50
Ker-Lindsay, James 41
Khan, Ayub 66–7
Kirklees Libraries 159
Kvist, Else 50

lack of work, education and other opportunities, reason for seeking safety and sanctuary 12–13
Lambeth Libraries and the Polish community, case study 130–2
Lawrence, Stephen 29
learning about 'new arrivals' experiences 105–11
  Maslow's hierarchy of needs applied to library provision 109–11
  new arrivals in your area 107–9
  people's needs 109–11
Leatham, Scott 11
Leicester Museums & Galleries 164–5
Libraries Improvement Fund, funding 157
Libraries of Sanctuary 99–100
Libraries Opportunities for Everyone (LOFE), funding 157
libraries' responses in the UK - historical background 73–100
  1940s and 1950s 76
  1960s and 1970s 76–84
  1980s 84–7
  1990s 87–93
  2000 onwards 93–100
  citizenship 90–1
  ethnic diversity 90–1
  Gloucestershire County Council, website for people seeking sanctuary 93–4
  information needs of refugee groups 91–2
  Lancashire 77
  Libraries of Sanctuary 99–100
  The Midlands 76–7
  The North of England and Scotland 77–8

Paul Hamlyn Foundation (PHF) 95–100
public libraries 90–1
'Public Library Policy and Social Exclusion' 92–3
refugee groups, information needs 91–2
The South 77
'Welcome To Your Library' (PHF) 95–100
Yorkshire 77
Library Advisory Council 80–1
Library Association 83
Library Association's Association of Assistant Librarians, 'Serving the Black community' 86–7
library materials supply 158–61
  Birmingham Library Service 158
  Cooperative of Indic Language Library Authorities (CILLA) 158
  current suppliers 159–61
  Polish Central Circulating Library 158
library services for new arrivals 116–20
library workers
  journeys to the UK 66–70
  offering support 71–2
lifetime impact of seeking sanctuary 20
Linley, Rebecca 89
Lipniacka, Ewa 76
Local Government Association 166
LOFE (Libraries Opportunities for Everyone), funding 157
Lowe, Kevin 17
Lynch, Bernadette 156

Macpherson report 29
Mahabir, Lynda 39–40
Makoii, Akhtar Mohammad 8
Malik, Nesrine 34
Mansour, Essam 115
Manzoor-Khan, Suhaiymah 26
Maslow's hierarchy of needs applied to library provision 109–11
materials supply, libraries' see library materials supply
Mayor's Commission on African and Asian Heritage 23

INDEX 237

Menendez, Elisa 15
Migrant Voice 50–1
Migration Observatory 16–17, 48–9
Mills, Geoff 78–9, 81
modern slavery/trafficking 18–19
Morrison, Marlene 90, 154
Mort, Lucy 57–8
Muddiman, Dave 92–3
Mulhall, Joe 4–5
music and new arrivals, case study
    127–30

National Crime Agency 18
new arrivals, perception and
    representation of 50–2

OAU (Organisation of African Unity) 10
Olden, Anthony 89–90
Oldham Libraries 124
'Operation Vaken' 34
Organisation of African Unity (OAU) 10
'overhauling' the immigration system
    47–8
Owen, Joe 37–8
Oxfordshire Libraries 125

Passarlay, Gulwali 61
Paul Hamlyn Foundation (PHF) 156
    'Welcome To Your Library' 95–100
people crossing the English Channel
    48–9
perception and awareness barriers to
    library services 102
perception and representation of new
    arrivals 50–2
perceptions of refugees 1–2
personal and social barriers to library
    services 101–2
PHF see Paul Hamlyn Foundation
Pinder, Sarah 8
PKV Library 124
Pohl, Julia Z. 13–14
Policy Action Team 156
Polish Central Circulating Library 158
political responses to new arrivals 146
Powell, Enoch 25
Pro Bono Economics (charity) 35
project funding 95–100, 156

'Project Welcome' 139–41
PSED (Public Sector Equality Duty) 36
Public Libraries in a Multi-cultural Britain
    83
'Public Library Policy and Social
    Exclusion' 92–3
*A Public Library Service for Ethnic
    Minorities in Great Britain* 83
Public Sector Equality Duty (PSED) 36
Pyper, Doug 36

Qian, Angela 20
Quarmby, Jacqueline 83
Quilon Library 124
Qureshi, Amreen 38–9

Race Relations Act 1965: 25
racism and hate crime 52–3
Rainbow Migration 14
reasons for seeking safety and sanctuary
    11–16, 20–1
    climate change 11–12
    environmental degradation 11–12
    gender identity 13–15
    Gypsy, Roma and Traveller people
        15–16
    lack of work, education and other
        opportunities 12–13
    sexuality and/or gender identity
        13–15
Redbridge Libraries 124
'Red Tape Challenge' 36
Refugee Action 115
Refugee Council 45, 54–5
'refugee crisis' 2015: 31–2
refugee resettlement programmes 7–8
refugees
    binary definitions 3–5
    current position 3
    definitions 5–6
    historical background 2
    terminology 3–5
Refugee Week 120–1
Renshaw, David 40
resettlement programmes 7–8
responses to people seeking sanctuary
    145–6
Roach, Patrick 90, 154

238   LIBRARIES AND SANCTUARY

Roache, Madeline 43
Rodenhurst, Kate 167
Rumsby, Seb 5
Ryder, Julie 95

sanctuary, terminology 5
Sandwell Library Service 98, 99, 100, 113–14, 146
Schools of Sanctuary 15–16, 99
SCONUL, library workers offering support 71–2
Scoop Media 53
Scottish Community Development Centre 167
Scottish Refugee Council 28
'Serving the Black community' 86–7
sexuality and/or gender identity, reason for seeking safety and sanctuary 13–15
sharing and learning 123–5
  'Building Bridges' projects 124
  CILIP Working Internationally Conference 123–4
Simsova, Sylva 84–5
Smith, David John 27
Smith, Reiss 13
sources of information, new arrivals 164
Southall Black Sisters 56
status quo 42–61
  UK 45–61
Surrey County Council 112
'survival migration' 4
sympathetic advice and signposting 115

Tanner, Claudia 59
Taylor, Diane 39
Taylor, Russell 32–3
terminology
  see also definitions
  binary definitions 3–5
  refugees 3–5
  sanctuary 5
  'survival migration' 4
Thimblemill Library 99
Thomas, Jonathan 51
Toronto Public Library (TPL) 143–4
trafficking/modern slavery 18–19
Traies, Jane 13, 14

Tsangarides, Natasha 35

unaccompanied children and young people 17–18
UNHCR (United Nations High Commissioner for Refugees) 2, 5–6, 7, 9–11
UNITED 43–4
United Nations High Commissioner for Refugees (UNHCR) 2, 5–6, 7, 9–11
United Nations Refugee Convention 9–10
University of Illinois, 'Project Welcome' 139–41
Urban Programme, funding 154–5

Varenna, Deborah 67–9
Vasagar, Jeevan 2
Velikova, Toni 69–70
Vickers, Tom 54
Vietnamese children and young people 19
Vincent, John 95, 107, 127–30
Vougioukalou, Sofia 127

Walsh, Peter William 7, 16–17, 48–9
Waters, Hazel 80
White Paper on Immigration from the Commonwealth 1965: 25
Wikipedia 26
Wilkinson, Jennifer 80
Williams, Liz 35
Wilson, Paulette 39–40
Winder, Robert 23
Windrush scandal 36–40
Wirral Schools' Library Service Library of Sanctuary Scheme, case study 126–7
Woodward, Sonia 59
work experience and work 116
'Working with New Arrivals', half-day course 162

Yeo, Colin 6, 28, 34
Younge, Gary 31
young people's access to the UK 49
Yusuf, Mohamoud 42–3